D1357776

The Millennial Advantage

How Millennials Can (And Must) Be the Next
Great Generation of Investors

By Jason Kirsch, CFP®

First Printing, 2016
ISBN-10: 0-9981189-0-7
ISBN-13: 978-0-9981189-0-1

GROW,LLC
500 N. Broadway
Jericho, NY 11753

www.GrowPlanning.com

Disclaimer

This book does not constitute investment advice from Jason Kirsch, any Registered Investment Advisory Firm (RIA) which Jason Kirsch is employed by or registered with, GROW, llc (GROW), the publishing company or any other affiliates.

This book contains statistics, examples and materials from sources believed to be reliable but we do not guarantee everything is accurate or complete. Neither party (Kirsch, Any RIA firm, GROW, Publishing Firm, or any other affiliates) can guarantee accuracy or completeness of any of the information in this book. There may be inaccuracies or omissions in the information contained within. Neither Kirsch, the RIA which he is registered with or employed by, GROW, the publishing company or any other affiliates are liable for any of the information presented in this book or any decision made from it. Neither Kirsch, the RIA which he is registered with or employed by, GROW, the publishing firm or any affiliate communicate any representations about the suitability of any recommendation or information in this book.

All information in this book is the property of Jason Kirsch or the information sources and is protected by copyright and intellectual property laws. No one shall reproduce, retransmit, disseminate, sell, publish, broadcast or circulate the information or material in this book without express written consent of Jason Kirsch or the other information sources.

Contents

Acknowledgements...*1*

Opening Words: The Value of Time..................................*3*

Introduction: Is the American Dream Still Alive?.................*7*

1: Time is On Your Side (But Not Timing)..........................17

2: A Nation of Investors...35

3: No Time Like the Present..55

4: The Market and You..71

5: Managing Risk..83

6: The Millennial Investor's Menu....................................105

7: Diversification..129

8: When Markets (and Investors) Don't Behave
   Rationally...153

9: Cycles...167

10: The Active vs. Passive Debate.....................................193

11: Beating the Market..209

12: Keeping Your Costs Low...231

13: Putting It All Together 251

Conclusion: Building Your Own Conclusion.....................275

Appendix *295*

Notes *305*

Acknowledgements

To my parents Leonard and Marilyn Kirsch, and my most beautiful wife Dana, who have always supported me and loved me unconditionally. It is because of them I consider myself the luckiest man in the universe.

This would not be the book it is without the assistance of my editor, Scott Doyle. His attention to detail, ability to research and gift for structure and narrative was invaluable. Without his work, this book would have never come to fruition.

I also offer a rousing round of applause for all those authors, educators, and artists in the world whose work educates, comforts, but most of all inspires us to be the best that we can be.

Opening Words

The Value of Time

Time is such an important theme in investing, in life and a constant theme of this book. Time allows for accomplishment in any field-and gives us the ability to generate substantial wealth.

Because the Millennial Generation, those of us born between the early 1980s and early 2000s, have time on our side, I've written this book mostly with Millennials in mind. But other generations will find value here as well.

After all, when I was only thirteen, I received gifts from friends and relatives that totaled roughly ten thousand dollars. Since my parents insisted that I place such a then-lavish sum (or so it seemed at the time) into long-term investments, I set about teaching myself the principles of investing. Soon I became fascinated by what I was learning. As young as I was, I already knew that I wanted the financial means to be in charge of my own destiny, and that I had been given a valuable asset, one that could help me move toward that goal – if I used it properly.

Because my family lived around the corner from the vacant offices of Stratton Oakmont, whose founder Jordan Belfort chronicled his rise and fall in the book The Wolf of Wall Street (also the film of the same title starring Leonardo DiCaprio), I had some notion early on of the stock market's volatility and the value of personal integrity. But I had no inkling of even the most basic investment terms. What, I wondered, was a mutual fund? I didn't know the first thing about tax deferred growth, fundamental analysis, compound returns or any other investment concept.

Wanting to learn how to turn my coming-of-age windfall into a far greater amount, I turned first to family members and older friends but their advice was, more often than not, confusing. The popular internet search engines of the day offered only slightly more valuable information. Eventually I found and read more than a hundred books on the topic – some good, some not so good – and distilled three key truths from my studies:

1. Investing is completely about the future.

2. The future is uncertain.

3. The skill of an investor is almost completely based on how that investor manages uncertainty.

A couple of years ago, I began writing down what I had learned in my youthful studies, and ever since. At first, it was only a pastime: I never imagined that I would write enough to publish a book. It seemed like a daunting task.

Nonetheless, six days a week I wrote, even when I didn't feel like it. Finally, when I had a 70,000-word manuscript, another truth hit me: Time is a vastly underrated force.

Just as, over time, I was able to complete a book by writing a little every day, so too can wealth grow over time. Take the principal of compound returns, which Albert Einstein once dubbed one of the wonders of the world. A penny invested so that its worth doubles each day will be worth sixteen cents in five days. While that may sound like much, give that penny thirty days to grow, doubling in value each day, and one penny can eventually be worth more than five million dollars.

This simple truth surprises many people, and it's easy to understand why. When we are working toward a goal, we only see the progress we're making on a short-term basis. Whether we're writing a book of investing small amounts of money on a regular basis, our progress can seem glacially slow. It's only when we stop to look at how far we've come and how much we've accomplished that we can begin to appreciate what a value commodity time can be.

Time, therefore, is a consistent theme in this book. Time, in partnership with consistency, allows for accomplishment in any field, including the effort to generate substantial wealth and build long-term financial security.

In ways that I'll explain soon, the Millennial Generation (those born between the early 1980s and the early 2000s) have a peculiar relationship with time. They have the advantage of time on their side, but the disadvantage of bad economic timing. This book is very much written with that generation in mind—focusing on the unique challenges and opportunities their place in history presents. But the broad principles of investing I outline are relevant to earlier (and later) generations as well.

In the pages that follow, I have tried to provide some clarity about the economic context within which we all live, so that no matter what year you were born, you can move forward and take real charge of your financial destiny. Money is just a means toward an end, and financial freedom is ultimately the freedom to lead the life you want to lead, to build your own American dream. It is my earnest hope that this book brings you closer to realizing that dream.

Introduction:
Is the American Dream
Still Alive?

On September 17, 2011, a group of protestors converged on a small public park in the heart of New York City's financial district, voicing their anger about a broad range of issues: from corruption on Wall Street and the need for banking reform, to the growing gap, not just between the rich and the poor, but between the rich and… well, everyone else. In fact, the group's catchiest slogan – **"We are the 99%"** – may be its biggest legacy. What would quickly become known as the Occupy Wall Street Movement was anchored by a two-month literal occupation of Zuccatti Park. It caught the imagination of disaffected young people in particular, both across the United States and the world. Sympathy protests broke out in more than 100 U.S. cities, and many more worldwide. "Income inequality" became headline news, and a topic of debate in the presidential campaign just then heating up. President Obama expressed a degree of sympathy with the protestors while his opponent Mitt Romney openly worried that some were trying to stoke the fires of class warfare.

That question has a special resonance in America which has always prided itself on being a **classless society:** a central tenet of what is sometimes called "American exceptionalism." The basic premise is that, unlike Europe and many societies around the world, the United States had no feudal past, no aristocracy, no kings or queens or princes. You can start out with nothing and, like the heroes of Horatio Alger's novels, pull yourself up by your bootstraps and go from rags to riches.

The reality has never been quite that simple but belief in social mobility and the American Dream is a powerful motivating force in American culture. The devastating Financial Crisis that began in 2007 (and which eventually became a full-fledged economic crisis that many call the Great Recession) dealt a serious blow to that belief, at least in the short term. Occupy Wall Street struck a chord for a while, with polls showing a growing number of people perceiving a fundamental conflict of interest between rich and poor. Yet the movement lacked organization and a clear focus, and failed to sustain its early momentum.

Years later, the movement has mostly disappeared, but the issue still resonates, even as the economy has slowly rebounded. Calls for income redistribution or radical economic reform have faded, but the question of income inequality remains part of the national debate. In 2014, *Capital in the Twenty-First Century*—a treatise on economic inequality by the French economist Thomas Picketty and not exactly a page-turner— became an unexpected bestseller when it was published in the U.S. Yale economics professor and Nobel Prize winner Robert Shiller praised the book and declared income inequality "the most important problem that we are facing today," while

President Obama has called the income and wealth gap[1] the "defining challenge of our time." Senator Bernie Sanders built a rather successful campaign by focusing on income and wealth inequality. And economist Joseph Stiglitz – whose May *2011 Vanity Fair column* "Of the 1%, By the 1%, For the 1%" helped introduce the 99% idea – recently released a collection of New York Times columns on inequality called *The Great Divide: Unequal Societies and What We Can Do About Them which,* like Picketty's book, argues that the problem is a global one.

A number of recent studies support the claim of a growing gap between the wealthy and the rest of us. According to the Federal Reserve, the poorest half of the U.S. population holds only 1% of its wealth, down from 3% in 1989, while the wealthiest 5% holds 63%. The Congressional Budget Office reports that the annual income of the wealthiest 1% has tripled since 1979 while that of the rest of the population (the 99%) grew less than 45%. A Pew Research Center analysis of Federal Reserve data shows that the median wealth of the nation's upper-income families is now nearly seven times that of middle-income families—the widest wealth gap in the 30 years this data has been collected. The same Pew study finds that, in the recovery that followed the Great Recession, upper-income families have recouped their losses and begun accumulating wealth again while wealth growth has been stagnant for everyone else.

---

[1]   While the two terms (income gap and wealth gap) are sometimes used interchangeably, it's important to distinguish them. The income gap is only one measure of inequality. Disparities in wealth (net assets minus liabilities) are another thing entirely. The income gap and the wealth gap don't always move in sync with one another. For the sake of clarity, I will sometimes use the term economic inequality as a general term encompassing both.

Share of US US adults living in
middle-income households is shrinking.

Share of US adults by income tier

	lower	middle	upper
2015	29%	50%	21%
2011	29	51	20
2001	28	54	18
1991	27	56	17
1981	26	59	15
1971	25	61	14

Figure A – Data Source: Pew Research Center

As a result, it seems clear that the middle class[2] is shrinking. The Center for American Progress reports that a majority of just over 61% of American households fell into that category in 1979; by 2015, that figure had dropped to 50%. Additionally, a number of studies suggest that upward mobility may in fact be lower now in the United States than in much of Europe.

• • •

Americans themselves seem to be of two minds on the subject. On one hand, the percentage of the public identifying themselves as "have-nots" doubled between 1988 and 2011. On the other hand, several fascinating studies reported in

---

[2] There is no standard economic definition of middle class. The Center for American Progress study cited here defines it as working-age households with incomes between 0.5 and 1.5 the median national income. The Pew Research Center has a different range: two-thirds to double the median national income (which in 2014 would have been between $42,000 and $126,000 for a three-person household).

Scientific American reveal that most Americans underestimate (by a good deal) the actual degree of economic inequality in the U.S.; while many believe the economic system unfairly favors the wealthy, a majority still believes they can overcome their circumstance through hard work.

Belief in the American Dream, it appears, is shaky but intact. And so is the ongoing debate about economic inequality. Economists, politicians and the public alike disagree about the extent of the problem and how to go about addressing it. I'd like to be able to say I'm going to present solutions to the big question of how to create an equitable society with equal opportunity for all. But that's beyond the scope of this book and beyond the scope of my expertise.

Instead, I offer something humbler but still powerful: the opportunity to take control of your own financial future and, perhaps, restore some balance to wealth distribution on a more personal scale. These remain unsure times, and that's unlikely to change anytime soon. A rapidly evolving economy driven by technological innovation has all but eliminated the certainties and securities of the past. Which makes it more important than ever for you to exercise control over what you can control: your money, how you make it, how you save it, how you invest it and how you grow it.

• • •

In the chapters that lie ahead, I'll discuss the nuts and bolts of putting together a customized investment portfolio. One of the key concepts we'll explore is asset allocation: how you distribute your investments among various "**asset classes**" (e.g., stocks, bonds, real estate, and cash). We'll get into that in depth at a later point. But it's important now to take a quick look at how asset allocation figures into the problem of growing economic inequality.

At the risk of oversimplifying... **One of the biggest reasons why the wealthiest among us are pulling ahead of everyone else is that they own more equity, whether through public stock ownership or private small business.** To some extent, of course, this is inevitable: they have more money, more disposable income, and can afford to invest more in private businesses and in the stock market. But it's also a question of habit: the habit of saving, first and foremost; and then of regularly taking some of those savings and investing them in the most important long-term wealth generator at our disposal—the stock market.

In a paper for the National Bureau of Economic Research, "Household Wealth Trends in the United States, 1962 – 2013," Edward Wolff found that wealth inequality remained largely unchanged in the years from 1962 to 1983—but rose sharply from 1983 to 1989. Why was this? During that six-year stretch, housing prices went up only 2% while the S&P 500 rose 62%. Stock ownership rates during this period were still only just over 30%, and even that figure doesn't begin to capture how much total stock ownership is concentrated in the hands of the wealthiest Americans. The bottom line: a small percentage of the population captured a disproportionate share of the booming stock market, and the wealth gap widened as a result.

Just how concentrated is stock ownership at the very top? Wolff finds that the top 1% own half of all stocks, financial securities and business equity; and that the top 10% account for 91% of all direct ownership of stocks and mutual funds.

No wonder the wealth gap widens when the stock market is booming!

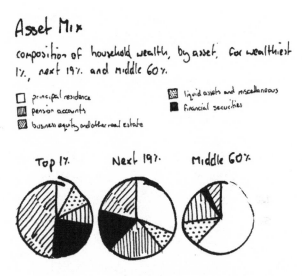

Figure B – Data Source: Edward Wolf, NYU

Wolff places a great deal of emphasis on differences in **household asset composition** (basically, the pie chart of what accounts for total household wealth), focusing on three key factors: 1) ownership of stocks and other investments; 2) The amount of household wealth tied up in a home; 3) household debt—specifically, the ratio of debt to net worth.

- For the **Top 1%:** three-fourths of household assets are invested in business, investment real estate, and financial securities like stocks, which alone count for 25% of assets. The primary residence accounts for only 9% of wealth, and their debt ratio is only 3%.

- By contrast, for the so-called **Middle 60%** (everyone between the top 20% and the bottom 20%): investments account for only 25% of assets (stocks are 10%), and 63% of total household wealth is tied up in their home. Their debt ratio is 65%.

The different financial make-up of the rich and the broad middle, Wolff argues, also explains the second spike in wealth inequality that took place during the Great Recession of 2007-2009. Although stocks took a slightly bigger hit than housing prices (26% and 24% respectively), the middle class was more vulnerable because so much of its wealth was tied up in home ownership, and because of its historically high levels of debt. **The very wealthy also experienced losses during this period; yet they were cushioned by a more diverse portfolio and, most important, lower debt. The vulnerable middle class saw its net worth plummet, and wealth inequality rose sharply once again.**

To sum up: a combination of a more diverse, equity-based portfolio and lower debt allowed the wealthiest to capture the upside of a major boom, and then protected it from the downside of a major bust.

• • •

The tone of this book is one of cautious optimism. Let's start with the cautious part of that equation. The wealth gap has widened significantly in recent decades and, according to some it's only going to get worse. Home ownership rates are down and student debt is up. Moreover, many Millennials have had the bad fortune to enter the job market during the worst economic downturn in recent memory—and studies indicate that starting a career during such a downturn has a long-term, negative effect on lifetime earnings potential.

For those and other reasons, I almost thought of naming this book *The Millennial (Dis)Advantage.* The challenges facing the younger generations are very real: both Millennials and Gen Xers have been put behind the economic eight ball, and are at a disadvantage compared to their Baby Boomer predecessors.

But I stand by the optimism of my current title because I do believe that, in the end, your advantages outweigh your disadvantages. In addition to the huge advantage of time, **Millennials have a number of qualities that put them in a great position to be terrific investors:** they are the most educated generation in history; they are more disciplined financially than many realize; they have a healthy skepticism of financial institutions and conventional wisdom; and they place a huge premium on customizing their financial decisions at a time when the options for doing so and pursuing an independent path have never been greater.

In the chapters ahead we'll take a look at how America has gone from a nation of savers to a nation of investors, and how we now need to rekindle both of these habits. We'll look at the changing world of retirement plans, and at how financial markets aren't always as rational as classical economics would have us think. We'll examine the question of risk, and how to manage it, and see that diversification is an important principle but not a guarantee of success. We'll look at the cyclical nature of markets and the economy, and how to avoid making big mistakes at the top and the bottom of those cycles. Finally, we'll review some sound principles for putting together and monitoring an investment portfolio that works for you and your life goals.

Throughout the book, I've made a real effort to avoid easy answers, and to give you both sides of some of the central dilemmas of investing. I provide you with different views on such questions for a couple of reasons. First, there is no "one size fits all" approach to investing. The approach that works best for you will depend both on your situation; and on your individual temperament: how comfortable you are with risk and volatility, how much research you're willing to do, etc.

Second, the world of investing (and of finance and economics in general) can be complicated. But that doesn't mean your approach to investing should be complicated. As Tony Robbins writes in his book about investing, "complexity is often the enemy of execution". "Simplicity is the ultimate sophistication," said the great Renaissance thinker Leonardo Da Vinci, and there's a lot of truth to that when it comes to investing. As you'll see later, some of the investors I most admire, while never forgetting the complexities and nuances involved, keep their focus on the essentials: they never lose sight of the forest for the trees.

So while my goal is certainly to educate and inform, it is first and foremost to inspire you to act: to begin saving (or if you've already started, to save more) and to invest that money in strategic ways that will allow it to grow over time into real wealth, real financial security. The key is to begin; to begin simple, but smart; and then to learn and evolve as you go along. In the Conclusion, I will stress that just as interest compounds, so does knowledge.

But first things first. It's time to start our journey, and you can't see clearly where you're going until you see where you've been.

Chapter 1

Time is On Your Side
(But Not Timing)

ime, time, time… is on my side, the Rolling Stones once sang. (Actually, they're still singing it.) It is obvious and perhaps redundant to point out that time is one of the advantages that comes with being young: you have time to plan a career and other life goals, to enjoy a certain freedom from responsibility before settling down, to travel, to pursue a passion project or volunteer work, to figure out what makes you happy.

Conspicuously absent from this list (and probably from the lists many Millennials might put together themselves) is this item: **time to invest.**

Which is unfortunate, for a couple of reasons. First, because of all that time you have on your side, Millennials are in the best position to benefit from the main tenets of this book. Second, Millennials are the generation that most needs to take control of their financial life, early and often. You (along with Generation X) are the generation most affected by growing economic inequality. You are also a generation growing up in an increasingly volatile economy which will force you to change jobs and even careers multiple times during your working life, and in which the safety net provided by Social Security and even pensions grows shakier by the year. The bottom line: **This generation's lasting and true wealth will come in large part as a result of smart investing.**

In future chapters, I will share with you the core concepts and insights and techniques that will allow you to take advantage of the time ahead of you and start building real wealth now—one strategic step at a time. But, for now, let's take a closer look at how Millennials view money and behave with regard to money, and also how their financial fortunes were affected by the Great Recession. You'll see there's both good news and bad news.

It's a Generational Thing

To begin with, let's define our terms: Who are these Millennials anyway? Who decides which generation is which? And why does it matter?

MONIKER	BORN BETWEEN
Millennials (Gen Y)	1986 - 2005
Generation X	1966 - 1985
Baby Boomers	1946 - 1965
Silent Generation	1926 - 1945
Greatest Generation	1901 - 1925

Figure C: Years are an approximation. Definitions of generations vary.

Although this book is primarily directed at Millennials (and, to an extent, Generation X), in this chapter and the next we're going to be looking at the previous three generations as well. The **Greatest Generation** was born in the opening 25 years of the 20th century, fought in World War II, and was given its moniker by newsman Tom Brokaw in a bestselling book of the same name. The **Silent Generation** followed—so called in a 1951 *Time Magazine essay*. They are sometimes also called "Depression babies. And since they were born at a time when, due to harsh economic conditions, the birth rate fell significantly, they were at an advantage during the prosperous post-WWII years simply because there were fewer of them.

Baby Boomers were the exact opposite. The term came about because there was quite literally a noticeable increase, or boom, in the birth rate in the years after World War II. So, sometime around 1970, the term started being used to describe the generation born between the mid-40's and early 60's. The Boomers came of age during years of great social change, and this has come to distinguish them from previous generations. And while they too benefited from post-war prosperity, they faced more competition among themselves.

The generation that followed became known as **Generation X**, a term popularized by novelist Douglas Coupland. As with all these categories, there is some disagreement about start and end dates—but in general Gen X includes those born between the mid 60's and early 80's. Like the previous generation, they tend to question authority, and are highly individualistic. (They are sometimes also called the slacker generation or the MTV generation.)

For the purposes of this book, there are three other things worth noting. For a long time it was assumed that each generation would be more prosperous than the previous one. This historical trend was reversed with Gen X as (adjusted for inflation) men in their prime working years actually earned less than their fathers, resulting in more mothers going to work and the now common phenomenon of the two-income family. Second, for almost a quarter of a century following WWII, income gains were equal for all segments of society—roughly doubling for the top 5%, the bottom 20%, and everyone in the middle. But, starting in the early 70s, that started to change as well. The income of the top 1% in particular grew at a startling rate (quadrupling between 1979 and 2007) while income at all other levels grew much more slowly. Finally, Gen X was hit by two traumatic economic events: the bursting of the dot-com bubble in 2000, and then the Great Recession that followed the collapse of the housing bubble in 2007.

The Financial Lives of Millennials

It would seem to make sense to call the generation that followed Generation Y, right? And, for a while, they were. Yet, in the late 80s, the authors William Strauss and Neil Howe (who have devoted their lives to studying the characteristics of different generations[1]) noted that those born in 1982 would be entering adulthood around the year 2000—they, and those after them, would come of age not just in a new century, but a new millennium. So they coined the term **"Millennials"** and it stuck.

Millennials are less consumerist than their predecessors and more focused on mission and meaning. Like the Baby

---

[1] In books such as *Generations, The Fourth Turning*, and *Millennials Rising*

Boomers and Gen X, they question authority. Partly due to the Financial Crisis and Great Recession of 2007-2009, and partly due to new options not previously available, they are highly distrustful of large financial institutions, banks especially. They are increasingly likely to be "unbanked"—avoiding traditional banks and instead opting to manage their finances through services offered by companies like Google, PayPal, Square, and Apple.

The newest generation also isn't counting on Social Security to be around when they retire (nor as I will explain later, should they). This, combined with their distrust of financial institutions (including Wall Street), has left Millennials cautious when it comes to their finances. They keep more than half of their investable assets in savings and only about a quarter in stocks: the complete opposite of the previous generation. And 43% describe themselves as "conservative investors" as opposed to only 27% from Generation X.

On the other hand, Millennials can be quite savvy when it comes to their money. They are accustomed to having their finances at their fingertips, and to using mobile technology to compare prices on the spot. They may distrust banks, but they are relentless connectors, and place greater faith in personal networks than in large institutions. It may seem antithetical but, while they don't like to take big risks, they are essentially entrepreneurial in spirit.

Be Comfortable Talking and Thinking About Money

The qualities I've just outlined can be channeled into turning Millennials into great, savvy investors. But first they've got to get over a certain discomfort over the idea of thinking and talking about money—especially the concept of accumulating wealth.

On the one hand, as I've already noted, Millennials are less materialistic than previous generations, and there's a lot of merit in that. The catch phrase for Gordon Gecko, the anti-hero of the 1987 movie *Wall Street,* was "Greed is good." Gecko's motto echoed the spirit of those times, as did a popular bumper sticker: "He Who Wins Dies With the Most Toys." The new generation is different. As a recent column in *Forbes* puts it, "Millennials Work for Purpose, Not Paycheck."

But let's not confuse money with materialism, or wealth with conspicuous consumption. In the end, money is a tool, a means to an end. For instance, Millennials are big on giving back. A 2013 study found that 20% of adults under 30 volunteered that year, up from 14% in 1989. But to give back, you need to have something to give back. Being smart with your money, and strategic about building wealth, will give you greater freedom to give back or pursue other meaningful projects down the road.

If you're a reluctant accumulator of wealth, it's time to leave that attitude behind. While this book is about accumulating wealth, it is not about building financial resources for a later ostentatious spending spree. No, building financial resources is an absolute necessity when nothing about the future is guaranteed, including the job you have today.

Be Smart About Money

The current generation is already pretty smart about money—and smarter than some in the media give them credit for. Yes, savings rates are down, but that's largely due to soaring student debt levels. The financial education firm Financial Finesse has found that Millennials actually do a better job of managing their day-to-day finances than Gen Xers.

And skepticism about the financial sector and caution about risk is healthy. In fact, it ties in completely with one of my core principles: Don't go after the big score. **First and foremost, adopt a strategy that grinds out modest gains while avoiding big losses.**

Allow me to make a brief digression into the world of poker...

Poker has exploded in popularity in recent decades and whether or not you're a part of that trend, there are some lessons to be learned from those who have lasted in the game long enough to make real money, and to hold onto it.

The game of poker is often mistaken as gambling. Well, it isn't; at least not in the long run. On any given day, of course even the best poker players can lose. But over time, the success rate of good poker players is astonishingly high... high enough to make it a legitimate and fruitful career choice of those select few that have the discipline. Read deeply into any poker guru's philosophy and, before odds and probability and learning to read the "tells" of your opponents, they will talk about something that doesn't sound especially exciting or glamorous: *bankroll management.* The long-term winner in poker knows when to cut his losses; is smart and patient enough to have the resources to maximize his gains, sometimes going all in when the right hand comes along; and understands that the winner is more often than not the one who makes the fewest mistakes.

As Matt Damon's character in the poker film *Rounders* sums it up: "You don't gamble, you grind it out."

And so it goes with investing as well. Like poker, investing is in many ways a so-called "loser's game"—you win mainly by avoiding big losses, and by capitalizing on the mistakes of others. In fact, it's mathematical. In both investing and poker, it takes an 11% gain to break even on a prior 10% loss. *The further you are in the hole, the harder it is to come out: a 25% loss requires a 33% gain to break even; a 50% loss a 100% gain.* These similarities have caused Wall Street traders to sometimes refer to the investments of institutional players like hedge funds as "smart money" and that of the general public as "dumb money." (Similarly, Vegas distinguishes between "public" money and "wise" money.)

The bottom line: you have to be smart about risk. *But you also have to be comfortable with the idea of SOME risk.* For some of you, that's a critical hurdle to get over. As one financial analyst puts it: "The preference for cash and aversion to the stock market among young adults is very troubling considering this age group has the biggest retirement savings burden. They won't get there without being willing to assume a little short-term risk in their long-term money."

A Note to Generation X

While this book is primarily directed at young investors just getting started in their careers, there's no reason to feel left out, Gen Xers. It's not like you're over the hill yet. And, in the current economic reality, people will need to keep working (and thus investing) later and later in life. You were also burned by the Great Recession of 2007-2009—and, in many cases (having already begun a family or purchased a house), you had more to lose. So you too may be wary of the stock market. Which makes my core principles – particularly my emphasis on aggressively managing risk, preventing emotional decisions, identifying and protecting against extreme behavior, and focusing on value – more timely than ever for you as well.

So, hang in there, and read on.

Generational Inequality

There are many ways to measure economic inequality. There is a difference between inequalities in *income* and inequalities in *wealth* or *net worth.* Somewhat surprisingly, these two forms of inequality don't always move in sync with one another. Depending on what's going on in the private sector and the housing and stock markets, wealth inequality can be growing even while income inequality is not. Of the two, the wealth gap seems to be the most important measure, because that's really the bottom line: in the end, how much are you worth. And whether you measure the difference between the top 1% and everyone else, or between the top 20% and the shrinking middle class, the wealth gap is growing.

So, that's one aspect of the wealth gap: the one between the classes, rich and poor, upper class and middle class, however you want to define it. But there's another aspect of the wealth gap that is starting to attract attention, and is indeed cause for some concern: that is **the wealth gap between the generations.** As Phillip Longman writes in "Wealth and Generations," a long examination of this problem in the *Washington Monthly*, "By focusing on the growing riches of the '1 percent,' we miss another form of inequality that is bigger, and arguably more dangerous."

Earlier in the chapter, I mentioned that one feature of the American Dream – the assumption that each generation would be more prosperous than the last – began slipping away with Generation X. In fact, the turning point came at about the middle of the Baby Boomer Generation: the year 1952, to be exact. In 1979, when those born after that year were in their twenties, their real income (that is, adjusted for inflation) was 20% lower than for twenty-somethings in 1969. A long-term reversal of the earlier pattern of generational progress had been set in motion, and was greatly accelerated during the Great Recession beginning in December of 2007. As a result, those born in 1955 (mid-wave Boomers) have 25% less real income and 40% less real wealth than those born in 1940 (the tail end of the Silent Generation). To measure it a different way: In 1989, the wealth of older families (62 years and up) was 7.6 times that of younger families (40 years or less). By 2013, that generational wealth gap had grown to 14.7 times. One final measure: In 2001, just under a fifth of the richest Americans (the so-called 1%) were 65-74 years of age; in 2013, that age group could claim nearly a third of the 1%.

THE LIFE-CYCLES OF WEALTH & INCOME

An important concept for financial planners, and one that becomes very relevant in our comparison of the financial wellbeing of the generations, is the natural financial cycle that most individuals and families go through over the course of their lives. **Income** tends to rise steeply during the twenties; grow at a slower but steady rate through the thirties and forties; plateau in the fifties; and then decline in the late fifties or early sixties.

Wealth, on the other hand, goes through a very different cycle. While younger families might see their incomes rise sharply in their twenties and thirties, they have fewer investment assets and higher expenses associated with raising a family and more debt. Thus, growth in wealth will lag behind growth in income, and won't usually peak until much later in life, in their sixties.

What stands out from a generational perspective is how those life cycles have changed in recent decades—and not for the better. As in the case of the wealth gap, a long-term trend that had been developing for years was aggravated and worsened by the Great Recession. Earnings are peaking earlier for each successive generation, and the apex or high point is declining. Whereas early Boomers (born 1946-1952) saw their earnings peak in their early fifties, mid-wave Boomers (1953-1957) peaked in their late forties. And for early Generation X, that peak came in 2007: the year the Recession hit, when they were in the 41-45 age range.

Impact of the Great Recession on the Millennial Generation

The dream that each generation would be better off than the one before has, as we have seen, been in slow but steady decline since that critical turning point of Boomers born after 1952. But it was the Great Recession (and the uneven recovery shortly after) that dealt a real body blow to Generation X Millennials, and greatly worsened economic inequality. And, as we look at the different ways the generations were affected by the Recession, we see more evidence of the point I touched on in the Introduction: that those with a deep and diversified investment portfolio and low debt are in a better position to absorb the blows of unexpected economic downturns.

Everybody was hit by the Great Recession, at least in the short term. But although the economy, including job prospects and wages, rebounded slowly during the recovery that followed, assets like stocks and housing bounced back more quickly. And the heart of the Silent Generation, those born between 1926 and 1935, came out in good shape: They experienced zero net loss during the Recession, and even as of 2010, when the recovery was just beginning, the net worth of older Americans was 53% higher than the same group in 1989.

For Baby Boomers, the timing wasn't great. Many were just approaching retirement age—not exactly the time you want to see your IRA or 401(k) drop in value. But for the majority of Boomers, their houses were paid for or mostly paid for, they could afford to wait for the market to bounce back, and their earnings dropped but not severely. In other words, they felt the pain, but it was manageable.

It was Generation X and Millennials who really got slammed by the Great Recession, although in different ways. For Gen Xers and early Millennials who had already purchased a home—but were at that early stage in a mortgage where debt is high and equity is low, and whose house was by far their largest asset—net worth dropped dramatically. Gen X lost 45% of its wealth in just a few years, and in 2010, those aged 25 to 49 (Gen X and the very first Millennials) had a net worth that was 32% less than that same group in 1989.

For later Millennials who had not yet bought a house and were perhaps just entering the job market or getting ready to graduate, their pain was different. The salaries of young workers are usually the most vulnerable during a recession, and that certainly was the case here: **while the average earnings loss for the general population was 12%, for Millennials it was 17%.** Second, younger Millennials experienced declining asset ownership during and after the Recession: they were more likely to put off buying a home (a significant tool for building long-term equity and wealth), less likely to start their own business, and less likely to invest in the stock market.

WHY HAVE GENERATIONAL FORTUNES BEEN IN DECLINE?

The reasons why older generations came out of the Great Recession in better shape are pretty straightforward: a deeper and more diversified investment portfolio and lower debt. But why late Boomers and younger generations had been losing economic ground even before the Recession is a little more complicated. We'll touch on some of these factors later, but here's a brief overview.

- *A Changing Economy* – With globalization and a competitive economy jarred by frequent "disruptions," it is harder for companies to maintain a long-term advantage and offer consistent employment and benefits. The lifetime financial security companies like General Electric used to provide is increasingly rare.

- *Social Security* – As late as the 1970s, retirees could expect to get more out of Social Security than they put in. Since then, the costs of the program have been increasing, putting the future benefits of the program in jeopardy.

- *Pensions* – For the first few decades after WWII, many companies offered generous pension plans, paid for entirely by the company. Now, while many companies offer a match for 401(k) plans, the responsibility and cost of retirement planning has shifted to employees.

- *Health Care* – With costs skyrocketing in recent decades, and employers passing on costs to workers in the form of co-pays and high-deductibles, a much larger chunk of the paycheck goes toward health care. In 1964, 78 hours of labor would pay for a typical family's annual health care expenses; in 2012, it required 452 hours. Note, however, that future costs will largely be determined by health care reform.

- *Student Loans* – The cost of a college education has skyrocketed as well, while subsidies in the form of scholarships and grants have gone down. In 1980, the average family paid only a third of the real cost of their children's education; in 2012 they paid half.

The Millennial (and Gen X) Disadvantage

I said at the beginning of the chapter that *time* was on your side, and I do believe that to be true. But your *timing,* on the other hand (while completely out of your control), hasn't been the greatest, and there's just no getting around that. And what makes the impact of the Great Recession even more devastating is that, in the preceding years, both Gen Xers and Millennials appeared to have a chance to reverse the slide in generational fortunes we've been discussing. While Gen Xers in their thirties and forties had a net worth that was slightly higher than that of late Baby Boomers, there was a catch: for many that wealth was measured at the height of the housing bubble. And in 2007, just before the Great Recession hit, older Millennials had incomes that were over 20% higher than those of preceding generations.

But there's no going back (at least for a while) to those rosy pre-recession days. The effects of the Recession are real and are likely to be long-term. Not only did Gen Xers lose 45% of their wealth—for many, their earnings peaked in their early forties (just as the Recession hit) and it remains to be seen whether they can get back to that level.

Older Millennials started out ahead of the game and finished behind. In 2001, their median wealth[2] was 134% that of previous generations. In 2013, it had dropped to 51%. "This means," as one study puts it in very plain language, "that the oldest Millennials – those entering what should be the prime

---

[2]   In any sample with huge extremes at either end, *statistical averages* can be misleading. This is certainly the case with "average" wealth, where large numbers at the top can distort the figures. So, the statistical *median* – a number right in the middle, where half of the sample is higher, and half is lower – is often a more meaningful figure.

of their working life and earning potential – **have on average amassed half the wealth of previous generations at the same age.**" It's going to take some time and effort for this group to catch up.

For younger Millennials who hadn't yet bought a house or were just entering the job market, the economic hit of the Great Recession was mainly in the area of earnings. That may also take some time to recover from. An economist at Yale University, Lisa Kahn, has found that recent college graduates entering the labor market during a major recession often experience lower earnings well into the future—even 14 to 23 years later.

So, that's the bad news, and I want to be straight with you about it. But the good news is you still have all that time I mentioned previously. Not only that, you have the tools, the temperament, and the habits to make up for a slow economic start.

"Encouragingly, Millennials seem to have learned some lessons from the Great Recession: they generally participate in retirement plans (when offered) at higher rates, tend to save at higher rates, and, generally, are financially more risk averse."

Some Closing Inspiration from the Oakland Athletics

I don't want to end the chapter on a sour note, so let's turn to America's pastime, baseball, for some wisdom and inspiration. For most of their history, the Oakland Athletics have operated at a severe disadvantage compared to their American League rivals like the Yankees and the Red Sox. Their total team payroll is often a fraction of those teams. And, for years, their performance lagged behind as well.

All that changed in 1997 when Billy Beane took over as the team's General Manager. Essentially, he took a disadvantage and turned it into an advantage. He couldn't afford the expensive free agents the Yankees and Red Sox were always fighting over, so he got smarter. He learned to underpay for underrated players rather than overpay for all stars. Michael Lewis (who not coincidentally has written a great deal about Wall Street as well) wrote a book about Beane and dubbed his smart and winning philosophy *"Money Ball."*

In the chapters ahead, I'm basically asking you, Millennials and Gen Xers, to adopt a Money Ball approach to investing and building wealth. The challenges are real – but so are the opportunities.

Chapter 2

A Nation of Investors

I n the next chapter (I promise) we'll start getting down to the nitty-gritty of investing and building long-wealth. But since we're taking a moment to look at the big picture, let's step back even further and examine how we went from a nation of savers to a nation of investors—and also at how both saving and investing have been threatened by the economic and financial turmoil of the previous decade.

Boom, Bust, Boom

The first half of the 20th century saw the American economy, along with the stock market, go through a classic boom-bust cycle—with high peaks, but also deep valleys. In 1914, World War I actually caused the New York Stock Exchange to shut down entirely for four months—the longest such shutdown in its history. The economy boomed in the post-war years, and the so-called Roaring Twenties were a time of high living, conspicuous consumption—and increasingly speculative investment on Wall Street, fueled by the growing practice of buying on credit, or margin. Even banks got into the game as "easy money" seemed impossible to resist.

But there is never, ever anything such as easy money. And in October of 1929, first on Black Thursday, then on Black Tuesday, it all came crashing down—first the stock market and, eventually, the entire economy. This of course was the beginning of the Great Depression, the longest sustained economic collapse in U.S. history. Thousands of banks closed, Gross Domestic Product plummeted, and unemployment soared.

The Depression did usher in a series of essential reforms to stabilize the U.S. financial system and prevent this kind of thing from ever happening again. In 1933 the Federal Deposit Insurance Corporation (or FDIC) was established to insure bank deposits. The following year, Congress passed the Securities and Exchange Act, establishing the Securities and Exchange Commission (SEC) to regulate the stock market, among other things. And the year after that, the Social Security Act created a social safety net, while the Banking Act strengthened the Federal Reserve System.

From Savings to Investing

Despite reforms enacted during the New Deal, Americans were slow to have their faith restored in banks, or Wall Street. You've probably heard about people stashing their money in a mattress—and in the years during and immediately following the Great Depression, that was literally quite true. My own grandmother, a self-described "depression baby," told me stories about living on bread and sardines during the thirties.

The frugal habits she developed during these years died slowly: decades later, her idea of splurging on a big gift for me was buying a U.S. Government Savings Bond that paid a whopping 3% interest.

It was only the belated American entry into World War II, and the incredible demand our intense involvement put on U.S. manufacturing, that finally jolted the national economy into high gear. And in high gear it stayed, nearly uninterrupted, for about a quarter of a century. As I mentioned in the Introduction, the prosperity of those post-war years was evenly shared, with all segments of the population experiencing a steady growth in income. Home ownership, increasingly seen as a cornerstone of the American Dream, soared during the 1950s.

A big step toward democratizing the stock market and helping us transform into a nation of investors came in 1974 with the enactment of the Employee Retirement Income Security Act (or ERISA). Among other provisions, the new law enabled the creation of several different varieties of Individual Retirement Accounts (or IRAs)—which allowed workers to contribute a certain amount of their annual income to a self-directed retirement plan, and write off the money against their taxes. Initially, the provision applied only to workers not eligible for an employment-based retirement plan. But in 1981 IRAs were opened to everyone.

Shortly thereafter, the SEC deregulated brokerage firm compensation—lowering fees for investors and increasing competition and choice. With declining interest rates, this more wide-open marketplace, along with the new IRA provisions, encouraged individual investors to explore and research the stock market on their own like never before. Low-cost brokerage firms like Charles Schwab began emerging. Through the eighties and nineties, a growing number of households and individuals moved away from strict reliance on conservative investments like CDs and government bonds, and into mutual funds and stocks.

The Bubble Bursts... Twice

Just as the Roaring Twenties came to a screeching halt with the stock market crash of 1929, the U.S. economy and financial markets have hit a couple of major speed bumps in the last two decades.

First, there was the bursting of the dot-com bubble in early 2000—which followed several giddy years when everyone and his brother seemed to be creating a new company and then cashing in a few years later for millions. Investors were banking on the promise that the Internet would utterly transform the economy and, for a while, things certainly seemed to be moving quickly. The first easy-to-use web browser was introduced in 1993, Amazon was founded the following year, then Yahoo. In 1998, Google. In January 2000, less than two months before the bubble burst, seventeen different dot-com companies took out expensive ads during the Super Bowl. Much of the investing frenzy took place on the tech-heavy NASDAQ[1] —which ballooned in value from 500 in 1990, to 1,000 in 1995, and peaked at 5,000 in March of 2000. By December 2000, the exchange had lost more than half its value. The Dow Jones Index of Internet Stocks fared even worse, losing 76%.

---

[1] The NASDAQ (short for the National Association of Securities Dealers and Automated Quotations) is an alternative to the New York Stock Exchange (NYSE). Founded in 1971, it is younger, and a purely electronic exchange.

Less than ten years later came the financial crisis of 2007-2009 (aka the Great Recession)—which started with the collapse of the sub-prime mortgage market, and then spread to take down financial giants like Bear Stearns and Lehman Brothers. In a sense, one bubble was building up just as another was bursting. Even as stocks plunged in 2000, housing prices were on the rise, easing and in some cases more than compensating for losses in the stock market. It was the rapid expansion of credit generated by surging home values that, in the eyes of many experts, fueled a renewed buying frenzy on Wall Street. The housing bubble began to deflate in 2007, and after hitting an all-time high of over 14,000 that summer, stocks (as reflected in the Dow Jones Industrial Average) also began to suffer. The market was down over 40% in 2008, bottoming out in March of 2009. What began as a financial crisis became a full-blown recession, with over 3 million jobs lost in 2008, and over 5 million in 2009, when the unemployment rate peaked at 10%. The entire global economy was eventually swept up in the downturn. Then Federal Reserve chairman Ben Bernanke called it "the worst financial crisis in global history, including the Great Depression."

Some people (including my grandmother) might disagree with that assessment. But it's indisputable that the Great Recession (as it came to be known) that followed, sent shockwaves through the U.S. and world economies, and that we're still reeling from those shockwaves.

Lessons from "The Lost Decade"

Just a few years after the Crash of 1929, economist Benjamin Graham wrote *Security Analysis*, a clear-eyed (if academic) assessment of the lessons to be learned from the boom and bust of the previous decade. His analysis was later refashioned for the general reader in his classic book *The Intelligent Investor,* which established him as the father of what came to be known as "value investing" and which famously attracted the attention of an aspiring investor named Warren Buffett.

Frank Martin is a fan of both Graham and Buffett, and draws on their insights repeatedly in his book A *Decade of Delusions,* his review of what investment professionals now refer to as "the lost decade"—a 10-year stretch when, after all was said and done, the stock market pretty much stood still. Because we are still dealing with the consequences of the two bubbles that burst during that decade, and because they have so much bearing on the challenges that Millennials now face in building long-term wealth, we will return to the lessons of those years throughout the book. Here are some of the highlights of the observations of Martin, Buffett and other reputable financial writers.

- **The stock market seems to move in roughly 17-year cycles.** There is nothing scientific or preordained about this pattern: let's be perfectly clear about that. But in a 1999 address to his Berkshire Hathaway shareholders, Warren Buffett (normally wary of making pronouncements on long-term trends in the market) devoted a good deal of time to these cycles, and so it's worth looking at. He noted that in the closing 34 years of the 20th century there was "an almost Biblical symmetry" between 17 "lean" (or bearish) years, followed by 17 "fat" (or bullish) ones. From 1964 to 1981, the Dow Jones advanced less than a single point, from 874.12 to 875. During the following 17 years, 1982 to 1999, it grew nearly ten-fold, closing at 9,181: the most impressive long-term bull market in history. That was followed, in turn, by the Lost Decade, 10 or so very bearish years. The market has rebounded nicely since then; but some contend we are still in a long-term bear market (there are rallies in long-term bear markets, and dips in long-term bull markets), and only the hindsight of history will tell us for sure. What we do know is that Buffett and other contrarian investors believe that bear and bull markets call for very different strategies. More on that in future chapters.

- **Survival is the wise investor's first priority.** This is a major theme of this book, and Buffett and other investors whose strategy has stood the test of time all agree on this point. As Buffett put it in 2006 (six years after one burst bubble, and one year before another): "A single, big mistake could wipe out a long string of successes." Or as Peter Bernstein, a lifelong student of risk and ruin, writes: "Survival is the only road to riches." Consequently, Buffett, Frank Martin, and other value investors were skeptical about the Internet hype even before the bubble burst; limited their exposure through large cash reserves; and were reluctant to join the buying frenzy when stocks again took off a few years later. They at times passed up what seemed like easy money, because they were in it for the long haul. "Sometimes it's not how much you gain in the good markets but how much you don't lose in the ugly ones that separates the winners from the wannabes," Martin writes in *A Decade* *of Delusion.* "The Lost Decade was a case study in the trade-offs necessary to win by not losing."

- There were warning signs. Dozens of books and hundreds of articles have been written about both bubble/busts, but a number of things stand out:

  1) **Investors were becoming less patient** and the industry was moving away from traditional "buy and hold" strategies. Stock turnover shot up from 46% in 1990 to 76% in 1999, and was three times as high on the NASDAQ. At the end of the decade, the average share of Amazon was being held for only 7 days. Day trading was in vogue.

  2) **IPOs (Initial Public Offerings)[2] were all the rage,** the hype and speculation around tech companies incentivized private tech companies to cash out big-time – a clear sign of a bubble. From a record 543 IPOs in 1999, the number dropped to 79 in 2003, only to shoot up again to 233 in 2004.

  3) **The dot-com rally was narrow,** and not broadly based. Tech stocks were behind 90% of the surge in the S&P 500, and more than half of all stocks experienced stagnant growth during this rally.

  4) **Accounting and financing tricks** were abundant. In the rush to keep pace with the Joneses, corporate and mutual fund managers engaged in various smoke-and-mirror accounting practices to pump up

---

[2] One of the most effective (and profitable) ways for a company to raise money is by issuing stock. When a company issues stock, it hires an investment banker to split up its equity into identical pieces called shares. *Shares* of stock are sold to public investors in what is known as an *initial public offering,* or IPO. Proceeds from the offering are used to invest in and grow the business.

and "smooth out" earnings so as not to lose investors to the competition. In 2003, the SEC (Securities & Exchanges Commission) reached a $1.4 billion settlement with ten Wall Street firms for "fiduciary misconduct" during the dot-com bubble. Similarly, increasingly complicated (and flimsy) real-estate financing (and re-financing) blew a lot of hot air into the later bubble.

5) During both bubbles, the stock market **was widely acknowledged to be overvalued**—but only a few contrarians had the courage and foresight to get off the runaway train. Frank Martin notes that behind the greed that fuels every bubble is a kind of fear: the "fear of falling behind the pack." During periods of "rampant speculative contagion," it is difficult to ignore the "rallying cry that everyone jump aboard the bandwagon or look like a fool." One key measure of this overvaluation (which we'll look at in depth later when we discuss value investing) is the market's overall **price-to-earnings ratio**—which peaked at an historic high of 44 in late 1999[3].

- **People have short memories.** In other words, one last lesson to take from the Lost Decade is that people often fail to learn the lessons of history. Investors tend to project only the very recent past (good or bad) into the future and lose sight of the long view. Warren Buffett calls this the "rearview mirror" mode of investing. In the 1999 address I quoted from earlier, he argued that the majority of investors were being swept up by an

---

[3] The P/E ratio of the NASDAQ, which closely tracks the technology sector, peaked at 175 in the year 2000.

"unsupportable optimism." He cited a recent poll showing that the least experienced investors were anticipating a 22.6% annual return in coming years—and even the most experienced were expecting a 12.9% return. They couldn't accept that the 17-year bull market just then coming to a close was the exception, and not the rule. In 2003, the market was heating up again, but Buffett was skeptical and maintained a conservative portfolio. In early 2007, fellow contrarian and value investor Mark Faber sounded the alarm: "In a selling panic you should buy, but in the buying mania that we have now... it's time to sell." All too few listened.

ORIGIN OF THE TERMS 'BULL' AND 'BEAR'

In fact, there is no consensus as to why hot markets with rising prices are called bulls, and cold markets with falling prices are called bears. Some theories point to the contrasting ways the two animals attack an enemy: bulls thrusting up with their horns; bulls swiping down with their paws. Others believe it is to do with how the two animals move: bulls are aggressive, charging animals; while bears are said to be more sluggish. (Yet bears like grizzlies can outrun a horse—so don't sleep on a bear!)

The most probable theory has to do with middlemen who bought bearskins from trappers and then sold them to traders. If they anticipated a price drop, they would sell the skins to traders at higher prices even before they'd purchased them: an early version of The Big Short.

The 'Charging Bull' is a three-and-a-half ton bronze sculpture in Manhattan's Financial District. The artist who created it, Arturo di Marco, installed it in under a Christmas tree in front of the New York Stock Exchange in late 1989, without the City's permission. It was soon impounded, but because it was an instant hit with the public, it was later installed a few blocks south of the Exchange, where it still stands today.

Money in Mattresses... Again?

One way we haven't yet recovered from the Lost Decade is reflected in our habits of saving and investing. In every year between 1998 and 2008 (with one exception) the percentage of Americans invested in the stock market was over 60%--peaking in 2007 at 65%. Since then, the number has dropped sharply, and stayed there. Despite a strong market rally over the last few years, the latest survey finds that only 48% of American adults have money in stocks.

As discussed in the previous chapter, Millennials tend to put investable assets into savings as opposed to stocks at a 2 to 1 ratio: the exact opposite of previous generations. The decline in stock ownership rates has been especially notable among Millennials. In 2001, 48% of young people between the age of 18 and 31 were invested in the market; **as of 2013, that number was only 37%.**

Moreover, a survey by American Express in 2015 found that Millennials have actually resorted to stashing savings in "secret locations" around the house as opposed to an actual savings account – just like people did in the thirties.

The Cost of Cash

Some pundits treat Millennials' preference for cash as an entirely negative trait but it's not. Contrarian investors like Warren Buffett often adopt a conservative wait-and-see approach during bear markets, or when they feel the market is overvalued. At such times they're willing to sit on more cash (or cash equivalents)[4] than conventional wisdom might dictate. As Buffett said in that same 1999 address: "Cash never makes us happy. But it's better to have the money burning a hole in Berkshire's pocket than resting comfortably in someone else's." (We'll get into the role cash should play in your portfolio in later chapters).

Yet there's no getting around the fact that there is a cost to cash. In a sense a dollar not invested is a dollar taxed. It's not a tax that is paid to the U.S. government. It's rather value that simply vanishes into thin air, due to **inflation**, and it is one of the biggest threats to Millennials in their quest to build long-term wealth.

Inflation is the rise in the price of goods and services, as measured by the Consumer Price Index, or CPI. Historically, the CPI has grown around 3% per year, which may not seem like a lot. But over time this 3% slowly but surely eats away at the "real" value or purchasing power of any asset. And it's a particular threat to cash or cash-like assets at a time when interest rates have, for almost a decade, been at historic lows. For example, 30 years into the future at the historic inflation rate, $100,000 held in a savings account will only be worth a little more than $40,000 in today's dollars. If inflation were to rise to 7% (which is possible, though unlikely), that real purchasing power would drop to $17,000 in today's dollars. **The longer your time horizon, the bigger the threat inflation poses.**

---

[4] In investing parlance, the term *cash equivalents* is used to describe not just cash sitting in a standard savings account but similarly liquid and low-risk assets like certificates of deposit, money market funds, and short-term Treasury bills.

The Stock Market Protects Against Inflation In the Long Run

Later on I will explain how investors in stocks expect to be compensated for taking on extra risk with what is known as a risk premium. Simply put, the risk *premium* is the rate of return over and above the current risk-free rate offered by government-backed Treasury bills. Historically, this risk premium has been large enough to substantially outpace inflation, allowing investors in the market to both preserve and accumulate wealth. Bonds, on the other hand, have historically offered investors a lower risk premium than stocks, which makes sense due to their inherently less risky cash flows. Over some periods, the returns on risk-free bonds have outpaced inflation but over other periods they have not. For example, from 1926 to 1980, the return on *short-term* government bonds called "Treasury bills" returned less than inflation after taxes. But by taking a little more risk and investing in *long-term* government bonds (Treasury bonds), long-term investors were able to preserve their wealth over the long-run, albeit barely.

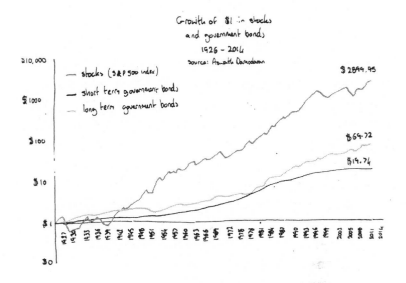

Figure D – For Illustration Purposes Only

Since stocks represent ownership in a company, it isn't an asset class that is especially vulnerable to inflation. If costs of raw materials increase, companies raise prices, often maintaining their projected profit growth (although this may not be the case if prices rise too quickly). Bonds, on the other hand, represent loans. Bond owners receives fixed coupon payments over a stated period of time. If prices rise, those payments will have less purchasing power. Bonds are an important tool in diversifying and reducing risk, but they will not protect you from inflation in the way that stocks will.

Don't Count On the Government (Or Your Employer) To Be There For You

More than any previous generation since the Great Depression, Millennials need to ensure long-term financial stability by building wealth through investments. In the beginning of this chapter, we looked back at the Great Depression and at how the federal government responded on a couple of fronts. First, through a series of reforms designed to bring stability and accountability to our financial system in general, and to the stock market specifically. Second, by setting up a social safety net that would protect people during tough economic times. The first set of reforms has functioned pretty well, and continues to do so. The second has had limited success.

On the one hand, we do have a network of programs in place to provide the most vulnerable members of our population with basic needs in the event of either individual or societal downturns. On the other hand, it is increasingly clear that the two programs designed to keep the middle class financially secure and healthy – Social Security and Medicare – are not sustainable. The long-term math just doesn't work.

When we get a paycheck, we all have a set percentage of our salary deducted for Social Security (6.2% of the first $118,500 of income, an amount matched by the employer) and Medicare (1.45%). The system is viable only if the money coming in as taxes or contributions keeps pace with the money going out in benefits. For a while, the math worked. As of the late 1970s, retirees could expect to receive more in benefits than they had contributed.

But, for a variety of reasons, the numbers have flipped. And as the massive Baby Boom generation retires, and as our population ages as a result of both demographic shifts and longer life expectancy, the math will get worse. According to the 2014 Social Security Trustees Report: "The annual cash-flow deficit will average about $77 billion between 2014 and 2018 and after, the deficit will rise as the number of beneficiaries (claimants) is projected to grow at a substantially faster rate than the number of taxpaying workers."

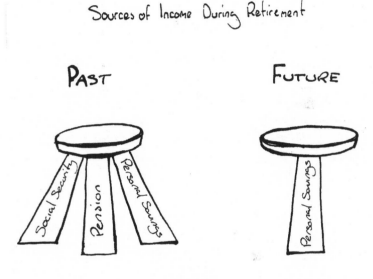

Figure E

The promise of a comfortable retirement used to rest on a three-legged stool: the safety net provided by Social Security and Medicare, the pension plan provided by your employer, and your own personal savings. As we'll examine in more depth in a later chapter, the pension plans (and gold watches) of an earlier era are vanishing. The so-called *defined benefit plans* of old (funded and managed entirely by the employer) have, for the last several decades, been phased out and replaced by *defined contribution plans* in which the financial burden and the decision-making is largely passed on to you, the employee.

So in the new realities of the 21st century, that stool has grown a bit wobbly. Fortifying it, and stabilizing your future, is your responsibility—and helping you do so is the ultimate objective of this book.

Investing in Your Future

As we've seen, anxiety about the present and future is real and rooted in actual events that have taken a toll on us as individuals and as a society. But this is the hand that's been dealt to us. We have to plan and prepare for the worst and make smart decisions based on reality, not fear. In the parlance of Las Vegas, we have to be on the "wise" side of the ledger, not the "dumb" side.

And what do the odds tell us?

- Wealth inequality is only going to worsen in coming years.

- Government programs like Social Security and Medicare are increasingly unsustainable and may not be there to catch you when you fall.

- The era of working for one company your whole career, and then collecting your gold watch and pension, is long over.

- Future inflation is uncertain. The government's recent quantitative easing program has pumped money into the economy. Eventually, an increase in money supply might lead to higher than expected inflation.

- The cost of real estate has bounced back since the global financial crisis. Low interest rates and international demand for populated locations are keeping prices inflated. Higher prices are preventing many Millennials from becoming homeowners.

In the well-known Serenity Prayer, the worshipper asks for the serenity to accept what cannot be changed and the courage to change what can be. Some of the seismic shifts you can't change. What you can change, what you can control, is how you invest in your future. In spite of the recent dip, investing in the stock market—in a deliberate, strategic manner—is one of the best ways to generate long-term wealth and take control of your financial future. So, in spite of the setbacks of the Lost Decade, it's time to get back to being both a nation of savers and a nation of investors.

Chapter 3

No Time Like the Present

So you've been wary about investing in the stock market and the concept of accumulating wealth hasn't been high on your list of priorities. Or maybe you were in the market for a while and pulled back during the recession, and have been reluctant to get back in. Or maybe, like a number of Millennials, you do set aside a certain part of your savings for retirement and other long-term goals—but not the 10%-15% of your income most financial experts recommend. I hope you can see that others are in the same boat, and that you have some understanding of why, and of how these things tend to go in cycles, just like the economy. The good news is that you're coming to these realizations and reading this book at an ideal time. There are some smart and well-financed entrepreneurs who are betting on the fact that the American people, Millennials especially, are getting ready to jump back into the market—but on their own terms, and in their own style.

Investing in the 21st Century

The financial world is complex. There are a lot of investing options out there, and those options are growing by the day. Since some of you may be relatively new to investing or have not been up to date on current trends, now is a good time to do a brief survey of the relevant topics within the investing landscape, and how it's changing.

- **Understanding Asset Classes** – There are several broad categories of investments. Within each category there is a good deal of variation, but also certain common characteristics and tendencies. The main ones are: 1) *stocks*, also referred to as *equities;* 2) *bonds* and *other fixed-income securities,* where you are essentially loaning money to the issuer (usually the government or a corporation) in return for regular interest payments; 3) *real estate* and other *commodities,* where you own or have a stake in an actual property or physical good; 4) *cash* and *cash equivalents* (like money-market funds) that are usually liquid and virtually risk-free, but pay very low interest. Each of these broad categories tends to behave differently under different market or economic conditions[1]. For example, stocks tend to perform well when the market is up, while bonds tend to do better when the market is down. For this reason, a basic understanding of asset classes will figure into our later discussion of *diversification* (the principle of "don't have all your eggs in one basket").

---

[1] The tendency of various asset classes to move in different directions is called *negative correlation*, and is a key part of the rationale for a diversified portfolio. In recent years, however, that negative correlation has faded and even disappeared at times—a development we will address later in Chapter 6.

- **Mutual Funds** – The principle behind mutual funds is simple: for a single lump-sum investment, you can own a piece of dozens or even hundreds of assets. It is thus a means of pooling investment money and spreading risk. Mutual funds have been around for a while, but the modern era of mutual funds, when they became a key option for the average investor, dates back to the early 1970s. Mutual funds really came into prominence during the extended bull market of 1982-1999, when their handsome returns convinced a growing number of Americans to make them the cornerstone of their retirement planning. Mutual funds can be devoted to stocks, or fixed-income securities, or cash equivalents, or a mix (so-called "balanced" or "hybrid" funds). Most mutual funds have a distinct investment philosophy. In general, they fall into one of two camps: *actively managed* funds attempt to beat or outperform the market; *passively managed* or *index* funds seek only to mirror the market as a whole, or a particular segment (or index) of that market. In recent years, the disappointing performance of many active mutual funds has become a hot topic, something we'll dive into in future chapter.

- **The Rise of Exchange Traded Funds (ETFs)** – ETFs are a relatively new innovation that has exhibited tremendous popularity over the past decade. And while some group them with mutual funds, their very distinct set-up warrants a separate category. They are in a sense designed to be an alternative to index funds, and as such the majority are passively managed. But ETFs – unlike mutual funds, which have to be purchased through an intermediary – trade on an exchange, and thus can be bought and sold directly. Without going into the mechanics of why, this lowers operating costs and brings certain tax advantages. These qualities, and their flexibility, make them an attractive option; but there are also some downsides we'll get into later.

- **The Changing World of Financial Advice** – For most of the 20th century, investors who wanted to invest in the stock market did so through so-called *full-service brokerages*: firms that evaluated individual stocks, made recommendations for clients, handled their transactions, and helped manage their portfolios. As a result of high commissions, uneven performance, and increased competition from discount brokers, the industry is moving away from the old commission model and toward fee-based services[2]. Technology continues to transform financial services, and one of the newest developments is he emergence of so-called *robo-advisors*: companies that use Google-like algorithms to suggest and manage investment portfolios based on a client's stated goals, risk tolerance, and other preferences. Robo-advisors are part of a wave of new products and services designed to channel that distrust and provide Millennials with financial services more in keeping with their style and philosophy. The emphasis is on customization, intuitive interfaces that work across various mobile devices, and 24/7 access and information.

Currently, robo-advisors manage less than 1% of Americans' investment assets. But a recent report predicts that by 2020, that percentage could grow to over 5%. "Robo-

---

[2] Commissions, because they are based on the sale of a particular product, can create a conflict of interest, or an incentive to make unnecessary trades. Fees (which come in various forms) ensure that the financial advice is independent of the particular investment that is recommended.

advisory services will become mainstream over the next three to five years," the report concludes. And a number of venture capitalists are betting on that: in just the last few years alone, over $3 billion has been invested in this new breed of financial services, revolutionizing the financial technology sector (or "fintech" as people now like to call it). Whether or not robo-advisors take off remains to be seen. Like any new business model, the potential is still largely unknown. There are downsides to removing the human element. As one New York Times writer advises, "For investors contemplating robo-advisors, perhaps the most important point is to fully understand their limits."

But regardless of whether robo-advisors continue to gain in popularity, **there's no question that the landscape of financial and investment services is evolving rapidly; and in the end that's a good thing for you, the consumer.** The range of options, and thus the competition for your business, will only grow as the new breed of companies supplement automated advice with old-fashioned personal counseling, and as traditional companies add automated services to their mix. In a sense, all this innovation is one of the many long-term consequences of the Great Recession: which exposed the inefficiencies and questionable practices of traditional banks and opened up the door for the current new wave of services.

Finance at Your Fingertips

Yes, Millennials do have a style all their own. But each individual also has his or her own investment style, or personality, as well—something we'll cover more in a later chapter. As I stated earlier, there is no such thing as good "one size fits all" investment strategy. Your individual style will stem from your personality (are you comfortable taking risk? are you a self-starter who likes doing your own research?) and also from your life goals, and the timeline for those goals. The investment needs of a single person are very different from those of a young couple saving to buy a house in the short-term, to fund their children's education down the road, and for their own retirement even further down the road. Money can seem like a cold and impersonal thing, but in fact, your finances are an extremely personal and individual matter, and require a unique and customized approach.

For just that reason, there's certainly something to be said for having a financial advisor. Advisors can walk you through the steps of building and preserving wealth, and some people can sleep better knowing they've got some expertise to fall back on. Most important, perhaps, financial advisors help protect people from their own worst enemy: themselves.[3]

On the other hand, steering your own investments provides a unique mix of competitive and intellectual stimulation. Again, investing is a personal and highly individual matter. But regardless of which route you go, or whether you choose a mix of the two, you will have access to knowledge like never before. A quick Google search can unearth information that previously required days of research. Beyond that, you can follow your company's CEOs on Twitter, read up on what it's like to work at a company on *Glassdoor*, ask experts questions for free on *Quora*, pull up a company's SEC filings on the *EDGAR database*, and effect trades online in a matter of seconds. Most

---

[3] In a later chapter about human nature, we'll discuss the exciting new field of *behavioral economics*.

of you reading this book have grown up as children of the new "information economy." You are as comfortable navigating it as you are navigating a car. You understand that information, *customized information*, is power, and expect to have it at your fingertips. It is part of your Millennial Advantage as investors.

For those who want to take direct control of their own investing, *discount brokers* provide cost-effective access to the stock market. Discount brokers have been around since the seventies, but the Internet has drastically altered the way these firms do business. Before the millennium, discount brokers primarily took orders by telephone. Today brokers do most of their business online. Discount brokerages don't recommend investments; they just provide an online platform for you to buy and sell what you want. In addition to implementing transactions, discount brokerages will help you manage your money by providing monthly statements, all the necessary tax documents, real-time data, research tools, and, finally, cash management plus debit and credit card services. Over the years, increased competition has pushed these firms to offer a larger variety of services at even lower costs.

The financial magazine *Barron's* publishes a very useful annual ranking of online brokerages. In addition to an overall ranking, they also rate services according to various other criteria—i.e., Best for Novices, Best for In-Person Service, etc. I'll say it again: Investing is an extremely individual matter, so do your research and find out what service is best suited to you.

In part to cater to information-hungry and tech-savvy Millennials, most of the brokerages listed by *Barron's* now routinely offer a range of online research tools to their clients, as well as educational services like free webinars. In addition to these tools, reputable sites like *Morningstar* can also be used to research financial services, mutual funds, and individual stocks.

The Qualities of Successful Investors

Whether you make use of a discount brokerage, a sleek new financial app or lean on the advice of a financial advisor, you have more freedom to research and explore the stock market than ever before. **But none of that guarantees good results.** As I've stated before, and it's a point worth repeating, investing is in some ways a so-called "loser's game" in which **the first key to winning is to avoid big mistakes.** Especially when the stock market is hot, individual investors all too often fool themselves into thinking they are smarter than they really are. They become infatuated with the latest trend, or with a "hot" investment tip and become convinced they can "beat" the market. Beating or outperforming the market is possible, and later we'll explore ways that investors have historically been able to do so. But it's difficult, and any attempt to do it should be approached with caution and humility.

This note of caution applies to professional investors as well—**many of whom not only fail to beat the market, but who under perform the market, sometimes by a good deal.** Yes, you heard me correctly. The investments of actively managed mutual funds, for example, are overseen by professional portfolio managers who closely monitor their funds and have access to the best available research. In any given year, many of these funds will successfully beat the market, and it is on that basis that they sell themselves to investors. Yet over a given 10-year stretch, most actively managed stock funds will fail to outperform their relative benchmark (the standard or average achieved by similar funds). A recent Standard and Poor's study found that zero out of 2,862 managed mutual funds consistently fell into the top quartile (or 25%) of performers from 2009-2016. This study, among others, has played a role in the current trend of investors leaving managed mutual funds for cheaper, more passively managed index funds.

The lesson I want you to take away from this is two-fold. First, even professionals, who devote their lives to investing and have access to the best information available, often fail. This basic fact is easy to lose sight of when the market is hot and everyone seems to be making money. It was said of the '82-'99 bull market that you could throw a dart at an investment board and probably pick a winner, and that isn't far from the truth. But success in the long term is a trickier affair, as the ups and downs of the last decade have shown. Second, and somewhat surprisingly, **individual investors have certain advantage over fund managers.** For reasons we'll explore later, these managers become locked into investment strategies that prevent them from adapting to changing circumstances and also encourage them to follow a dangerous "herd mentality."

So, given that investing is such a tricky affair, what, you might ask, makes for a successful investor? If you scan through the studies on past performance, and also glean the advice of superstar investors like Warren Buffett, you will find four major traits common to the successful individual investor:

1. They started investing early in life.

2. They minimized their tax burden.

3. They refrained from short-term speculation and held their investments for a long time, not unloading positions when the markets were near its bottom.

4. They invested in quality companies that were trading at reasonable prices and were conscious of the cost of professional management, often purchasing low-cost investment funds.

And the good news is that Millennial investors – with the chance to begin early, with their skepticism and cost-savvy habits, and their ability to research and form independent opinions – are in a perfect position to excel at all four.

Compound Returns

Excelling at the four essential traits of the successful investor is a question of consistent habits, sustained over a long period of time. And the test of time, and the power of time, is, it turns out, the key to just about every aspect of investing.

Let's look at why starting early is such a powerful thing over the long term. Albert Einstein (who knew a little something about numbers) famously said, "Compound interest is the eighth wonder of the world. He who understands it, earns it… he who doesn't… pays it."

When earnings from an investment (whether it's a bank account, a bond, or a stock) are reinvested and added to the principal or initial investment, and go on to generate their own earnings, even a modest rate of return compounds over time, creating a powerful, exponential snowball effect.

The size of the snowball is based on two things: time and rate of return. Let's look at a few examples.

If, at the age of 25, you put $10,000 into an investment earning 6% per year, you would, without investing an extra dime, have a little more than $100,000 by the time you turn 65. But time is money, so what happens if you put off making that investment for 10 years, and did so instead at the age of 35? That same $10,000 investment would only be worth about $57,000 when you turn 65. The gains over a 40-year period are nearly twice as great as over the 30-year period because the effect of compounding becomes exponentially more powerful as time goes on. You can see the effect in "Figure F."

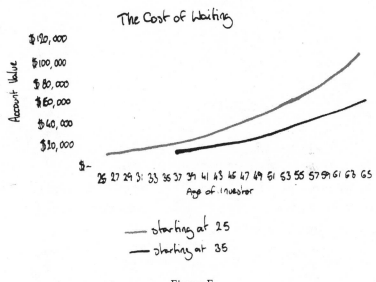

Figure F

The previous example was based on an investor holding a portfolio split 50/50 between stocks and bonds, and earning a consistent annual rate of return of 6%. Yet historically, the average return on the S&P 500 (i.e., a representative stock portfolio) has been a little over 9.5%. So if over that same forty-year period you had invested that same $10,000 in stocks and stock-based funds whose performance kept pace with the S&P 500, you would have more than $375,000 by the time you turn 65 (much more than the return of a 50/50 portfolio).

It's important to note that these examples are for the purpose of illustration only, and are based on historical data. As any investment advertisement will tell you: **Past performance is not necessarily indicative of future results.** The short-term and long-term fluctuations of both the market and the economy make it impossible to project into the future with any accuracy. Yet I hope you can see how, because of the phenomenon of compound returns, even a modest annual yield, if consistent, can have a tremendous impact over time.

Compound Habits

The same power of consistency over time applies to the habit of saving and investing. Try this mental exercise as a case in point: If you were given a choice between taking $3 million in cash today or a single penny that doubled each day for 31 days, which would you choose? For most people who haven't heard this before, the choice seems obvious: they would take the $3 million. It turns out, however, that taking the penny is the better choice. And, as with compound returns, the key is taking what seems like a small change and extending that change over time.

Let's say you take the cash and your friend takes the pennies. On the 5th day, your friend will have $.016 and you will have $3 million. On the 10th day, your friend will have

$5.12 and you will have $3 million. And, on the 20th day, your friend will have $5,243 and you will have $3 million. But, come day 30, your friend will have $5.3 million and on day 31, he will have $10.7 million.

Day 1	$ .01	Day 16	$ 327.68
Day 2	$ .02	Day 17	$ 655.36
Day 3	$ .04	Day 18	$ 1,310.72
Day 4	$ .08	Day 19	$ 2,621.44
Day 5	$ .16	Day 20	$ 5,242.88
Day 6	$ .32	Day 21	$ 10,485.76
Day 7	$ .64	Day 22	$ 20,971.52
Day 8	$ 1.28	Day 23	$ 41,943.04
Day 9	$ 2.56	Day 24	$ 83,886.08
Day 10	$ 5.12	Day 25	$ 167,772.16
Day 11	$ 10.24	Day 26	$ 335,544.32
Day 12	$ 20.48	Day 27	$ 671,088.64
Day 13	$ 40.96	Day 28	$ 1,342,177.28
Day 14	$ 81.92	Day 29	$ 2,684,354.56
Day 15	$ 163.84	Day 30	$ 5,368,709.12
		Day 31	$ 10,737,418.24

Figure G

Obviously, doubling your money each day isn't realistic. But it drives home the power of basic financial arithmetic over time.

Let's look at the more modest example of instance of a 26-year-old who commits to set aside $100 every month for her retirement. That's a good start. But let's say she decides to skip a single restaurant lunch costing $33 each month and adds that to the previous $100. Fast forward to age 67, and that monthly skipped lunch has become $330 a month in retirement income: $4,000 a year, and more than $99,000 over a 25-year retirement.

I'm not suggesting that you deprive yourself of life's pleasures. I am simply making a point that your decisions today (and even more so, the habits you develop) can make or break your future. Cutting costs, in many ways can be just as (if not more) effective as actively trying for investment gains. It should be your goal to focus on both!

When Now *Isn't* the Time

Clearly, there's no time like the present to put in place the financial habits that will pay off in the long run: saving money, paying down debt, and investing some of that savings for retirement and other long-term goals. But exactly what that investment should look like isn't a simple or obvious matter. Some books and articles about investing adopt a certain sunny optimism about the stock market. They point out how much, say, $10,000 invested on the first day of 1970 would be worth on the first day of the year 2000. That's all very well and good—but it doesn't take into account that in real life, the exact timing of your *investment horizon* (i.e., when you put the money in, and when you're going to need it) is crucial.

For example, if you had paid attention to the optimists at the end of 1999 and invested your $10,000, anticipating a 15% annual return and counting on that money for your child's education 10 years later, you would have been sorely disappointed when you checked your account in 2009. While I strongly believe that stocks are the most powerful tool for building wealth in the long run, timing is critical. You would have been better off with an all-bond portfolio during the "lost decade." In fact, even cash outperformed stocks during that period.

As we'll explore later, bull markets and bear markets demand different investment strategies. It's usually not a good idea to try to outsmart the market by timing its short-term ups and downs. But it is a good idea to take the general pulse of the market.

The market, you see, is a powerful tool, but also a tricky one that should be approached with a certain degree of caution. So let's take a closer look at the market, and at different theories about why it behaves the way it does.

Chapter 4

The Market and You

Now that we're ready to start delving into the details of investing and building long-term wealth, it's time to take a look at this thing we call "the market." The term itself has several different levels of meaning. As an abstract idea, it simply refers to any medium that allows buyers and sellers to engage in transactions for goods and services. It can be a physical place, like the corner grocery or the New York Stock Exchange; or more of an aggregate, like the housing market. The term also relates to the overall economic philosophy of a country like the United States which, because it operates according to modified free market principles of supply and demand, is categorized as a "market economy." Finally, the term is often used as shorthand for the stock market, a very specific market designed for the buying and selling of equity securities.

In this book, "the market" mostly means the stock market. But, even here, there is a range of meaning. In general, we'll be referring to the U.S. stock market as a whole – but remember that this aggregate market is composed of many individual markets known as exchanges. The two largest being the New

York Stock Exchange, which is a physical place; and the NASDAQ, which is not. And although the market as a whole displays certain broad characteristics, each of these exchanges has its own personality.

There are two general schools of thought about how and why the market behaves the way it does. And from these two schools of thought come two very different approaches to investing.

Just How Rational Is The Market?

The short answer: some say very rational; others say, not so much.

The foundation of the rational school is the Efficient Market Hypothesis, or EMH, largely credited to Nobel Prize-winning economist Eugene Fama. Fama was part of a new generation of economists who helped establish finance as a legitimate academic pursuit, and who developed theoretical models about the market that would greatly influence the practice of investing. For his contributions, Fama is often referred to as the "Father of Finance."

His central argument, that the market is "informationally efficient," means that the price of a stock (or any other investment asset) incorporates all relevant and available information, and thus will accurately reflect its true or intrinsic value.

This claim of market efficiency rests on four assumptions:

- **Number of Rational Participants:** Participants are mostly rational, and the more such investors there are, the more efficient a market is.

- **Availability of Information:** Essential information is widely available and easily accessible.

- **Impediments to Trading:** There are few trading restrictions, which allows profit-seeking investors to quickly pursue and close profitable opportunities.

- **Transaction and Information Costs:** Transaction costs are low, which drive price to better reflect fundamentals.

According to this theory, short-term fluctuations of a stock's *price* above or below its intrinsic value will be random and unpredictable. Changes in a stock's intrinsic *value* are also random and unpredictable because they will be based on future developments and new information that are impossible to anticipate. In a 1965 article, Fama described what he called the "random walk" behavior of stock prices (the analogy of a drunkard's "random walk" had already been used in probability theory and a number of other fields).

The upshot for the investor? **If the Efficient Market Hypothesis is true, then consistently outperforming the market is extremely unlikely and, in the long run, nearly impossible.**

Why? For active investors, the market is a "zero-sum" game. In any given trade, the seller believes the stock is overpriced, and the buyer believes it is underpriced. They can't both be right and, to the extent that one of them is (at least in the short term), the winner's gain will mirror, exactly, the loser's lost opportunity.

But if Fama is right, and stock prices accurately reflect a company's real value, neither the seller's nor the buyer's gambles will consistently pay off. Short-term stock price movements are, according to this view, random and unpredictable, and therefore impossible to predict. And if it is too difficult to consistently outperform the market, there is no reason to try.

An Opposing View

The other school of thought has emerged out of a relatively new field called *behavioral economics*, which takes findings from psychology and other social sciences and applies them to how people make economic decisions both in general and in the stock market. One of the leaders in the field is Daniel Kahneman, who sums up his research (alone and with others) in the book *Thinking, Fast and Slow*. Supported by a wealth of detailed behavior studies, Kahneman argues that most of our decisions are a result of a fast and intuitive thought process that is very easily colored by emotions and unconscious bias— and that even the judgments of our slow, rational side are influenced by the assumptions of our intuitive side.

According to this view, since participants in the market are anything but rational, the market is anything but efficient. Those arguing against a rational market seem to be gaining the upper hand in the debate. Kahneman also won a Nobel Prize for Economics, and others like Robert Shiller (*Irrational Exuberance*), Richard Thaler (*Misbehaving: The Making of Behavioral Economics*), and Justin Fox (*The Myth of the Rational Market*), building on his work, contend that the ups and downs of the stock market in recent decades are more pronounced and volatile than should be the case if the Efficient Market Hypothesis was true.

We keep coming back to the Great Recession—because it was such a game changer in so many ways and it was a key turning point in this debate as well. Some claimed that the proponents of the Efficient Market Hypothesis were in part to blame for the crisis. Even those who didn't go that far acknowledged the crisis "could drive a stake through the heart" of the belief in a rational market.

The "Random Walk" School of Investing

In 1973, economist Burton Malkiel published *A Random Walk Down Wall Street*, still one of the most influential books on investing. Malkiel helped bring the theories of Fama and others to a wider audience. He echoed the EMH thesis that stock price fluctuations are random and unpredictable, and that in the long run it is folly to try to outperform the market. The old saying, 'If you can't beat 'em, join 'em,' was basically Malkiel's advice: Instead of trying to *beat* the market, be content with *riding* it and taking advantage of its long-term upward trend.

The advice was met with some resistance from investment professionals because Malkiel was essentially questioning whether they were providing real value for their clients. But his book arrived at a critical time for the field of investing. First, the stock market was in the middle of a long slump, and skeptical investors were open to new ideas. Second, institutional investors (like mutual funds and pension funds) were responsible for a growing share of the stock market (from 34% in 1969 to 43% in 1978), and were looking for predictable performance with low risk. Finally, the new field of finance economics, with bases at schools like the University of Chicago and MIT, was finally being taken seriously on Wall Street.

Malkiel would spend 28 years at the Vanguard Group, a leader in developing and promoting so-called "index funds" that use formulas to mirror the market (or a segment of the market) rather than trying to beat it. We'll go into this in more detail in future chapters, but this kind of "passive" investment strategy (in addition to arguably reducing risk) comes with a lower cost to the investor, as well as certain tax advantages. It is thus no coincidence that Malkiel is now affiliated with Wealthfront, the largest of the new "robo advisor" services that employ algorithms to provide investors with low-cost, largely passive investment strategies.

The Problem (and Opportunity) of Anomalies

Even EMH purists acknowledge that there are certain scenarios where price doesn't seem to accurately reflect value—a departure from the market's "informationally efficient" character. Believers in a rational market refer to these departures as *anomalies*: exceptions that prove the rule, and thus don't challenge the overall rational and efficient nature of the market. Skeptics, on the other hand, don't view these instances as isolated exceptions, but as just one piece of evidence that the Efficient Market Hypothesis is fundamentally flawed.

Anomalies of all sorts have been identified, studied and debated. Some (like those having to do with Super Bowl winners and the length of hemlines) are fun but ultimately silly superstitions. Other anomalies have to do with timing: such as the *momentum effect*, in which an investment that has performed well (or poorly) in the recent past (3 to 12 months) is more likely than not to continue its good (or poor) performance in the short term. By contrast, there is the *reversal effect*, in which good or poor performance over a longer time period is likely to reverse itself. These anomalies are a problem for EMH because, theoretically, positive or negative price momentum should have no bearing on intrinsic value. Even Fama acknowledged the persistence of the momentum effect, and some argue that a smart investor can make money from these anomalies. But doing so is always a short game, and I strongly recommend against any effort to take advantage of short-term term fluctuations. Also, as we will see later, the most frequent traders are rarely the most successful investors.

Similarly, there are a number of intriguing *calendar effects*. Prices tend to go down on Mondays, to rise on the last day of the month, and the first three days of the next month. Then there is the so-called *January effect*, where the stocks of small companies tend to outperform other stocks during the first two or three weeks of the new year. This is the calendar effect with the most logical explanation: small-cap stocks tend to be more volatile, and are thus more likely to be sold at the end of the year at a loss for a tax write-off, and later to bounce back. These effects are all intriguing—but again, I suggest staying away from such-term plays.

There are a few other anomalies that are in my view more substantial, and which don't involve trying to time the market:

• **The Small Firm Effect** – Historically, smaller companies have outperformed larger ones. It makes sense intuitively as companies, like humans, seemingly go through a life cycle of their own. Young, unproven companies often have more growth opportunities and potential for greater upside, particularly on a percentage basis. For a huge company like Microsoft or Google to grow 10%, earnings have to increase in the billions. For a small company, a much smaller jump in earnings can produce significant percentage growth.

• **The Neglected Stock Effect** – Because such stocks trade at a lower volume, they generate less buzz and support from professional analysts. Less interest in these stocks reduces the chances that the investment is overvalued. This is a close cousin to the small firm effect because smaller companies tend to fly under the radar as well. But, if the company is solid, it can represent a significant opportunity for the savvy investor.

• **The Value Effect** – In these cases, a company's underlying value (as measured by earnings, book value, dividend yield, or cash flow) isn't fully reflected in its market price. According to this theory, a low ratio of price-to-earnings (P/E) and/or price-to-book (P/B) is a good indicator of such an under-valued company. This kind of mispricing can occur when a company seems to be out of fashion (such as non-tech stocks during the tech bubble of the late 90s) or has taken a dip based on short-term bad news, but still has strong fundamentals.

While I'll have more to say later about these anomalies, according to the Efficient Market Hypothesis, once an anomaly is studied and identified, it becomes new information which will eventually become incorporated into the price, thus ultimately nullifying the anomaly and the opportunity it represents. And indeed, the effect of some anomalies seems to have faded in recent years. Yet some have persisted, and there is disagreement as to how much, and as to whether the average investor can consistently make money from these mispricings.

Contrarian Investing and Beating the Market

When you start out with a belief in a largely rational and efficient market where price fluctuations are random and unpredictable, the logical extension is an investing philosophy that mainly seeks to *ride* the stock market. In the words of John Bogle, the founder of Vanguard and an early advocate of passively managed index funds, the investor's aim should be modest: to capture his or her "fair share" of the long-term rising tide of the stock market. Attempts to outsmart the market might work in the short term but will more often than not backfire in the long run.

Contrarian investors, on the other hand, believe that market inefficiency and irrationality are far more prevalent than the EMH School acknowledges. Irrationality may not be the rule but it is hardly the rare exception. They also contend that human psychology is a major factor in the ups and downs of the market—and is often the driving force behind the bubbles and panics that have created and then destroyed so much wealth in recent decades. While specific price fluctuations may not be predictable, the human response to them is "predictably irrational." **Passive investing, contrarians argue, will leave an investor vulnerable to the manic-depressive mood swings of the market.** It may not be a good idea to try to forecast the market: but it is possible, contrarian investors believe, to take the general temperature of the market; to identify irrational herd mentality, and at the very least avoid the mistakes of others; and ideally, to profit from them.

There are two general approaches to contrarian investing. One is geared to the *technical* analysis of things like the timing anomalies discussed above. Technical analysis focuses on the patterns and trends of price movements, not on the underlying value of a company. In other words, it is a study of the *behavior* of the market, not the *merits* of a particular investment. While there are some important insights that can be gleaned from technical analysis, it can all too easily lead to over-trading and to disastrous attempts to try to "time" the market, and I recommend maintaining a skeptical view of such methods.

The other approach focuses on *fundamentals*, an assessment of the underlying value of a particular investment. This is, in my view, the contrarian philosophy with the longest tradition and the most solid track record. **Value Investing**, as this approach is known, goes back to Ben Graham and the tough lessons he learned from the Crash of 1929. His book *The Intelligent Investor* became the bible of the value investor, and caught the eye of a young Warren Buffett, who would become Graham's protégé and later emerge as one of the most successful contrarian investors of all time.

We will further discuss the value investing approach over the course of the book. But its essence is simple: Any investing decision must start with an assessment of the underlying or intrinsic value of a stock or other asset, and then consider that value in relation to its current price. For a variety of reasons (most of them involving institutional impediments to trading, human psychology and irrationality), an investment can at a given time be priced well below its intrinsic value. **It is these undervalued assets that are the primary target of the value**

investor, who believes that, while irrationality can result in under and overpricing in the short term, the market will in the long run reflect real value. As Graham put it: "In the short run, the market is a voting machine but in the long run, it is a weighing machine."

Because value investing involves going against the crowd, and against trends, it isn't for everyone. Two other things should be noted about value investing, and most other forms of contrarian investing.

One of the central tenets of the Efficient Market Hypothesis is the importance of *diversification* (which will be the focus of Chapter Six). The basic principle of diversification is not to put too many eggs in one basket: to spread risk across a variety of investments in order to reduce the negative impact of any single investment going south. There is considerable merit to the idea of diversification, and contrarian investors don't entirely dismiss it. But the more diversified your portfolio is, the more likely it is to mirror the market, and you can't beat the market by mirroring it. **A broadly diversified portfolio is one without much concentration. Contrarian investors, by contrast, often have a good deal of concentration in their portfolios.** Warren Buffett, for example, once had over half his money in Geico, which his Berkshire Hathaway company would later take sole ownership over. In other words, contrarian investors *are* often willing to put a lot of eggs in one basket.

Second, we observed earlier that, while an index like the S&P 500 rewarded investors with handsome returns during the extended bull market of 1982-1999, that same index would have lost money during the "lost decade" that followed. Contrarian investors believe strongly that bull markets and bear markets call for very different strategies. Even if your objectives are modest and you are mostly seeking to capture the long-term upward trend of the market, **it is one thing to ride a bull, and another thing entirely to ride a bear.**

The Two Schools

Although it's overly simplistic to reduce the vast and varied world of investing to these two schools, in practice, the line between them is often blurred. I'll argue later that you as an individual investor don't have to make an either/or choice between them. Strict EMH adherents concede that it is possible to beat the market at the margins, and contrarian investors like Warren Buffett acknowledge the merits of passive investing.

But if it's a simplification, it's a useful one. Beneath all the number-crunching, investing is ultimately a question of philosophy. There is no one correct path but the most successful investors have a coherent philosophy and stick to it. These two points of view – of a rational market that one can at best hope to ride, and of an irrational market that is beatable – are the North and South poles of investing philosophy. And, in the next couple of chapters, you'll see how these contrasts play out in very different approaches to two key questions faced by every investor: managing risk and diversification.

Chapter 5

Managing Risk

I stated previously that **one of the biggest keys to succeeding as an investor is avoiding big losses.** As with poker, investing is in many ways a "loser's game" where the players who come out on top in the long run are often those who avoid big mistakes and capitalize on the mistakes of others. And in this sense, the fiscal caution typically associated with Millennials can be a positive attribute.

On the other hand, I also pointed out that if you avoid the stock market altogether, you're taking this caution too far. **Building wealth requires some short-term risk in the interest of long-term financial security.**

So let's take a close look at risk: at the various kinds of risk investors can be exposed to, and when and why you need to be concerned about those risks. We'll find that the two schools of investing introduced in the previous chapter view risk in contrasting ways, and thus take very different approaches to dealing with risk. We'll also see that risk, like everything in investing, is a highly individual, personal matter: what is risky for one investor may not be for another. Finally, I'll argue that

Millennials are generally in a position to assume more risk than other investors.

A Brief History of Risk

The concept of risk is so central to modern life that we take it for granted. Without the ability to measure or at least estimate risk, and on that basis make informed decisions about the future, life as we know it would be impossible. It's not just the stock market that depends on this inexact but crucial science. International trade and currency exchange, insurance, and fields as varied as engineering, physics, and medicine: all involve the theory and practice of risk. Without actuaries estimating the probability and risk of certain undesirable events, we wouldn't have health, life, or property insurance.

Yet risk, and the forecasting it makes possible, wasn't always a part of our vocabulary. For much of human history, the future was regarded with a mixture of fear and superstition, a mystery subject to the "whim of the gods." Calculus and advanced mathematics weren't possible until we replaced Roman numerals with Arabic ones. And it was only when Renaissance thinkers like Galileo questioned old beliefs that a new view of the world and the universe began to take shape. The Renaissance was also the Age of Exploration, and thus the birth of a new kind of international trade, requiring new forms of bookkeeping and finance.

In this book I make periodic reference to poker, and it's interesting that hypothetical gambling problems were the starting point for the development of *probability theory* in the Renaissance and of *game theory* in the 20th century. Both are too complicated to go into here. But the essence of the field is to try to estimate probability, and thus risk, in situations involving multiple players, as well as a mix of measurable factors and uncertainty: a perfect description of the stock market. The field is responsible for the development of a number of advanced mathematical models in finance and investing, which is why over a dozen thinkers have won the Nobel Prize for Economics for their work in game theory—including John Nash, the subject of the movie A *Beautiful Mind*.

Varieties of Investment Risk

There are many kinds of risk an investor might be exposed to and, for our purposes, we're going to talk mainly about the first two which are Market Risk (systematic risk) and Company Specific Risk (Idiosyncratic risk).

- **Market Risk** – Frequently referred to as *systemic risk*, this is the risk of loss due to overall poor performance of the financial markets. Diversification can help hedge against such risk but ultimately can't protect you: the larger forces affecting the market will come down on every investor.

- **Company Specific Risk** – Also called *idiosyncratic risk*, this is the risk associated with the upside and downside of a particular company. And this is a risk you largely *can* negate through diversification.

- **Inflationary Risk** – Inflation (the rise in the price of goods and services) has a complicated relationship with the market and the economy in general. On the one hand, it reduces consumers' purchasing power while at the same time increasing the cost of inputs for business, thus putting a drag on the economy. But if inflation is steady and predictable, it can actually encourage consumer spending and stimulate the economy. Studies have shown that it is *unexpected inflation* that tends to have the most adverse effects on the economy and the stock market. The market performs best when inflation holds steady between 2-3%, which, according to many analysts, it is expected to do in coming years.

- **Liquidity Risk** – We have already addressed this to some extent in the discussion about certain small stocks that, because of their size and the fact that they fly under the radar, experience lower turnover and trade volume and thus are somewhat less liquid than more active stocks. Liquidity also applies to bonds and other securities whose full benefit isn't reached until maturity. In general, if your money is in any way "tied up" and you either can't redeem it, or there is a cost in doing so, that is a form of risk.

- **Fixed-Income (Bonds)** – Although there is a whole category largely associated with bonds (credit risk, taxability risk, call risk, reinvestment risk) that I can't discuss here in depth, interest rate risk is a particularly important factor in relation to bonds. In a way that may seem counterintuitive, interest rates have an inverse relationship with bond prices: rising interest rates push bond prices lower, while falling rates are good for bonds.[1]

- **International** – Finally, there is a set of risks faced by the investor in foreign securities—mainly related to possible political instability, but also uncertainty around exchange rates.

So basically, the relationship between risk and return portrayed in the following graph is an elaboration on the old adage, "Nothing ventured, nothing gained."

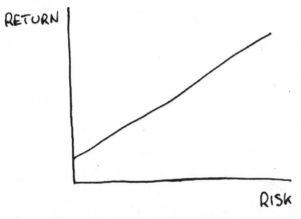

Figure H - The standard view of the relationship between risk and potential or expected return.

As you can see, the upward sloping line in this graph doesn't start at 0% return—it begins instead at what is known as the risk-free rate. The proxy for the *risk-free rate* at any

---

[1] Most bonds available to the individual investor are existing bonds bought on the so-called *secondary market*. (The primary market for new bonds is dominated by institutional investors.) The face or *par value* of an existing bond is fixed, but its trading price may fluctuate. A bond with a 5% yield, for example, will be less attractive if interest rates go up, thus pushing its price down.

given time is usually the interest rate on the ten-year Treasury Bill. The idea here is that, given the extreme unlikelihood of the U.S. government defaulting on its own loans[2], the interest rate offered on such loans is virtually risk-free.

Extremely cautious investors might be willing to settle for the risk-free rate, keeping most of their money in cash and government bonds. Most investors, however—while keeping some of their money in such safe, liquid assets—are looking for a greater rate of return, and are willing to accept greater risk. The difference between the potential or expected return on a riskier asset and the risk-free rate is what finance professionals calls a *risk premium* or (in the case of stocks specifically) the *equity risk premium*, or ERP. It is **the compensation the investor expects in return for assuming greater risk.** It makes sense: If riskier investments didn't have at least the potential for higher returns, rational investors would avoid them.

Investment advisors often use two different versions of the above chart—the Securities Market Line and the Capital Market Line—to gauge the pros and cons of a specific investment, and to assess the "efficiency" of an individual portfolio (how well it achieves a targeted rate of return while minimizing risk). But the assumption of a direct relationship between risk and reward is central to both—an assumption questioned, as we will see, by many contrarian and value investors.

---

[2] Academics assume that U.S. Treasuries are free of default risk since it can simply print money to payback debt. While there may be negative consequences to "printing money", they are likely less harsh than those that would arise if the country defaulted.

Although first developed in the 1950s by Harry Markowitz while still a graduate student in economics (a decade earlier than Fama's work on the Efficient Market Hypothesis), Modern Portfolio Theory and EMH share the same basic view of the market as fundamentally rational and efficient. Markowitz proposed that an investment's *idiosyncratic or specific risk* (its individual downside) could essentially be eliminated by grouping it with other investments with contrasting kinds of risk. Because the various investments would behave differently (one going up while another went down, for example), their specific risks would cancel one another out if the overall portfolio was sufficiently diversified. (We'll explore this concept of diversification more fully in the Chapter 7.)

Markowitz shared Fama's belief that it was folly to try to outsmart the market. And because investors are naturally risk-averse, it stood to reason that the only risk a rational investor should assume was *market risk*, which cannot be eliminated by diversification. Although this is the risk associated with the market as a whole, it is not uniform across all investments. In other words, individual investments have varying degrees of sensitivity to shared market conditions.

Markowitz's key (and ultimately controversial) contribution was to suggest that this second kind of risk could be quantified. As an approximation (or proxy) for an investment's market risk, he proposed its *volatility*: the degree to which its returns fluctuate above or below the market's statistical midpoint or mean. This deviation from the mean would later be termed the investment's beta risk. *Beta risk* varies according to the investment's sensitivity to market conditions. An investment that moves exactly as the market does as a whole is said to have a beta of 1; if the investment moves up or down 10% more than the market, its beta is 1.1; and so on. If a particular investment is less volatile than the market as a while, its beta will be below under 1. Investments that move in the opposite direction of the market as a whole can actually have a negative beta.

This measure of beta risk was later developed into a formula (called the Capital Asset Pricing Model) for determining the rate of return a rational investor should expect from a given asset. Assuming a certain expected rate of return for the market on average, this formula uses the investment's beta to determine its expected rate of return over and above the current risk-free rate.

Without breaking down the formula in detail, here's how a specific calculation would play out: If the risk-free or Treasury rate is 3% and a stock's beta is 1.5 and the S&P 500 is expected to return 7%, the stock should, over the long term, be expected to return 9%. So, in this case, the stock's risk premium is 6%.

The essence of this model is two-fold. First, an investment's risk can be quantified as its volatility. Second, its expected rate of return is directly related to its degree of risk: the higher the risk, the greater the return.

The Contrarian View

Contrarian investors, mainly those who adhere to the Value school of investing, have a very different view of risk. **They contend that equating risk with volatility is flawed on a number of levels.**

First of all, deviations above and below the mean are treated the same. So if a stock is up 50% one year, down 2% the next, and then back up 25%, it is still defined as a volatile (and thus risky) stock, even though it's consistently beating the market.

Second, if volatility were an accurate reflection of risk, one would expect higher risk (i.e., a higher beta) to be rewarded with higher returns. Yet studies show that low volatility stocks often outperform high volatility stocks: in a number of instances, low-beta investments had higher than expected returns and high-beta investments lower than expected returns.

Third, critics argue that Modern Portfolio Theory is preoccupied with *probabilities* that can be quantified and turned into formulas, as opposed to *uncertainties* that cannot. Yet the "prevalence of surprise in the world of business," writes Peter Bernstein in his book Against the Gods: *The Remarkable Story of Risk*, "is evidence that uncertainty is more likely to prevail than mathematical probability." Elroy Dimson of the London Business School, for example, encourages his students to view risk in a different way: the simple fact that more things *can* happen than actually *will* happen. This is a deceptively simple but profound insight. In hindsight, we construct narratives as to why 'x' happened and 'y' did not. But the truth is that uncertainty in the present is always greater than we realize. For this reason, Dimson and value investors like Howard Marks approach risk as a range of possible future outcomes—and as risk grows, so does the uncertainty about those outcomes. Instead of presenting the relationship between risk and reward as a simple upward slope, they characterize risk as a widening range of uncertainty, as in the following chart:

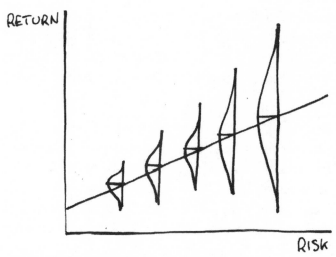

RETURN

RISK

Figure I - Potential return grows with risk. But so does uncertainty and the possibility of substantial loss.

This is one of the glaring weaknesses of Modern Portfolio Theory: **an insufficient emphasis on the possibility of large (and in some cases permanent) loss.** In the end, this is the biggest risk any investor faces. A single, big mistake could erase any previous successes. But volatility is a major risk only if one is forced to sell a stock on the low end of a downward dip. Otherwise it is the less significant measure of risk.

Finally, equating risk with volatility ignores the crucial question of price. Theoretically, according to the MPT model, a stock selling at $100 a share is no riskier than the same stock when it was $50 a share as long as the beta remains the same. Howard Marks sees this as preposterous. "For a value investor," he writes, "price has to be the starting point." Often, the greatest risk is of overpaying for a stock at a time when the market is irrationally optimistic. **"High risk comes primarily with high prices."** And because it is often psychology that fuels irrational bubbles, "The biggest investing errors come not from factors that are informational or analytical, but from those that are psychological." Instead of engaging in forecasting and trusting mathematical models for probability, Marks suggests taking the "risk temperature" of the market: if optimism is high and skepticism low, tread carefully.

Warren Buffet, a contrarian investor, who has always advocated paying close attention to price and value, as opposed to volatility notes, finds it absurd that "a stock that has dropped very sharply compared to the market... becomes 'riskier' at the lower price point than it was at the higher price." If the fundamentals of a company haven't changed, the lower price presents the investor with a built-in margin of safety, making the investment less risky and more appealing. Buffett suggests that investors should search not just for wonderful companies, but for wonderful companies trading at low prices. For instance, when the financial sector tanked in 2008, he invested $5 billion in financial powerhouse Goldman Sachs—an investment that is believed to have made him and his shareholders a return of over 40% or $2 billion.

Risk and Time

Time is an important factor in considering risk. A key concept in investing is the idea of a *time horizon*. This is the length of time you expect to hold an investment before you liquidate or cash in. In the case of a certificate of deposit (CD) and other fixed income securities, that term is usually quite explicit. You either can't touch the money until your investment's maturity date or, if you do, you'll pay a penalty.

With stocks, the time horizon is a little less defined. It's basically a question of how long you're willing to stick with an investment and (depending on the level of risk) its inevitable ups and downs before you sell. In general, the greater risk, the longer your time horizon should be. As your holding period increases, the chances of losing money in the stock market decreases.

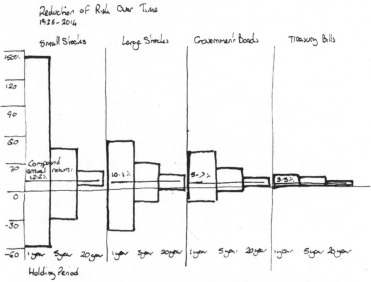

Figure J - The distribution of returns (for different asset classes) for 1yr, 5yr and 20yr time periods. Data Source: Ibbotson

In a sense, your acceptable time horizon is a question of *goals*. If you're looking to fund *short-term* goals (those less than five years in the future), you'll want to make conservative investments like Treasury bills, CDs and money market funds. *Intermediate* goals are those in the five to ten year range, and are best funded through a balanced portfolio of bonds and cheap, dividend paying stocks.

The assumption I'm making in this book is that most of my readers are young, at a relatively early stage in their careers, and that most of their investment goals are *long-term* in nature. You should be thinking long term because as we've discussed, due to today's ever-changing economy and the fact that you can't count on Social Security or pensions to provide for you down the road, it is more important than ever for your generation to begin the process of building wealth early and often.

That said, you will, as an individual have your own unique mix of time horizons. If, for example, you plan on buying a house seven years from now, that's an intermediate goal, and you'll want to adjust your investment portfolio accordingly. **In other words: risk is a highly personal matter.** What may be low risk for one investor could be high risk for someone with different goals and different time horizons.

Value Investing: Volatility as Opportunity

According to the Efficient Market Hypothesis, the market quickly incorporates all relevant new information on any given investment asset, information which will then be reflected in that asset's price. Contrarian value investors put a very different spin on this process. Yes, Howard Marks acknowledges, the market is efficient in that it is quick to incorporate new information—but a lot of that 'information' is subjective perception, which may result in a price that is a poor estimation of real value. For example, in January, 2000 the market valued Yahoo stock at $237 a share; fifteen months later, in April of 2001, that same stock was selling for $11 a share. Clearly, the market was not 'right' in its estimation of value in both cases.

Therefore, Marks restates the EMH thesis as follows: **The market is efficient at reflecting a consensus view of what all current information means—yet that consensus view may also very well be wildly inaccurate.** And that inaccuracy presents the smart investor with an opportunity. If you can accurately assess the intrinsic value of an investment (easier said than done) and purchase it at a price well below that intrinsic value (also easier said than done), you will build in a *margin of safety* that creates the possibility of a very different relationship between risk and reward. **The Value investor sees volatility as an inefficiency to be exploited—but does not equate that volatility with risk.** If you do your homework and guess right, you will set yourself up for healthy returns without assuming unnecessary risk. (If your margin of safety is sufficient, you will actually reduce your risk.) You will benefit not only from the stock price eventually (and *eventually* is the key word) returning to its intrinsic value, but also from any future increase in that value.

Of course, if it was obvious what these undervalued stocks were, everyone would take advantage of that mispricing. Later in this book, I'll offer some tips about how to do your homework in the elusive art of Value investing. But Marks and others argue that the ability to question consensus opinion, and to go against the grain of the crowd is just as, if not more important. If you can do that, you can profit from the irrationality of the market's ups and downs.

Risk Revisited

So if, in the eyes of contrarian and Value investors, volatility is *not* a good measure of risk, how *should* one gauge risk?

The Value approach views risk **not as a probability that can be measured or quantified but as varying degrees of uncertainty that cannot be captured in numbers or formulas.** We can and should prepare for uncertainty, and can sometimes anticipate when it is more likely—but we cannot measure or quantify it.

The greatest threat this uncertainty poses to the investor is the possibility of a major downturn (for a specific investment or company, for the stock market as a whole, for the economy, or for a particular sector of the market or economy) that could result in permanent loss of capital (the 2007 Financial Crisis saw a confluence of all of these possibilities[3]). Modern Portfolio Theory acknowledges these events but views them as rare, and doesn't account for them in its formulas for measuring risk. Value investors argue that these formulas consequently create a false sense of security, and that Efficient Market proponents underestimate the possibility of such events in the future.

Contrarians like Buffet and Marks put little emphasis on beta scores for three reasons. They (beta scores) encourage investors to confuse volatility with risk. Second, the attempt to quantify risk leads to overconfidence: a belief that risk can be known precisely, when it cannot be. Third, it distracts investors from paying attention to real risks. Again, first and foremost among those is the risk of permanent loss.

---

[3] A collapse in one segment of the housing market triggered a bursting of the housing bubble; which in turn led to a larger crisis in the financial sector; a major downturn in the stock market; and ultimately the worst recession in decades.

> *More money has been lost through the mismeasurement of risk than by the failure to measure risk. It would be safer to drive a car without a speedometer than a speedometer that understates true speeds by 25 percent. If you had no mechanical gauge of speed, you would be conscious of that absence of information and take extra caution as a result. If, instead, you are relying on a speedometer you believe is providing correct readings but, in fact, is significantly understating actual speed, you will be more prone to an accident.*
>
> – Jack D. Schwager, Market Wizards

Contrarians point to several other risks investors should be mindful of. **One is the risk of disappointing returns, particularly those that result in a loss of purchasing power.** Put simply, a loss of purchasing power means your investment is failing, at a minimum, to keep up with inflation. As of the writing of this book, historically low short-term bond rates are below the historical average rate of inflation, so investing in them is likely a losing proposition[4]. Even if you keep up with inflation, **sub-par returns can constitute a significant risk if they threaten your ability to fund major life goals,** such as the purchase of a house, your child's education, or your own retirement. As stated before, risk is a highly personal, individual matter—the nuances of which can't be captured in clear-cut formulas.

The other risk we haven't addressed is that of missed opportunities, what economists call opportunity cost. Anytime

---

[4] Given this basic fact, some analysts argue that there really is no such thing as a truly "risk-free" rate.

you make a decision, you forego or pass up the potential benefits of the alternative options. By investing $1,000 in a 5-year Treasury, for example, you risk losing the potentially higher returns of a more aggressive investment. Value investors are at times willing to accept the risk of missed opportunity in the name of caution and prudence. Warren Buffet knew he was likely passing up short-term gains when he refused to jump on the dot-com bandwagon in 1999, but that was a risk he was willing to take.

The other risk we haven't addressed is that of missed opportunities, what economists call *opportunity cost.* Anytime you make a decision, you forego or pass up the potential benefits of the alternative options. By investing $1,000 in a 5-year Treasury, for example, you risk losing the potentially higher returns of a more aggressive investment. Value investors are at times willing to accept the risk of missed opportunity in the name of caution and prudence. Warren Buffet knew he was likely passing up short-term gains when he refused to jump on the dot-com bandwagon in 1999, but that was a risk he was willing to take.

Risk, Value, and Price

This is where the contrast between Value investing and traditional theories really comes into focus. **In Modern Portfolio Theory, price in and of itself is not a risk—only the *movement of price* up and down, i.e., an investment's volatility.** The Value perspective is the exact opposite. In this view, volatility is only a risk if you have a short-term time frame; otherwise, it is an opportunity. **Price, on the other hand, is at the very heart of risk.**

For the contrarian investor, price and risk are inseparable. While high risk may often come from high prices, low prices, on the other hand, can potentially reduce risk—dramatically. **The central question for the Value investor is always what the price of an asset is in relation to its underlying value. If price exceeds or is even comparable to that value,** the investment is risky, regardless of its beta. High prices increase the likelihood of sub-par returns; the law of *reversion to the mean* suggests that high-flying stocks will eventually come back to earth. And if that high price reflects an excess of enthusiasm in the market and a bubble waiting to burst, it also carries the possibility of a significant and possibly permanent loss of capital.

This is where the Value investor's emphasis on uncertainty comes into play. Good value investors know that there are things they don't (and can't) know. Multiple variables that can bring down a stock or the market as a whole are beyond the individual investor's control and forecasting ability. Understanding and respecting that uncertainty, the Value investor insists (in all but the most conservative investments) on a margin of safety that is the difference between a stock's underlying value and its current market price. This margin of safety represents an alternative to the traditional equity reward premium—one that rejects the assumption that greater reward necessarily involves accepting greater risk.

Again, this is easier said than done (or everyone would be doing it). Value investing demands you do your homework (or hire a trusted advisor to do so), and requires a temperament comfortable with going against the crowd. And it carries its own set of risks: the risk that you have misjudged the company's fundamentals and picked a losing stock (what one might call *valuation risk*), or that its price takes longer than expected to return to its true value.

"Risk Temperature"

Value investors stress the importance of taking the overall risk mood or temperature of the market. Although there are statistical measures that can indicate an overheated market in danger of collapsing, this is primarily a question of market psychology—a factor that both Value and contrarian investors attach great significance to. Most successful investors acknowledge that it is impossible to predict precisely when the market will swing one way or another. Yet assessing the general mood can be very instructive—providing clues as to when it's a good time to be cautious and when the time is right to be more aggressive. **Different market moods carry different risks.**

When the market is riding high, as it was during the dot-com boom in 1999, greed rules the day and the public develops a high comfort level with risk. People stop worrying about losing money and are mainly concerned with missing out on the action. During such times, even low-quality investments can appear attractive. The "father" of value investing, Benjamin Graham, wrote that some of the worst losses come from such decisions—with investors mistakenly assuming "that prosperity is synonymous with safety."

Sentiment-based risk also comes into play in a different way when the market is down. For instance, when the Financial Crisis was in full bloom in 2007 and 2008, people worried about losing money when should have been worrying about missing out on opportunity. Caught up in panic of the moment, they were overly cautious at precisely the time they should have been willing to take some strategic chances. **All too often, people worry about missed opportunity at the top of the market (when in fact they should be worrying about losing money), and worry about losing money at the bottom (when in fact they should be worrying about missed opportunity).**

The Biggest Risk(s)

Remember **that substantial and possibly permanent loss of capital is the greatest risk faced by any investor.** Keeping this in mind, also realize that sometimes you win simply by not losing.

We saw how much wealth was lost during the Financial Crisis of 2007-2009; how quickly it was lost; and the long-term ripple effects of those losses, especially for Millennials and Gen Xers. What's at work here is a brutal math that may not be readily apparent. If you're down 10% one year and then up 10% the following year, you're still behind. **The bigger the loss, the harder it is to make up.** A 40% loss requires a 67% gain just to come out even; a 50% loss, a 100% gain.

Yet, **the next biggest risk for young investors is playing it too safe and remaining on the sidelines of the investing game.** Call it the risk of inaction. There are reasons for your skepticism about the market, and your caution is healthy—up to a point. But as I wrote earlier, the Millennial Disadvantage is very real. As a result of the Great Recession of 2007-2009 and its ripple effects in the years since then, many of you are off to a slow start in saving for retirement and other major life goals. And because of growing economic inequality, long-term problems with Social Security, and a changed work environment, you more than any previous generation need to take responsibility for your own economic destiny. So, while not putting your money to work may appear to be a cautious move, it is in fact quite risky: you are putting your long-term financial security at risk.

The balancing act I'm challenging you to make isn't an easy one. Warren Buffett's two rules of investing are:

✓ No. 1 – Don't lose money.

✓ No. 2 – Don't forget rule #1.

I don't want you to forget either. But if I could throw in two more rules, they would be:

✓ No. 3 – Don't count on anyone else to provide for your long-term financial needs.

✓ No. 4 – Don't settle for below-average returns. It's a risk you can't afford to take.

The Two Schools, Part II

While it is somewhat of an oversimplification to separate the world of investing into two distinct schools, you will see two very different philosophies of how the market works, what constitutes risk, and how to deal with it as you investigate the option open to you[5].

---

[5] Modern Portfolio Theory has responded to its critics and modified some of its models, while contrarian investors acknowledge some merit to its analytic tools.

In Chapter 7, we'll see that tension continue to play out in contrasting approaches to the question of diversification, seen by some as the ultimate form of risk management for investors. While diversification can absolutely help manage risk, it isn't the magic bullet many make it out to be. The challenge of diversification is developing the right balance of different kinds of investments. So it's time now to take an in-depth look at the growing menu of options you have to choose from.

Chapter 6

The Millennial Investor's Menu

I n Chapter 3, I briefly introduced the idea of *asset classes*—
broad investment categories that share certain general
characteristics, and which tend to behave similarly in the
market. They are: 1) stocks, or equities; 2) bonds and other
fixed-income securities; 3) real estate and other commodities;
4) and cash and cash equivalents.

It is essential that the investor have a solid understanding
of these categories, of the opportunities and challenges,
and the strengths and limitations that come with each. That
understanding will help you come up with the *asset allocation*
that is right for you. (Think of asset allocation simply as the
pie chart showing what percentage of your total investment
dollars falls in each category.)

I've said it before and I'll say it again: Investing is a
highly personal matter, and there is no such thing as a "one size
fits all" strategy. Your own strategy, your individual investing
personality, will largely come down to your decisions regarding
asset allocation. Will you, for example, be heavily invested in
stocks, or will your portfolio lean more towards bonds? Your
strategy, and that pie chart can and should change over the

course of your life, just as your goals, financial situation, and risk tolerance will change. The portfolio of a single person in their twenties won't typically be the same as that of someone approaching retirement.

Asset allocation is a critical question in almost every topic we explore in this book. It plays into the previous chapter on risk because some asset allocation strategies are riskier than others. It will play a huge role in the next chapter on diversification. We discussed how strategies that work in bull markets don't necessarily work in bear markets and that is partly a question of asset allocation. A later chapter focuses on the challenge of beating the market, and asset allocation comes into play here, too. Finally, at the end of the book, we'll take a look ahead at how your investment needs and strategies might evolve over the course of your life, and modifying your asset allocation is a big part of adapting to changing life circumstances.

Mutual Funds: An Overview

To be perfectly clear: mutual funds are *not* an asset class. They are a vehicle that allows you to invest in various asset classes, either separately or in combination. For example, some mutual funds are invested mainly in stocks, others mainly in bonds. Other hybrid funds—described as *mixed asset, balanced,* or *blended*—mix and match asset classes. A typical balanced fund might be 60% stocks and 40% bonds, for example. Most mutual funds also keep a certain amount of their assets in cash reserves, in part so they can pay investors selling all or part of their shares in the fund.

The sheer variety of mutual funds is dizzying, as is the variety of labels used to indicate their focus and philosophy. There are growth funds, income funds, value funds, emerging market funds, small cap, mid cap, large cap funds. Entire books have been written about mutual funds; I could easily devote several chapters to the topic in this one. My purpose here is to introduce you in a broad way to mutual funds as one of your many investment options—and in particular to highlight their advantages and disadvantages.

Mutual funds really began taking off in the 1970s, when new laws were enacted allowing for Individual Retirement Accounts (IRAs) and 401(k) plans. The vast majority of households owning mutual funds do so as part of a tax-deferred retirement plan. Currently, just over 43% of U.S. households are invested in at least one mutual fund—down slightly from 45% in 2010 but a huge jump from just under 6% in 1980. Over half (56%) are equity funds, 21% are bond funds, and the remaining 23% are hybrid and money market funds. Hybrid funds have grown in popularity in the last decade. Among equity funds, domestic funds have been losing ground to global, international ones.

The 1970s also saw the introduction of *index funds*: passively managed mutual funds that—in contrast to actively managed funds that try to beat the market—use a set formula to mirror the market, or a particular segment or index of the market (sometimes called a *benchmark*). For example, the first index fund, still one of the most popular, is set up to mirror the S&P 500 (the 500 biggest companies in the U.S., as measured by total capitalization). Ever since, there has been a debate among investment professionals about whether actively managed funds beat the market often enough to justify their higher fees; or whether it's a safer bet to just ride the market. We'll dive into that in a bit. For now, suffice to say that the passive, indexed approach is currently gaining ground. In 2015, active funds experienced a net "outflow" for the first time since 2008—in other words, more money was withdrawn than invested. Active funds lost $207 billion while index funds gained about twice as much. And in the last fifteen years, passive funds' share of the equity mutual fund market has more than doubled: from less than 10% to over 20%.

The merits of a mutual fund are pretty straightforward. It's a kind of one-stop shopping option on your investing menu. With a single lump-sum investment, you can own a piece of dozens (or even hundreds) of companies or other assets. If, for example, you want to ride the long-term growth of the top companies in the U.S., you can buy into an S&P 500 index fund. If you then want to balance that investment in domestic stocks with a sampling of international stocks, you might invest in an Emerging Markets fund. Throw in a bond fund and you would have a fairly well-rounded portfolio. In each of these instances, you don't have to research individual stocks. You are counting on the index you are tracking, or on the manager of your fund, to make your investment decisions for you.

And this is where the debate about actively managed funds comes in. The argument for such funds is as follows... Say you're an investor who is serious about building real long-term wealth. You're not content to simply ride the market. With at least some of your investments, you'd like to outperform the market, and you are willing to pay higher fees for the opportunity to do so. On the other hand, you don't have the time or inclination to research individual stocks, and you're willing to pay someone a reasonable fee to do that homework for you, in return for a decent chance that they will be able to beat the market over time.

Sounds like a good deal, doesn't it? And during the bull market of the 80s (1982-1987) and 90s (1987-2000), it was an attractive and increasingly popular option with investors. Mutual funds routinely reported returns in double figures, and high-profile fund managers like Fidelity's Peter Lynch (who, over a 10-year period, beat the S&P 500 by an impressive 150%) achieved almost superstar status. Hundreds of new funds were created and the competition between them was intense—yet more people were winning than losing

But then the dot-com bubble burst, followed by a decade with big gains at some times and big losses at others. **It now appears that the 90s were the exception rather than the rule, creating unrealistic expectations about the stock market in general, and mutual funds in particular.** Moreover, a growing number of studies question whether the performance of actively managed funds justifies their higher fees.

The Underperformance of Actively Managed Funds

In the last couple of chapters, one of the things we've found is that there are two very different views of how the market works, two contrasting schools of thought. According to the Efficient Market Hypothesis, the market is for the most part "informationally efficient"—prices reflect all relevant information, and thus are pretty close to intrinsic value. Price fluctuations are random and unpredictable. Therefore, it is folly to try to beat the market; the wisest course is to simply ride it.

John Bogle, the founder of Vanguard and creator of the first popular index fund, is a big proponent of the EMH view, and has been arguing for passive investing since the 1970s. In 1995, even while actively managed funds were flying high, he wrote an article entitled "The Triumph of Indexing." And as of 2010, his boast seemed to have come true. Increasingly, investors have been taking money out of active funds and putting them into passive indexes. And in 2010, his Vanguard Group passed Fidelity (known for actively managed funds like Magellan) as the world's largest mutual fund company.

Moreover, a number of studies appear to support the case against active management. Foremost among these is Standard & Poor's comparison of index and active funds— the SPIVA Scorecard (S&P Indices Vs. Active). Issued twice a year, the most recent scorecard for 2015 finds that 66% of large-cap, 57% of mid-cap, and 72% of small-cap active funds,[1] failed to meet their benchmark (the index they would track if they were passive funds). The numbers are even worse when extended over a 10-year periods. S&P also issues a Persistence Scorecard to assess whether funds are able to maintain above-average short-term performance over time. Again, the numbers aren't pretty. Of the 678 domestic equity funds that were in the top quartile (25%) in September 2013, only 4.28% were similarly ranked two years later. SPIVA also found a very high "mortality rate" for actively managed funds. In the past five years, a fourth of all active domestic equity funds either merged or were liquidated.

---

[1] The "cap" here refers to *market capitalization*, or the total value of a company's stock shares. Large-cap companies have a stock valued at $10 billion or above; mid-cap are between $2 and $10 billion; and small-cap below $2 billion.

Why are "expert" fund managers, with all the research tools in the world at their disposal, so consistently bad at beating the market?

• **Size** – Simply put: the bigger a ship, the harder it is to change course. Markets are cyclical and investors can become irrational. The best investors learn to quickly adjust, and to protect their portfolio from market extremes. Large funds are for the most part unable to do so. Also, because of their size, investing in small, dynamic companies often isn't worth the trouble—effectively shrinking a fund's universe of investment-worthy stocks.

• **Psychology** – Fund managers are generally compensated based on how they perform relative to their benchmark, so they often have an incentive to play it safe and simply try to stay even with (or even slightly behind) the pack, as opposed to trying to beat the market. This herd mentality is especially evident during a heated bull market. If a given index is surging (such as what happened with tech and internet stocks in the late 90s), the majority of managers end up riding the wave and investing in the same popular stocks (in the business we call this "chasing performance").

• **Timing** – As we'll discuss later, sometimes the smartest investing move is the non-move: knowing when to hold off, rather than (in baseball terms) swinging at a bad pitch. Professional fund managers usually don't have this luxury. As new money comes in, they can't just sit on it, even if they suspect the market is overvalued and overpriced. It's a particular problem during a bull market when, because of recent performance, a fund attracts a lot of new investors—a phenomenon called forced buying. Timing can adversely affect investors another way. A fund might, for instance, report a 20% annual return in a good year. But, unless you were on board from the beginning, you're not going to see all or even most of that. Individual investors also chase performance, jumping on the bandwagon of a hot fund, not at the bottom, but as it nears its peak. One study estimates that this "timing penalty" costs individual investors 5% in returns each year.

• **Concentration (not enough of it)** – In the next chapter, we'll explore how diversification (the principle of not putting all your eggs in one basket) can be a good thing... up to a point. The limits of diversification are nowhere more evident than in the world of mutual funds, especially the biggest, most popular ones. Despite studies showing that the benefits of diversification drop off greatly once you hit 20 to 30 stocks, many funds insist on maintaining dozens, even hundreds of holdings. At a certain point, this "excessive diversification" (as some call it) is self-defeating: you end up mirroring the market and losing any chance of beating it. And, if all you do is match the market, your returns (once you factor in the higher fees charged by active funds) are bound to disappoint.

Making Sense of the Active vs. Passive Debate

Armed with the findings of the SPIVA Scorecard and similar reports from financial research firms like Morningstar and Lipper, some experts and commentators are ready to declare the debate over, and to name passive indexes the winner. "Active fund management is outmoded," writes respected *Wall Street Journal* columnist Jason Zweig, "and a lot of stock pickers are going to have to find something else to do for a living." As we've seen, investors certainly continue to vote that way with their money.

But is the issue really so cut and dry?

A lot of it comes down to how you define a truly "active" fund. As I pointed out above, a number of funds are so broadly diversified that they are active in name only. Researcher Antti Petajisto calls such funds "closet indexers" and has been working on ways of identifying them and distinguishing them from truly active funds. He and his colleague Martijn Cremers have developed a measurement of a fund's "Active Share"— that part of a fund's portfolio where managers are making strong individual choices, rather than just following the crowd or an index. They have found that funds with an Active Share rating of 90% or higher actually do stand a good chance of beating the market. Morningstar and Lipper provide active share ratings to subscribers, and Fidelity now tracks the active share of all its funds.

Analyst and fund manager Thomas Howard also questions the conventional wisdom about the under performance of actively managed funds. His research concludes that the returns of such funds are held back by three factors he combines into a *Portfolio Drag Index.* Closet indexing is the most significant of these, followed by over diversification. Related to both is a third he calls "asset bloat." Fund managers are not only compensated based on performance relative to a benchmark, but also on how big the fund is: total Assets Under Management (AUM), as it's known in the industry. As the fund grows and (over)diversifies, the quality of its investments becomes diluted. Howard finds that most of a fund's chance for superior performance can be found in its first 20 investments: these are its best ideas, its "high-conviction" picks. But, with the average fund now comprising over a hundred holdings, it has four or five times more low-conviction stocks than high-conviction ones.

It Doesn't Have to be Either/Or

Most investors are not served by an either/or approach. A number of high-profile articles have appeared in the last year or two offering a contrarian view to the prevailing wisdom that index funds are necessarily superior: And, while Vanguard is known for championing passive indexing, about half of its funds are actively managed. In some years those active funds outperform its passive ones; and Vanguard has conducted extensive research on the keys to a successful active fund.

Here are a few key things to keep in mind when choosing a mutual fund:

- In general, index funds perform best in long, steady bull markets—during which they are an excellent instrument for riding a rising tide.

- When markets are highly volatile or experience sudden downturns, a good active manager has the ability to "play defense" against the market's irrationality while an index fund may well be swept up in that irrationality.

- In certain areas requiring prudent judgment—especially foreign stocks and municipal bonds—actively managed funds consistently outperform passive ones.

- If you choose to explore active funds, you don't need a lot of them: the more such funds you have, the more your overall portfolio will look like a passive index.

- Active funds tend to do better when interest rates are rising, and also when there is a large performance gap between the best and the worst funds (known in the industry as "dispersion").

- An advantage of index funds is that they require very little research, something that can be appealing to the novice investor. They also come with less emotional strain because there is no expectation of beating the market.

I've spent a lot of time examining mutual funds and the ongoing debate about the merits of active vs. passive management. Not because I think they are necessarily the best investment vehicle available to you but because they are a popular and easy way to get your feet wet in the market. As is one of the biggest innovations to hit the investing world in recent years: the Exchange Traded Fund, or ETF.

The ETF Revolution

Exchange Traded Funds are similar to mutual funds in that they are not an asset class themselves—but simply a vehicle for investing in different asset classes, separately or in combination. In a way, they are kind of an evolution of the mutual fund, one that introduces increased accessibility, ease of trading, and liquidity.

Like mutual funds, ETFs pool investors' money and diversify by holding a "basket" of assets: sometimes narrowly focused on one sector or asset class, sometimes broadly diversified like many of the popular index funds. However, unlike a mutual fund, an ETF trades on an exchange, making it easy to buy and sell shares without an intermediary[2]. This results in lower operating costs, and tax benefits (we'll get into

[2] Parties called "Authorized Participants" ensure that ETFs trade near its fair market value.

those in a later chapter). At the turn of the century, there were only 90 ETFs with holdings of $70 billion. Today, world-wide, there are almost 7,000 ETF products, valued at $3 trillion.

ETFs have helped close the gap between institutional and individual investors, which is a good thing. The exchange traded securities **are an easy way for investors to branch out into asset classes like real estate and commodities.** For decades, the standard portfolio was split 60/40 between stocks and bonds. Institutional investors have for some time been breaking out of that two-dimensional mold, and now the individual investor can as well. Also, the low cost of ETFs and their growing popularity has helped push down costs for all mutual funds, active and passive.

When they were first introduced into the market, ETFs embraced the broadly-based, passive index approach espoused by Vanguard's John Bogle. The first such fund, symbol: SPY, tracks the S&P 500, much like Bogle's first index fund. It is by far the biggest ETF, with $166 billion in assets, and trails only Vanguard's Total Stock Market Index Fund as the largest fund in the world. But, in an investing environment where above-average returns have been rare, and in which companies are competing for the attention and business of skeptical and wary investors, **many ETFs have departed from their roots and become increasingly specialized.** Broad funds now account for only 20% of the ETF market. Yet ETFs are still often marketed as passive investments.

The ease with which ETFs can be traded also comes with a dark side, tempting investors to make short-term bets in a bid to try to "time" the market. While Vanguard and other proponents of passive indexing actively discourage short-term trading, ETFs come with no such restrictions. To the contrary, they are sometimes marketed to so-called "day traders"—speculators who move quickly in and out of securities to exploit momentary price advantages. ETFs typically experience a high *turnover* with an average *holding period* of only six months. At the time of writing this book, the SPY ETF is the world's most traded security, with an average daily trading volume four times that of Apple, the second-most traded security. On August 24, 2015—Black Monday, when the market fell over 5%, its worst day in four years—ETFs (which typically make up 25% of total trading volume) accounted for 40%. The SEC is currently looking into the role ETFs played in that day's market panic.

Buyer Beware

Exchange-traded funds are a valuable addition to the investor's menu. As with any tool, they are only as smart as the person using it. Keep the following things in mind as you investigate your options in this area:

- ✓ For the most part, use ETFs as a vehicle for broadly-based, index-like investing. Products with names like "total stock" or "total market" are more likely to stick to this approach.

- ✓ As with index funds, in areas like foreign stocks and municipal bonds, actively managed funds which allow for judgment calls may be a better bet than an ETF, and in some cases can actually be cheaper as well.

- ✓ ETFs can also be a problematic way to invest in certain commodities. Commodity ETFs usually hold so-called "futures contracts"[3] which can leave them vulnerable to speculative ups and downs.

✓ Take a buy-and-hold approach to ETFs, and resist the temptation to overreact to price fluctuations or to try to time the market.

Robo-Advisors and Smart Beta

Another significant new innovation available to the investor is the so-called "robo-advisor"—a low-cost, customized, auto-pilot approach to building and maintaining an investment portfolio. After clients input their stated goals, risk tolerance, and other preferences, a Google-like algorithm puts together an appropriate mix of investments—largely composed of ETFs. The approach has some appeal to Millennials who are distrustful of financial institutions, are open to non-traditional financial services, and enjoy the 24/7 access and mobile-friendly interface. There is also some evidence that algorithms and other "rules-based" approaches to investing can help take irrationality and emotion out of the equation.

On the other hand, just as with the ETFs they utilize, **it appears that some robo-advisor services have strayed from an early emphasis on passive indexing** and moved toward more targeted and aggressive approaches that resemble actively managed funds in some respects—yet without the

---

[3] In this book I stay away from the area of investing involving *futures, options,* and *derivatives*. Basically, these involve placing bets on future price movements, and, in many cases are more speculation than investing. While it is possible to hedge against risk and make money with these approaches, I recommend you steer clear of them.

critical human element, the ability to make judgment calls. They may not be the passive investing option they are sold as.

In a related development, some financial advisors have been marketing all-ETF portfolios to their clients that they claim are the best of both worlds: based on indexes, yet with the potential to beat the market. These "managed ETF accounts," as they are called, are thus somewhat of a contradiction: an active portfolio composed of supposedly passive instruments. "Is a managed ETF investment any better than an actively managed mutual fund?" asks one investment manager, Lawrence Glazer. **"In effect you are doing market timing, and most of the people who got into ETFs did so because they didn't believe in market timing."** Such accounts are growing in popularity, and heavily marketed. But a *Barron's* study finds they underperform non-ETF portfolios more often than not.

Strategic robo-advisors and managed ETF accounts both utilize a trendy concept known as "smart beta"—tactical risk factors that can be used to take advantage of small inefficiencies in the market. While some of the ideas have merit, the strategies don't have a long enough track record for investors to put too much confidence in them. And some would argue they are marketed under false pretenses: **offering investors the supposed safety and low risk of passive indexes, while at the same time promising above-average performance.**

In any event, robo-advisors and ETFs are a growing and evolving part of the investing menu. Funds under robo-advisor management have shot up sharply in just a few years: from $2 billion in 2013 to $53 billion in 2015. Part of this growth is due to more established players like Vanguard and Schwab entering the field with their own auto-pilot offerings.

Some of the early robo-advisors are experimenting with adding a human element to the mix, and such hybrid services will likely become a major part of the investing landscape.

ETFs, for their part, are poised to challenge mutual funds as the dominant investment vehicle: the *Journal of Financial Planning's* 2015 Trends in Investing Survey found that ETFs had overtaken mutual funds as the most popular product used and recommended by financial advisors. Robo-advisors and ETFs are both useful tools that can play a part in a comprehensive investing strategy, as long as you understand their limitations.

Bonds and Other Fixed-Income Investments

Bonds and other *fixed income securities* differ from stocks in a few key respects. With a stock you are buying a small piece of a company; with a bond, you are essentially buying debt. An institution (a government or corporation) needs to raise money, and does so by offering investors a proposition: in return for making a loan to the institution by buying a bond (at set denominations like $100 or $1000), the investor is guaranteed a set rate of return (in contrast to a stock). The "fixed" part of the definition refers both to this set interest and to a set maturity date: the time when the issuer promises to pay back the principal (again, very different from a stock, which comes with no pre-determined period of ownership).

Bonds in general carry less risk than stocks (and promise lower return). Its cash flows are more predictable and bondholders have a more senior claim to assets if the company goes bankrupt. *Corporate bonds* are the riskiest, because there is always the chance that the company seeking to raise money will go out of business or declare bankruptcy and thus default on its loan, risk (and return) is measured on a sliding scale according to the company's *credit rating,* with AAA being *high-grade.* Credit ratings of BB to C are on the bottom end of the scale, and are designated as so-called *junk bonds*—with high risk, but also, potentially, substantial returns.

The federal government issues three kinds of bonds: short-term *Treasury bills* (with maturity terms of 3 months to one year); *Treasury notes* (1 to 10 years); and long-term *Treasury bonds* (10 or more years). All three are at times collectively referred to as "Treasuries." States, counties, and cities raise money for various projects by issuing *municipal bonds* (sometimes called *muni bonds* or simply *munis*) whose term can be a short as a year, or as long as 30 years or more. Because they are backed by the government, Treasuries and munis[4] carry little risk of default (although the credit risk for municipal bonds can vary a good deal depending on the financial health of the local government). The main form of risk here is a loss of value if inflation and/or interest rates go up unexpectedly. Also note that municipal bonds come with substantial tax benefits, making them an attractive investment for high income earners in taxable accounts.

Since 1997, investors have had a new option added to the fixed-income menu: Treasury Inflated-Protection Securities, or TIPS. These are a variation on the standard Treasury note issued by the government. Like traditional Treasuries, they come with very little risk, and so are a great way to protect

---

[4] Municipal bonds are either backed by taxes or revenue from a certain project (such as toll collections on a bridge or tunnel). In either case, municipal bonds are often considered more risky than Treasuries, and that risk varies depending on the city and state involved.

capital, especially in volatile markets. But whereas an unexpected rise in inflation can erode or even eliminate the real return on a standard Treasury note, TIPS are indexed to the rate of inflation, as measured by changes in the Consumer Price Index, or CPI. While rates of return are modest for TIPS, they protect both your principal, and your purchasing power.

As we'll explore more in the next chapter, *fixed-income securities aren't going to make you rich, but they're an important element in a diversified portfolio.* For the most part, they behave differently than stocks, providing some protection in the event of a volatile or down market. Like stocks, bonds and Treasuries can be purchased directly, or through a mutual fund or ETF that specializes in that asset class. In general, the individual investor should prefer to look for low-cost bond funds that are broadly based, and steer clear of highly specialized funds promising above-average returns. Beating the market is a legitimate goal—but the way to do that is through stocks, not bonds.

Real Estate and Commodities

Commodities (a broad asset class that includes real estate) are, after stocks and bonds, the third major category in the investor's menu. As part of a diversified portfolio, they are attractive because their behavior in the market is distinct from both stocks and bonds. They can help protect you from volatility and inflation because the price of commodities tends, over time, to match inflation.

Commodities are sometimes also referred at as *real assets* (in contrast to financial assets). When you buy a company's stock, for example, you indirectly have a stake in the real assets under its control—like factories, trucks, or infrastructure. But you're also investing in a lot of intangibles: the value of the company's brand and the quality of its management, among other things. A commodity, by contrast, is something you can put your hands on.

Non-real estate commodities fall into broad categories such as energy (oil, coal, natural gas), agriculture (grains, livestock), and metals (both industrial metals like copper, and precious metals like gold). Some smart people argue that such commodities have a place in your portfolio, and that because they are tied to tangible goods society needs to survive they will, in the long run, provide solid performance. There are certainly many index funds and ETFs to choose from in this area. But I would argue that, especially for the individual investor just starting out, the disadvantages of commodities outweigh their advantages. They can be extremely volatile—a great deal more than the average investor can tolerate.

Real estate, on the other hand, is an asset that can help balance your portfolio *and* protect you from inflation without undue risk. Real estate assets are unique because they combine a fixed-income component with one of growth. Property can, over the long term, be expected to appreciate in value, offering opportunities for growth. And by issuing mortgages or collecting rent, investors can collect regular income.

As we saw earlier in our look at growing economic inequality, one of the reasons the 1% came out of the financial crisis and recession in better shape than most was the diversity of their holdings—which often include non-residential real estate. Obviously, this may not be feasible for the average investor who is probably happy to afford a primary residence.

But, in 1960, Congress added a new option to the investor's menu: the Real-Estate Investment Trust, or REIT. A kind of a mutual fund for real estate, a REIT is a pooled investment vehicle that allows you to buy into a company that owns a diversified array of income-producing commercial real estate: including office buildings, apartment buildings, shopping centers, and hotels. Over the long run, real estate returns yields that don't quite match those of stocks, but are superior to those of bonds. Low-cost index funds and ETFs both offer a range of options for investing in broad-based REITs.

Cash and Cash Equivalents

There's nothing new about cash as the ultimate safety option for your money. Many responded to the bank runs of the Great Depression by hiding their money in mattresses; and in recent years, Millennials have shown a tendency to keep more of their money in cash than previous generations.

But there's nothing exciting about cash either. You're not going to build real wealth through a savings account. So I'm not going to spend a lot of time on cash here, although, as a hedge against volatility and economic downturn, cash does play a role in your overall portfolio. Even aggressive investors like Warren Buffet have sometimes taken the temperature of the market, found it unappealing, and concluded that the wisest course was to stay on the sidelines and keep a substantial sum in cash.

Cash can be literal (cash in your mattress or a savings account) or in what are termed *cash equivalents*: high liquidity, low risk, and low return vehicles like money market accounts and short-term Treasuries.

Last, And Certainly Not Least: Stocks

Whether held individually, through a mutual fund, or ETF, stocks (or equities as they are often called) should be at the heart of your portfolio. During an extended bear market (such as the one after the bursting of the dot-com and Internet bubble in early 2000), an equity-heavy portfolio may underperform one weighted more toward bonds and cash, and we'll discuss strategies for surviving bear markets later in the book. But, for the most part and definitely over the long haul, **stocks will and should be your primary means for building long-term wealth.**

Aswath Damodaran, a professor at the Stern School of Business, annually updates historic returns for stocks (as measured by the S&P 500), 10-year Treasury Bonds, and 3-month Treasury Bills. As of the end of 2015, and going back to 1928, Professor Damodaran found returns for stocks, 10-year Treasury bonds, and 3-month Treasury bills as 11.41%, 5.23% and 3.49% respectively. Even during the last ten years, an uneven stretch for the stock market, stocks returned 9.03% compared to long-term bonds (5.16%) and short-term T-bills (1.16%).

There are a number of ways of categorizing stocks:

- **Size** – As measured by a company's *market capitalization* (the total value of its stock), they are seen as small-cap, mid-cap, or large-cap.

- **Style** – Stocks are usually seen either as *growth* (a company expanding at an above-average rate) or *value* (a company whose fundamentals are solid and its shares priced below those of its peers). Some might add a third style, *income* (stocks such as utilities that may not be attractive in terms of either growth or value, but which pay regular dividends).

- **Sector** – Standard & Poor's breaks up the economy and thus the stock market into ten broad sectors including: energy, telecommunications, information technology, health care, and financials. Each of these sectors can, in turn, be broken down into a handful of discrete industries.

- **Region** – American investors generally make the bulk of their investments in the *domestic* market; but in the interest of diversification, are also increasingly spreading out into the foreign or international market. Foreign markets are usually categorized as either developed (such as in Europe or Japan) or *emerging markets* (a developing country with a lower per capita GDP, but which is in the process of transitioning and thus may have great growth potential).

You will see these categories whether you are looking into individual stocks, mutual funds or ETFs. Morningstar has developed a widely-used "style box" that classifies stock funds according to varying combinations of style and size—so you could have, say, *large value, or small growth,* etc.

Stock-based or equity mutual funds and ETFs are a great way for beginning investors to get their feet wet in the stock market. Any of a number of popular, low-cost S&P 500 index funds or ETFs can efficiently buy you a diversified sampling of the U.S. stock market and allow you to capture a share of its overall long-term growth. Such broadly-based holdings should play an important role in any portfolio.

But, I also want to encourage you to consider modest investments in individual securities. Since the 2008 Financial Crisis, there has been a sharp and steady decline in directly owned equities; and Millennials in particular have been reluctant to get into the market. While I understand and appreciate the caution and wariness behind this trend, it has meant missing some major opportunities. As we saw with the few active fund managers who consistently win above-average returns, the greatest long-term success in the market comes from making strong, high-conviction investments and sticking with them. Warren Buffet may now promote the value of index funds but he made his wealth by, for example, investing over half his holdings in a little-known company called Geico at one point, and not by mimicking the rest of the market.

Investing in individual stocks definitely isn't for the faint of heart, and it is essential that you do your homework first. The online resources for doing that kind of research have never been greater. Those same online resources can allow you to develop your stock-picking abilities without risking any money. Many brokerages, as well as sites like Yahoo Finance, allow you to construct make-believe or hypothetical portfolios and then track their progress. This two-pronged approach is perfect for the beginning or tentative investor: You can use a broad index fund to get a foothold in the market, and develop the habit of regular savings and investing while using your virtual portfolio to develop stock-picking skill and confidence.

Putting It All Together (Preview)

Later on, I'll offer some tools and thoughts for evaluating individual stocks, and some things to look for when it comes to active funds, passive funds, and ETFs. For now, I hope you can appreciate (and aren't completely overwhelmed by) the menu of options available to the modern investor.

The sheer variety of choices can, in truth, be overwhelming at first. The art and science of putting it together—what we call *portfolio construction*—is something I'll also address in a later chapter. The important thing is to start simple (perhaps with an equity index fund and a bond fund), and then build your portfolio as your knowledge and confidence grow.

This chapter has introduced you to the idea of asset allocation. In the next chapter, we'll examine asset allocation as it relates to another key concept in investing: diversification.

Chapter 7

Diversification

In the previous chapter, we began to look at the concepts of *asset classes* and *asset allocation*. In the chapter before that, we examined **risk**. Diversification is where those two topics come together. You'll recall that, in Chapter 5 on Managing Risk, I introduced Harry Markowitz's ground-breaking assertion that the risk associated with an individual stock can be mitigated through diversification of one's total portfolio. This was a new approach to investing where the value of an investment was viewed, not just on its individual merits, but also by how it fit into an overall portfolio. The various investments in a portfolio, Markowitz argued, should complement one another by behaving differently in the market so that potential losses in any one investment will be "cancelled out" by gains in others. In essence, he was proposing a way for maximizing return while minimizing risk.

Diversification takes place both within and between asset classes. As a general rule, certain asset classes tend to behave differently in the market. Traditionally, for example, stocks tend do well during a bull market while bonds do better when the market is slumping. So in your asset allocation strategy, you will seek to have a mix of asset classes that complement one another in the way that works best for you. But you also want some diversity *within* each asset class. For example, you don't want the stock or equity portion of your portfolio to be weighted too heavily in any one sector. An investor who went all in on tech stock in 1999 was doing well for a while but then came crashing to the ground in 2000.

So in this chapter we'll consider the principles behind diversification and some strategies for carrying it out. Because diversification isn't a magic bullet, and doesn't represent the final word on portfolio management, we'll look at its limitations and critics as well. Just as there are two different schools of thought about what risk is and how to manage it, there are different views on diversification.

Many Boats, Many Routes

A balanced and diversified portfolio is akin to having a fleet of boats roaming the world and searching for profit. If all of those boats are in the same waters, traveling the same route, they will be exposed to the same potential threats (like storms and pirates), leaving you vulnerable. The essential principle of diversification is to spread risk and be diversified across as many different categories as possible: sectors of the economy, asset classes, and national markets.

> *"Ship your grain across the sea; after many days you may receive a return. Invest in seven ventures, yes, in eight; you do not know what disaster may come upon the land."*
> –Ecclesiastes 11:1-2

A broad S&P 500 index fund, for example, will diversify you across various sectors of the U.S. economy. But your money will all be tied up in stocks so if stocks take a dive, so will you. Bonds, on the other hand, tend to perform well in a down market, which is why for many years financial advisors recommended a 60/40 split between stocks and bonds. Today, bond yields are lower than they have been in a while, making them an unfavorable long-term investment. As we saw in the last chapter, modern investors have many more options at their disposal, making the 60/40 formula outdated. But the basic principle of trying to diversify across a broad range of asset classes and sub-categories holds.

Exactly how to split your investments across various asset classes and, how to manage your fleet of boats, is the challenge of asset allocation. As you begin to assemble your portfolio, be guided by the following basic principles.

- **Don't be afraid to start simple.** Like the pharmacy aisle with dozens of toothpaste brands, the sheer variety of investing options can be overwhelming. It's possible to put together a reasonably well-diversified portfolio with just three basic index funds or ETFs: a broad sampling of U.S. stocks; an international stock index; and a bond index. As we'll see later, many investors get carried away with the principle of diversification and create unnecessary redundancy and confusion in their portfolios.

- **Take advantage of the full menu of investing options.** Again, today's investor needn't be limited to the old asset allocation model of 60% stocks and 40% bonds. A wealth of index funds and ETFs offers ready access to asset classes like international stocks, real estate, commodities, and fixed income securities.

- **Diversification can be counterintuitive.** While later in the chapter we'll explore the flaws and limitations of diversification, it remains a powerful tool. Even if you question volatility as a proxy for risk, it is still remarkable that, **in a well-diversified portfolio, the rate of return will be the average of the individual investments while the volatility will be *far less* than the average.** This is due to the magic of negative correlation, which produces another surprise: investments that might be seen as risky on their own can actually reduce the risk of the total portfolio. For example, riskier emerging market stocks reduce overall portfolio volatility more than safer ones.

- **Diversification is a discipline.** The core idea of diversification is that some of your assets will be up while others are down, and vice versa. This can be a difficult thing to accept during a heated bull market when the pressure is on to "chase performance" and put all your money into the hottest assets. At such a time, diversification can appear unnecessary and even a drag on your portfolio, tying your money up in slow-growing or stagnant assets. As *Wall Street Journal* columnist Jason Zweig writes, "Whenever one sector of the stock market is hot, diversifying your money across other assets will always feel like a waste of effort—an umbrella you never seem to need... But no matter how many times you carry an umbrella without needing it, you will be very glad indeed to be carrying one when a downpour finally hits."

- **Asset allocation should be fluid, not fixed.** In general, the younger you are, and the longer your investment timeline, the more risk and volatility you can tolerate. In other words, you can (and should) have a portfolio more heavily weighted toward stocks, because that remains the most powerful tool for building wealth in the long run. But your needs and risk tolerance will change and evolve over the course of your life, and so should your asset allocation. There used to be an old rule-of-thumb that the percentage of your portfolio devoted to bonds should equal your age. While this is now seen as an outdated concept, the basic principal holds: As we near retirement, most of us will get more conservative with our investments. (Chapter 13 is devoted to the art of assembling and modifying your portfolio.)

Diversification and Correlation

The "many boats, many routes" metaphor is folksy way of explaining *correlation*: the extent to which any two assets, or asset classes, behave similarly in a given market. This relationship is measurable and quantifiable. If two investments over time mirror one another exactly, they are said to be perfectly correlated and to have a *correlation coefficient* of 1.0. At the opposite end of the scale, if they are mirror opposites (with one going up just when the other goes down, and to the same degree), they are said to be *negatively correlated*, with a correlation coefficient of -1.0.

Both of these concepts are central to Harry Markowitz's vision of a balanced and diversified portfolio. He is of the school that views the up and down fluctuations of individual investments as random and as unpredictable as the flipping of a coin. Diversification offers the promise of relative security in an uncertain environment. "It would be like flipping a large number of coins," he wrote. "We cannot predict with confidence the outcome of a single flip; but if a great many coins are flipped we can be virtually sure that heads will appear on approximately one-half of them." Thus, to the extent that assets and asset classes are not correlated, combining them in a single portfolio is a way of "canceling out chance events" and creating stability so the portfolio as a whole is superior to any one investment.

So let's see how the primary asset classes I introduced you to in the last chapter can complement one another in a balanced, diversified portfolio.

• **Domestic Stocks** – As I emphasize throughout the book, stocks or equities should be at the heart of your portfolio. In spite of their short-term ups and downs, over the long haul they will be the real engines of building wealth. Whether you invest in them individually, through mutual funds and ETFs, or a combination of these approaches, U.S. stocks should, in most cases, be your featured asset class. Both active and passive mutual funds are typically defined by an index or benchmark: basically, a cross-section of the stock market, sometimes very broad, and sometimes narrowly focused on a particular sector or industry. If you're going to go with the index approach to investing, at least to start with, the most basic is one that tracks the S&P 500—Standard & Poor's index of the 500 biggest companies in the U.S. market. Because these companies account for 70% of the domestic stock market, buying into that index is your best bet for "riding" the market long-term.

The past decade or so has seen a definite trend: toward passive index funds and away from active funds, and also away from direct investment in individual stocks. There are good reasons for this trend, and passive indexing has a place in just about any portfolio. But many experts also feel that this trend creates new opportunities for the smart contrarian investor can take advantage of irrationality in the market—something we'll explore a bit in this chapter and in more depth in the next chapter. **Beating the market by trying to time it or outsmart it is generally a bad idea. But avoiding its irrationalities and using them to your advantage is another matter**—and investing directly in individual stocks is the best way to pursue this contrarian path. So I encourage you to at least dip your toes in direct ownership of stocks.

• **Foreign or International Stocks** – Whether it's out of patriotism, or a belief in the strength of the U.S. economy, or simply the greater comfort level and familiarity with the domestic market, many investors are reluctant to stray too far from home and explore the international market. In the past, Americans had a good excuse for being highly concentrated in U.S. stocks. There were few affordable and accessible ways for the average investor to invest overseas; there were concerns about the financial accounting of foreign firms and it was more difficult to research distant markets. Now however, international accounting standards and a range of affordable options make it far easier for average investors to broaden their horizons.

Indeed, in the last three decades, Americans have begun to overcome their investing "home bias." In the past decade in particular, foreign index equity funds have gained at the expense of domestic ones. Broadly-based mutual funds are invested 25% overseas now as compared to only 8% in 2000. Yet investment overseas tends to fluctuate wildly, depending on how foreign stocks are doing at any given time. In January 1993, for example, after a long slump in the international market, foreign stocks accounted for only 5% of Americans' total equity investment. Foreign stocks then rallied, and in October1994 they hit a then all-time high of 14% of total equity. Currently, Americans keep about 70% of their assets in domestic equity although that market amounts to only about 50% of total global equity.

There are a number of reasons for investing overseas. Many of the world's fastest-growing companies are in other countries. And, although the U.S. still has the world's largest economy, in 2014 it accounted for only 22% of global GDP, down from 33% in 2001. Most important, because foreign stocks respond to very different economic conditions abroad, they tend to be negatively correlated to domestic stocks, often moving in opposite directions. For example, while the U.S. stock market took a nosedive in 2009, emerging market stocks prospered in the years immediately following the financial crisis, meaning that a portfolio with a healthy dose of foreign stocks would have done a better job of weathering the storm. Conversely, foreign stocks lagged in 2014 while domestic stocks soared. The undisciplined investor can easily grow impatient with the negative correlation that makes foreign stocks a valuable asset in the long run. So, if you're going to make international stocks a part of your portfolio, be prepared to weather their ups and downs.

• **Bonds and Fixed-Income Securities** – In the last chapter, we reviewed the range of fixed-income investing options available. What's important for the purposes of this chapter is to understand their negative correlation with stocks, and with one another.

There are arguments to be made for the merits of corporate bonds, domestic and foreign, and for municipal bonds. Some have made substantial profits in high-risk "junk" bonds. But remember that you are not going to build long-term wealth through bonds. Their purpose in your portfolio is to add stability and diversification. And, on those grounds, most experts agree that U.S. Treasury bonds offer the most reliable safe haven against the stormy ups and downs of the stock market. A Vanguard study agrees. One of the distressing aspects of the financial crisis was how risky assets started to move together, "in lockstep," in contrast to traditional negative correlations. In the years since, "only U.S. Treasury bonds," Vanguard found, "have proven to be a true diversifier, correlating at -0.3 to U.S. equities."

While some investing experts lump all fixed-income investments together, I suggest classifying Treasury Inflation-Protected Securities (or TIPS, which I previewed in the last chapter) as an asset class unto themselves, based on their very different relationship with inflation. Bonds have a unique connection with inflation. Basically it comes down to expectations. Assuming other factors stay equal, if inflation is higher than anticipated, bond performance will suffer, if it's lower, bonds will thrive. TIPS, however, have exactly the opposite relationship, protecting you against higher than expected inflation. Therefore, a mix of TIPS and regular Treasury bonds in your fixed-income portfolio will help you weather economic and market downturns, and unexpected volatility with inflation.

• **Real Estate** – As discussed in the last chapter, real estate is just one of many investments that fall into the broad category of commodities[1]. And while there are those who argue for the merits of investing in non-real estate commodities, and every few years someone seems to make a new case for investing in gold, the volatility and speculative quality of these assets makes them unsuitable, in my opinion, for the average investor.

Real estate—easily purchased through the pooled investment vehicle called a Real Estate Investment Trust, or REIT, however—is a valuable addition to any portfolio. It offers returns that are at times competitive with equities but with a low to moderate correlation with other assets. Moreover, it is positively correlated with inflation which makes it a good hedge against it. Finally, REITS are required to return the bulk of their earnings to shareholders in the form of dividends—which can either be reinvested or serve as a source of regular income.

The low correlation that has historically made real estate a terrific diversification tool sometimes fails to hold up during periods of severe economic stress. On the one hand, when stocks fell 9% in 2000, real estate went up 34%. In 2008, conversely, both fell sharply (real estate slightly more)—yet the stock market rebounded more quickly. Its correlation with stocks peaked at 80% in 2013, and has since fallen.

One last note about REITS as a diversifying tool: since 1990, they have shown 23% more volatility than stocks. That means they're a bit of a roller coaster, a roller coaster you

---

[1] Many analysts will treat real estate and commodities as two distinct asset classes. While there are important differences, they are both what we call "hard assets." And both tend to appreciate or go up in value during inflationary times, and depreciate or go down during deflationary times.

don't want to exit impulsively. This is where the discipline of diversification comes in. **It's a healthy thing that some of your non-equity assets will be going down as stocks go up,** and you need to resist the temptation to chase performance and divert the money into some temporarily hot asset.

A Brief Look at Portfolio Construction

Now that we've seen the primary asset classes and how they complement one another, the question becomes how to put them together? This challenge is the art and science of portfolio construction. I'll devote a later chapter entirely to assembling and maintaining a balanced portfolio. But for now let's take a look at a sample asset allocation strategy.

o   35% in U.S. Equities

o   15% in Foreign Equities (Developed)

o   15% in Foreign Equities (Emerging Market)

o   15% in Hard Assets (REITS and Commodities)

o   10% in U.S. Treasuries

o   10% in TIPS

Note that there is no ideal, one-size-fits-all approach to asset allocation. The portfolio that works best for you will depend on your goals (short-, mid-, and long-term) and the time horizons for each of them, as well as on your risk tolerance and risk capacity. The make-up of your portfolio will also evolve and change over the course of your lifetime.

I treat foreign stocks as two categories—developed and emerging market. This is because (as previously noted) they are often negatively correlated, moving in different directions as they respond to very different economic realities.

Specialized Index Funds and ETFs: Buyer Beware

As I mentioned in the previous chapter, index funds in their early years were grounded in the conservative, passive approach to investing espoused by Jack Bogle and others: Don't try to beat the market, just try to capture your "fair share" of its long-term upward trend. And Exchange-Traded Funds or ETFs at first took that approach as well[2].

Yet the last decade or so has seen the rise of what Bogle calls a "new breed of indexers" who try to beat the market using a variety of strategies (sometimes marketed as "smart" or "alternative"). A growing number of ETFs have also followed this specialized route. A particularly bad sign is that these ETFs are marketed to day traders—who exemplify the worst market-timing impulses—and that these ETFs experience high turnover and short holding periods.

There's absolutely nothing wrong with trying to beat the market. But one has to approach the challenge of doing so humbly, cautiously, and strategically—knowing how difficult it is to do, and fully appreciating the pitfalls along the way.

---

[2] While I believe investors can and should do better than just riding the market, the caution and prudence of the passive index approach has its merits: it helps investors avoid the rash and impulsive decisions that all too often result from attempts to time or outsmart the market. As we'll see in the next chapter, investors can, without realizing it, be their own worst enemies.

The problem with this new breed of "smart" index funds and ETFs is that investors often assume they are pursuing a low-risk, diversified, passive strategy—and the way these new products are marketed may encourage that perception, lulling investors into a false sense of security and into taking on greater risk than they realize. Index funds and ETFs are terrific investing tools—but best used in a broadly based, rather than narrowly targeted, strategy.

The Contrarian View of Diversification

Contrarians, especially those who advocate for Value Investing, don't entirely dismiss the virtues of diversification. There's no denying the value of constructing a portfolio of investments which complement rather than duplicate one another—smoothing out both the lows and the highs of individual fluctuations. Yet contrarians contend that diversification is not the magic bullet the Efficient Market school believes it to be. As a guiding principle of asset allocation, they argue, diversification is a flawed and vulnerable strategy.

Here are the four major issues with diversification as the cornerstone of an investing strategy:

1. **Risk ≠ Volatility.** As we discussed in Chapter 5, there are serious flaws to the idea of equating risk with volatility, and diversification (as a risk-mitigating strategy) is built on this assumption. The biggest risk is permanent loss, and volatility results in loss only when you have a short time line and are forced to sell when prices fall. If you can wait out that dip, your "losses" will be paper losses only, not real losses.

2. **Diversification cannot protect you from market risk.**
   While it might "smooth out" the ups and downs of your
   total portfolio, diversification doesn't protect you from
   the kinds of permanent losses often suffered during major
   market downturns like the ones that occurred in 2000 and
   2008. Contrarians even contend that diversification can,
   actually increase your exposure to market risk. If you
   take diversification and the Efficient Market Hypothesis
   to its logical conclusion and adopt an indexing approach
   to investing, you will be mirroring the market—which is
   usually a good thing in the long run, but can be disastrous
   in the short term. ("In the long run, the market gets it
   right," one economist writes. "But you have to survive
   over the short run, to get to the long run.") Warren
   Buffett and others survived The Lost Decade essentially
   by *abandoning diversification*—temporarily moving out
   of stocks and into safer investments. As Frank Martin
   writes, sometimes the key to successful investing isn't
   "how much you gain in the good markets but how much
   you don't lose in the ugly ones."

3. **Correlations aren't constant.** Negative correlation is
   essential to the soundness of diversification as a way to
   mitigate risk. The idea is that, at any given time, losses
   in one asset class will be "cancelled out" by gains in
   another. Yet if those negative correlations break down
   and all your assets are moving in the same direction at the
   same time, diversification suddenly loses a good deal of
   its power. We already saw how the negative correlation
   between real estate and equities suddenly disappeared in
   2008. And, in the years since the financial crisis, many
   historical correlations have shifted. This has happened
   before during bear markets, but some experts worry that

correlations may be altered indefinitely, thus making diversification far less effective than it used to be.

4. **You can't earn abnormally high returns through diversification.** Not every investor is up for the challenge of trying to outperform the market. There's nothing wrong with settling for riding the market; while it's not the optimal strategy, it is preferable to impulsive and ill-advised attempts to time and outsmart the market. But, if you do want to achieve superior performance, the only way to do so over the long run is by making concentrated bets, and by going against the crowd and conventional wisdom (something we'll explore further in Chapter 11). If you make diversification the cornerstone of your investing philosophy—and thus more or less pursue a passive, index approach—you are essentially tying yourself to the crowd.

Diversification, Passive Investing, and Behavioral Risk

In the next chapter, we'll explore irrationality in the market—and how herd behavior and cognitive bias can lead investors to act against their best interest, and sometimes to be their own worst enemy. While diversification certainly has its shortcomings, and is hardly a magic bullet, it does have considerable value in helping to mitigate what might be called *behavioral risk*: the likelihood of making bad decisions under uncertain conditions.

Daniel Bell, Richard Bernstein and others have researched "decision regret"—which applies not only to decisions resulting in losses, or bad outcomes or missed opportunities but also to *anticipating* decisions that might produce such a result. In the world of investing, decision regret can come into play when we invest in something and it loses money—but also when an investment option we pass up on does better than the one we chose (the regret of a missed opportunity). These researchers found that we are more likely to regret a path that is less conventional, that deviates from the norm. Bell found that people are sometimes willing to make trade-offs to avoid possible regret in the future, in other words, to sacrifice potential profits in order to avoid potential regret.

Bernstein and Bell conclude that diversification and indexing meet an emotional need in addition to a financial one: even if an investment takes a turn for the worse, our regret will be less intense if others are experiencing that same loss, if the decision to make the investment reflected the wisdom of the crowd, as opposed to going against the crowd. While this can lead investors to make unproductive herd-like decisions, it can also prevent them from panicking and making rash decisions to sell at the wrong time.

John Rekenthaler, a vice president of research at Morningstar, agrees. "I think passive funds are easier to own…Investors will have a better experience, in general, with passive funds because it gives them fewer reasons to make a bad decision."

The danger of making such quick short-term decisions is a major pitfall facing the individual investor. In a classic study entitled "Trading Is Hazardous to Your Wealth," researchers found that investors who traded most often had consistently poor performance. So, again, while the passive index approach isn't optimal, it is preferable to impulsive overtrading, and is a sound strategy if you feel you are vulnerable to such decisions.

Yes, diversification and index investing can protect investors from overtrading and overreacting. They can also help timid investors sleep better at night—which is no small thing. The danger, on the other hand, is to be lulled into complacency, into the assumption that your portfolio is less risky than it really is.

Can You Be Over-Diversified?

The conventional wisdom, that diversification is an unqualified positive and the key to successful investing, avoids this question. But the answer is: yes.

As we saw earlier, the most successful mutual fund managers are those who make concentrated bets, and who build their portfolios around a smaller number of "high-conviction" investments. Despite all the bad press about active managers, their first choices, the stocks they invest the most in, are often good ones. Studies have found that, even an average active fund manager's top five stocks consistently exhibited strong performance. The underperformance that mutual funds are criticized for occurs when, due to a variety of institutional pressures, managers add on more and more stocks because they have to.

Contrarian and value investor Frank Martin of Martin Capital Management is a strong believer in making just a handful of high-conviction, well-researched picks. Beyond a dozen or so such "thoroughbreds" as he calls them, he worries about a "dilution of quality." He cites research finding that **the risk-mitigating effects of diversification diminish greatly once a portfolio contains 15 or 20 stocks.**

> *"The idea of excess diversification is madness. Wide diversification, which necessarily includes investment in mediocre businesses, only guarantees ordinary results."*
>
> – Charlie Munger, longtime associate of Warren Buffett

For the average individual investor who might mix selective stock-picking with index investing and ETFs, the danger of over-diversification comes mainly through redundancy: owning funds that duplicate one another and cover the same ground. For example, owning a solid S&P 500 index fund or ETF gives you broad exposure to the heart of the U.S. stock market. There's no need to supplement it with additional sector- or industry-specific funds.

I suggested earlier that there is a case to be made for actively managed mutual funds as at least part of your investment strategy. If you decide to go this route, keep in mind that **owning more than a few active funds might make your overall portfolio resemble a passive index fund**—defeating the whole point of choosing an active fund in the first place, and making it less likely that you'll be able to outperform the market.

Passive Investing and Agility

Diversification and passive investing are not equivalent. Embracing diversification, up to a point, doesn't necessarily imply adopting a passive indexing approach to investing. Even active and aggressive investors acknowledge the central merit of diversification: holding investments in several different asset classes, investments that ideally will complement one another, behave somewhat differently under the same market conditions, and thus lend a portfolio stability and reduced volatility.

On the other hand, you'll recall that diversification, as we typically talk about it is grounded in the Efficient Market Hypothesis, and shares the same philosophical foundation—a belief in a rational and efficient market whose fluctuations are unpredictable and therefore can't be profited from and the assumption that volatility is a reasonable proxy for risk. If you take this philosophy to its logical extension, you will adopt the passive, index-based approach espoused by John Bogle and others. According to this view, it is folly to try to beat the market; so the wisest course is to try to ride it.

Again, this is not the worst approach to investing, not by a long shot. It can protect you from the worst mistakes investors are prone to, and may represent the most prudent, mistake-free and anxiety-free path for some. Yet I would argue that, even if you choose to adopt a cautious and conservative strategy for the most part, you can significantly improve your odds by going against the crowd and against conventional wisdom at least some of the time—and a purely passive, index-based approach will prevent you from doing so.

I stated before that diversification not only *doesn't protect* you from market risk, it can actually *increase* your vulnerability to such risk. To illustrate that point, let's return to the "many boats, many routes" analogy from earlier in the chapter. When you adopt a purely passive, index-based approach to investing, you essentially become a tiny dingy tied to the huge ocean liner that is the market. You rise and move forward when the winds and waters are favorable; but your hands are tied when stormy weather hits. You are married to the market, sink or swim.

This is not a question of theory but of cold hard mathematics. Most passive indexes, whether they be mutual funds or ETFs, are what is called *cap-weighted*. That's a fancy way of saying the bigger the company and, the higher its *market capitalization* or the total value of its stock, the more heavily your index fund will be invested in it. So when the market becomes irrationally enthusiastic about a given stock or sector, so will your index fund.

Go back to 1999, when internet, dot-com and tech stocks were all the rage. Contrarian investors like Warren Buffet and Howard Marks were skeptical, sensing a bubble ready to burst. They refused to jump on the bandwagon (even though they sacrificed short-term profits by doing so), and adopted a more conservative approach.

When you are married to the market, when you take the principle of diversification to its logical extreme, you give up this option. You lack agility.

Agility is something we'll explore in detail in Chapter 10: The Active Vs. Passive Debate and Chapter 11: Beating the Market. But, basically, it comes down to *flexibility*, and *adaptability*: the freedom to pull back when the market is overheated (playing defense); to jump in when the market is undervalued (playing offense); and to sit on the sidelines when the water is murky and the options are unclear (exercising patience). Passive index funds don't have that freedom, that flexibility, that agility. They are set up to let the market make decisions for them, under the assumption that human decisions are inherently untrustworthy. Passive funds miss out on the benefits of both judgment and restraint. One of the biggest advantages of active investors (and active management) is not what they can buy, but what they can avoid.

One last word on this subject ... Although I briefly discussed cash (and cash equivalents) in a previous chapter, the Millennial Investor's Menu, I did not address it earlier in this chapter as one of your primary asset classes. And, indeed, cash is often thought of as dead weight in an investor's portfolio: money that's just sitting there, under-utilized. In a low-interest environment such as the one we've experienced in recent years, cash (whether in savings or money market accounts) may fail to keep up with inflation and lose purchasing power over time.

Yet cash—and the tendency of Millennials to keep more of their assets in cash than previous generations—can come in handy as well. Cash might lose a small amount of purchasing power against inflation and it's certainly not going to help you build wealth over time. But it will protect you against an investor's biggest risk: the permanent loss of capital and it will allow you to invest a larger portion of money when investments are less expensive. Remember... over the course of the "lost decade" of 2000-2010, cash outperformed the S&P 500, and the best contrarian investors kept unusually high cash reserves over this stretch—not only to preserve capital but as spending money (what investors call *dry powder*) to tap into when bargains presented themselves.

RESILIENCE. AGILITY. OPTIONALITY.

Mohamed El-Erian is chief economic advisor at Allianz, one of the world's largest financial services firms, a former deputy director of the International Monetary Fund, and a savvy observer of international markets. He argues for the importance of cash in a world where market volatility is likely to increase, and where traditional correlations between asset classes are breaking down. In most strategic asset allocations, he says, "cash plays no role whatsoever." It's seen as a "dead asset." It's not, he says—especially not in today's world. "You need resilience. You need agility. And you need optionality. The only thing that gives you these three things is cash. Suddenly cash becomes a part of the strategic asset allocation, putting conventional wisdom on its head."

Making Sense Of It All

Clearly, the model put forward by Modern Portfolio Theory has holes in it. Some defenders of the classical approach have attempted to modify and update the initial formulas, replacing volatility (beta) with factors like momentum and book/price ratio. Diversification still holds considerable merit as long as you keep the following in mind:

o   Diversification demands discipline: requiring you to remain patient while one asset class loses value, even while others are gaining.

o   You can't diversify away market risk and are still vulnerable to major downturns in the overall market.

o   The only way to avoid losses during such downturns is to follow contrarian strategies and make substantial adjustments to your asset allocation.

o   Diversification as a guiding principle will not allow you to outperform the market.

Chapter 8

When Markets (and Investors) Don't Behave Rationally

In previous chapters, we've discussed how the Efficient Market Hypothesis (the basis for a lot of thinking about economics in general, and investing in particular) is built on a number of assumptions—one of which is that those participating in the market are rational, and make decisions based on an objective assessment of risk and reward. We've also seen how a growing number of contrarians, many from the field of *behavioral economics*, question this assumption, and make a convincing case that there are times when the market and its participants are anything but rational.

In this chapter, we'll examine these beliefs in greater detail: the science and research behind behavioral economics, and the consequences for the market and for you as an investor. You will hopefully walk away from this chapter understanding:

1. How emotion and irrational thinking can cloud your judgment as an investor

2. How these same forces can distort the market as a whole

3. How you can avoid, or even profit from, the common mistakes of others

Know Thy Enemy, Know Thyself

A slim text from ancient China called *The Art of War* has been used in military academies for decades. But when Michael Douglas's character Gordon Gekko quoted the book in the movie *Wall Street* ("every battle is won before it is ever fought"), sales of the book soared. Suddenly political strategists and business gurus were quoting a Chinese general who walked the earth 2,600 years ago.

Investing is its own kind of war, and there is an art to that war. Investors would do well to pay close attention to another quote from the book: "If you know the enemy and know yourself, you need not fear the result of a hundred battles. If you know yourself but not the enemy, for every victory gained you will also suffer a defeat. If you know neither the enemy nor yourself, you will succumb in every battle."

Our first instinct is to think of any war as a battle against an outside opponent. And, in the case of investing, a battle against other investors, the market, the odds, conventional wisdom. But it is first a battle against ourselves. Or, to put it another way, a challenge to understand ourselves and how we react to uncertainty.

A central theme of this chapter (and something increasingly taught in the best business schools) is the brain function. The past few decades have seen huge leaps in neurological research. Particularly interesting, for our purposes, is research into how financial matters (thinking about money, worrying about money) affect the brain. By understanding our reactions to certain events and circumstances, we can avoid the same pitfalls that we and others have made in the past and will be tempted to make in the future.

"Animal Spirits"

Although human beings have been around for about 200,000 years, it wasn't until about 11,000 years ago that our ancestors began making the transition from hunter-gatherers to what we now call civilization. And, while the environment we have built for ourselves has rapidly progressed since then, especially in the last few centuries, the human brain has evolved at a glacial pace. Our brains today aren't much different from when we were hunting bears, fighting lions, and gathering crops.

We like to think of ourselves as beings of reason and logic, but our decisions are driven largely by instinct. How we behave in the world of finance and investing is no exception. John Maynard Keynes, a famed early 20th century economist who was well aware of this phenomenon wrote about what he called "animal spirits"—the "spontaneous optimism" driving markets and economies in good times. His observations anticipated contemporary research into how our everyday financial decisions are distorted by cognitive bias, overconfidence and emotion.

Benjamin Graham wrote *The Intelligent Investor* years before anyone spoke about "behavioral economics", but his investing philosophy was shaped by the tough first-hand lessons of the 1929 Crash and the Great Depression. He watched (and, like most people, lost money) while the market briefly rallied; crashed again in 1930; rallied again; and crashed once more in 1937. To drive home the human element inherent in investing, he wrote of the market not as a distant impersonal force but as an imaginary character he called Mr. Market—one subject to frequent mood swings, sometimes acting logically but occasionally, irrationally.

Slow and Fast Thinking

Behavioral economics is sometimes oversimplified as exposing the emotional underbelly of the so-called rational market. But it's not as simple as pitting emotion and reason against one another. The truth is more complicated, and more interesting.

A leader in the field is Daniel Kahneman, a psychologist by training who found that his research into decision-making had a special relevance to economics and the stock market, and who would eventually go on to win a Nobel Prize in Economics. In his book *Thinking, Fast and Slow*, he identified two styles or modes of thinking. The first works quickly and intuitively, relies heavily on association, and is easily swayed by emotion. The second is deliberate, methodical, and logical—but also very slow. Neither is better, and we need both of them. Every day, every hour, we process huge amounts of information, and make hundreds of decisions, both large and small. We don't have time to work through it all slowly and carefully, which is where our intuitive, instinctual thinking comes in to play. Intuitive thinking has emerged as an evolutionary necessity, and it's spot on a good deal of the time.

But, because it relies on taking shortcuts, it's also vulnerable to what scientists call *cognitive bias*—ways in which those same shortcuts lead us to flawed conclusions. Experts have detailed as many as 58 different varieties of cognitive bias that can lead to poor business decisions. Many stem from the "narrative fallacy"—the tendency of the brain to create coherent stories based on random facts, and to see cause and effect where there is none.

Behavioral economics is a fascinating area, and although we'll touch on some of these biases as we go along, we can't go into it in depth. Former trader and award winning author Nicholas Nissim Taleb's book *Fooled By Randomness* is another important contribution to the field, and I've listed some other books in the Recommended Reading section in the back of the book. But the bottom line, as Daniel Kahneman puts it, is this: **"Learn to recognize situations in which mistakes are likely and try hard to avoid significant mistakes when the stakes are high."** We are most prone to mistakes in situations marked by a high degree of uncertainty. And, as you're hopefully well aware by now, the stock market is chockfull of uncertainty.

Emotion and Money

The shortcomings of intuitive thinking aren't simply a case of emotion vs. reason. But emotion does come into play, and is a major focus of economist Meir Statman's book *What Investors Really Want*. Like Kahneman, Statman isn't out to demonize intuition or emotion. "Emotions complement reason more often than they interfere with it," he says. But he also wholeheartedly rejects the premise of a rational market driven by participants acting solely on the basis of objective self-interest. "We want higher returns," he writes, "but so much more." Just as our jobs are only partly about earning a living, he contends that our relationship with our investments can't be viewed in purely economic terms.

Obviously economic motivations are a big part of why we invest (Statman terms these *utilitarian benefits*). But we are also, he says, seeking *emotional* and *expressive benefits*. Emotional benefits revolve around how our participation in the market makes us feel. There is a certain thrill to taking a chance on a risky stock, and if that stock performs well, we feel smart and proud. By contrast, following a conservative strategy heavy in bonds might make us feel safe and secure. Expressive benefits have more to do with our identity, and our values. Accumulating funds for our kids' education fuels our sense of passing on a legacy to the next generation. Investing in companies known for a high degree of social responsibility is a way to express our concerns for society and our community—a particularly relevant factor for many Millennials.

Danger at the Top...

Our most important investment decisions will likely take place at the extremes of the stock market: when the market is riding high or when prices are sliding and panic starts to set in. These are precisely the moments when emotion and cognitive bias are liable to get the best of us. At these times, try to remember Sun Tzu's motto, "Know thy enemy, know thyself."

Our portfolios can go on an upswing for any number of reasons. Sometimes, we're just riding the rising tide of the market as a whole. At other times, sheer luck plays a role. While there are always cases of portfolio managers outperforming the market each year, sustaining that performance over several years is another thing altogether. But, when our portfolio is doing well, we tell ourselves that we're on a hot streak (what psychologists call the "Gambler's Fallacy"), or we overestimate our own skill in picking investments—even though, more often than not, skill has little to do with it.

In a word, we become overconfident. Even seasoned businessmen and investors aren't immune. Former General Electric CEO Jack Welch admitted he bought the brokerage firm Kidder Peabody (even though he knew "diddly" about it) because a run of successes had left him feeling lucky. And, in a phenomenon known as "chasing performance," professional fund managers are often guilty of trying to ride the wave of a hot market by acquiring assets whose recent performance makes them appealing and popular—even when a more sober examination might reveal them to be overvalued. Chasing performance is sometimes a symptom of overconfidence and sometimes its opposite: doubt and insecurity. **A fear of missing out can lead you to make a trendy investment without the necessary due diligence, or to jump on the bandwagon of a rising stock whose hot streak is bound to come to an end**, probably sooner than later.

Additionally, **overheated stock markets quite literally overheat our brain**. In a study published in the journal Neuron, researchers using magnetic resonance imaging (or MRI) found that sudden financial gains stimulate the brain in ways similar to "euphoria-inducing" drugs like cocaine, and that these brain patterns also resemble those experienced during sexual arousal. Moreover, even the anticipation of such gains was enough to fire up the brain's pleasure center.

... And at the Bottom

While greed leads investors to be overconfident (and thus over-purchase) during a rising or "bull" market, fear can paralyze those same investors during a falling or "bear" market. Interestingly, the brain reacts even more strongly to loss than to gain: the pain of a $100 loss is equal to the pleasure of a $200 gain. Kahneman calls this "loss aversion," and it leads investors to be overly cautious during down markets.

The fear that grips many investors during a down market not only prevents them from taking advantage of bargain prices—it also leads them to hold on too long to a bad investment (which is different from riding out a dip in an otherwise solid investment). If an investment is radically underperforming its benchmark and similar investments, it might be wise to cut your losses and sell (and benefit from the tax write-off). But a common behavior is to rationalize holding onto a losing proposition because of the money and time we've already invested (the so-called "sunken-cost fallacy"), and because it hurts to admit a mistake.

Compound Psychology: Bubbles and Panics

When the market is calm, irrational decisions by individual investors might very well offset one another. In other cases, the effect of those decisions can add up in a cumulative way.

And in more extreme cases, those decisions become mutually reinforcing. As Meir Statman puts it, "Sometimes our behaviors collectively compound rather than merely sum." The result is a kind of herd mentality, producing bubbles on the upside and panics on the downside.

In a 1996 speech, then Federal Reserve Chairman Alan Greenspan used the term "irrational exuberance" to describe the collective optimism of the dot-com boom driving the stock market upward. Sure enough, that boom turned into a bubble and eventually burst. Several years later, Nobel Prize-winning economist Robert Shiller wrote a book of the same name about the forces of unreason in the market. In the book's second edition, published in 2005, he openly worried about the bubble in the housing market—and two years later his worries were realized in the sub-prime mortgage crisis.

Bubbles inevitably burst, often producing panics in their wake. "Herds inflate bubbles, pumping stock prices far above their values," Statman wrote, "and herds deflate bubbles faster than they have inflated them." The net effect, is that individual investors commit more money to the markets as it rises and less as it falls, which is exactly the opposite of what investors should be doing. **In other words, despite the well-worn adage to "Buy low, and sell high"… all too often, investors do just the opposite.**

Staying Smart in an Often Irrational Market

Right now you're probably wondering: If the market is so unpredictable, so subject to the influence of emotion, irrationality and herd behavior, how can I ever hope to succeed? All of the above is indeed sobering, and it is meant to be—like a cold, bracing splash of water to the face. But it shouldn't paralyze you or discourage you from participating in the market, and even taking some calculated chances. You just have to be smart about it.

And being smart means, first and foremost, understanding the pitfalls that so many individual investors and even professionals fall for, and doing your best to avoid them. **If you follow a set of guiding principles, you can minimize your mistakes, make more good choices than bad ones, and maybe even profit from the mistakes of others:**

1) Be A Healthy Skeptic.

This is such an important point. In his book *The Most Important Thing*, Howard Marks stresses the importance of contrarian, "second level" thinking. This mean not going against the crowd just for the sake of it but looking critically at what seems to be the consensus point of view. You will outperform the market, he claims, only by being successful at "non-consensus" strategies.

A big part of being a healthy skeptic is being selective, and a bit suspicious about the media you consume. A good deal of media coverage of the financial markets appeals to the twin demons of emotional investing: greed and fear. Learn to identify and stay away from market reporting characterized by these two extremes.

2) Don't Trust Forecasters.

An essential part of skepticism is a distrust of forecasters who almost invariably pander to our emotional response to the market. They tend to be either unbridled optimists, promising rich returns for modest risks, or doom-and-gloom pessimists. Whether they're peddling hope or fear, stay away from them. As the famous economist John Kenneth Galbraith said: "We have two classes of forecasters: Those who don't know – and those who don't know they don't know."

Although some people credit him with predicting the collapse of the sub-prime market in 2007, Nassim Nicholas Taleb (author of *Fooled By Randomness, The Black Swan, and Antifragile*) isn't a fan of making predictions. Instead, he argues for what he calls "non-predictive decision-making"—a stance that is very similar to Meir Statman's advice to *prepare* rather than *predict*.

3) Know What You Don't Know.

We began this chapter with Sun Tzu's motto, "Know thy enemy, know thyself." We return to it now because one of the most important kinds of skepticism is the one that is turned inward: at one's own pre-conceptions and cognitive biases. **A central insight of behavioral economics is our tendency to see cause and effect where there is none, to think we know more than we know.** Guarding against this is crucial.

Even George Soros, one of the world's great investors, with a cumulative rate-of-return that rivals that of Warren Buffett admits he is "overwhelmed," by the persistent reality of uncertainty. "I'm constantly on watch, being aware of my own misconceptions, being aware that I'm acting on misconceptions and constantly looking to correct them."

4) Avoid Impulsive Decisions.

As we discussed earlier, often the most important decisions an investor makes occur when the market is at an extreme: in the grip of an optimistic bubble or a pessimistic panic. It is at those extremes when an investor is mostly likely to make a rash decision driven by emotion or cognitive bias.

Our vulnerability to impulsive decisions can be gauged in part by how frequently we buy and sell investments. Overtrading is a common pitfall for both the individual, and the professional investor. The more we turn over our portfolio, the more we expose ourselves to errors of judgment. One researcher, Terry Odeon, found that the most active traders generally had the poorest results—and, interestingly, that men were more prone to such overtrading than women.

5) Stick To Process.

This might be the most important rule of the bunch. A clearly defined process, governed by simple but flexible rules and principles, is the best way to guard against impulsive decisions. Figure out your short-term, mid-term, and long-term goals– determine a set of sound principles for meeting those goals, and then stick with them. That doesn't mean you don't adapt and occasionally reconsider your strategy or realign your portfolio. (We'll discussing portfolio rebalancing in the final chapter.) But it does mean you err on the side of buy-and-hold and stay away from overtrading—from constantly tinkering with your portfolio and trying to "time" the market just right.

For example: You might build an investment strategy around a core of index funds or ETFs that you think are strategic yet reasonably diversified. And, instead of trying to "play" the market and be smarter than you really are, you set up a schedule of automatic investments into those funds. You trust that a well-conceived system, over time, will be smarter than your day-to-day self.

Beware the Pendulum

In the next chapter we'll examine the cyclical movements of the economy and the stock market. We'll consider how to navigate those movements, and not get burned by them. But the point of *this* chapter is to understand that it's not just the numbers that swing (sometimes dramatically) from high to low but the emotions and psychology of investors—even seasoned and professional investors who should know better.

It bears repeating that avoiding mistakes is especially difficult at the extremes of the market. **When everyone else is buying, it's hard not to join in.** (And harder to sell investments that are overvalued but still doing well.) **And when everyone is selling, it's hard not to join the panic.** (And even harder to be an active buyer.)

At the high end, the market is gripped by blinding optimism and certainty; at the bottom end, by crippling doubt. Smart investors learn to be skeptical during the peaks and to recognize opportunity in the valleys. It's about monitoring the pendulum of the market, and being mindful of how that pendulum affects your own decision-making.

Because in the end, as Ben Graham wrote decades ago, "investing isn't about beating others at their game. It's about controlling yourself at your game."

Chapter 9

Cycles

There are cyclical patterns that emerge in the economic and financial behavior of a nation. As an individual investor, you need to understand how these cycles can affect your portfolio. Most important, you need to be aware of the potential dangers and traps that lurk in both the highs and lows of these cycles. Trying to actually profit from them is a tricky matter, and one best approached with caution.

While the terms given to these cycles are sometimes used interchangeably, and while they are certainly interconnected, they are also quite distinct. The *business cycle* (sometimes also termed an *economic cycle*) revolves around whether Gross Domestic Product or GDP is rising or falling, and by how much. A *financial cycle* has to do with the availability of credit, the accumulation of debt, and related phenomena such as interest rates. *Market cycles* concern the specific question of whether stock market prices are rising or falling. Some of the cause and effect connections between the three different cycles are obvious, others not so much.

There are a lot of theories about how to predict these cycles and how to profit from them. It is good to have a basic understanding of some theories, but acting on them is another thing entirely. As a general rule of thumb, I advise you use this understanding mainly to avoid costly mistakes. Profiting from these cycles is, again, a tricky matter—thinking you can somehow "outsmart" the market is more often than not an invitation to disaster.

Business Cycles

A business cycle describes the long-term up and down movement of a nation's economy as measured by its Gross Domestic Product. In the simplest terms, the economy is either in a growth (expansion) phase or a recession (contraction) phase. The generally accepted definition of a recession is two consecutive quarters of decline in GDP.

There are various models for further breaking down a business cycle. Economist Joseph Schumpeter's model of: 1) a period of expansion; 2) a crisis (stock market crash, high-profile bankruptcies, etc.) halting the expansion; 3) recession; 4) recovery (during which the economy and market slowly rebound from the low point, or trough). The economy has completed a business cycle when it has gone through all four stages. The National Bureau of Economic Research (NBER) has classified eleven such cycles in the post-WWII economy of the United States.

Economist Joseph Ellis argues that consumer spending (which accounts for 70% of GDP, with capital and government spending sharing the remaining 30%) is the primary engine of growth. He argues that increased consumer spending leads to increased production which, in turn, leads to increased capital spending, or capital expenditure (a company's investment in property, equipment and facilities). Increased production and capital spending both generate higher corporate profits and these are ultimately reflected in a rising stock market. Higher profits also generally result in high wages and levels of employment which reinforces a growth or expansion phase.

There is a good deal of disagreement as to the nature and cause of business cycles. I don't recommend that the individual investor get too caught up in these debates, or in the day-to-day forecasting chatter about the economy and the market (what Ellis calls the "noise" of the financial press). Just be aware of these broad movements and what they can mean for the market and your portfolio—something we'll examine more closely in a bit.

Financial Cycles

If business cycles are about the expansion and contraction of GDP, financial cycles are about the expansion and contraction of credit and debt. Financial cycles tend to run longer than business cycles. Where a business cycle might go from peak to trough over a period of 5-7 years, a financial cycle might do so over a much longer period. Since the 1960s, the duration of the average financial cycle has been about 16 years. As with anything having to do with economics or finance, there is considerable disagreement about the factors driving financial cycles, and also their effect on both business cycles and market cycles.

Economist Hyman Minsky, believing that all three cycles (business, financial, and market) were deeply connected, proposed a "Financial Instability Hypothesis" that described a boom and bust cycle for credit markets that overlaps with (but isn't equivalent to) business and market cycles. In prosperous times, healthy corporate cash flow results in looser credit requirements. Banks lower their own interest rates and chase profits and market share by lending out more money and financing increasingly risky investments. Companies that borrow money from banks follow suit. The net effect is a speculative euphoria that produces a bubble which, as all bubbles do sooner or later, bursts. In the subsequent financial crisis, credit suddenly tightens up and the economy contracts. Companies find it difficult to borrow money, which stunts their growth, and leads to layoffs and, in some cases, bankruptcies.

During much of the post-WWII era, economists didn't pay much attention to the relationship between financial cycles and business cycles. But, with the sub-prime mortgage crisis of 2007, Minksy's ideas came back into favor, even though he had passed away in 1996. Contemporary Claudio Borio defines cycles as "self-reinforcing interactions between perceptions of value and risk... which translate into booms followed by busts." The peak of a financial cycle almost always produces a financial crisis, he says. And a business cycle recession that coincides with a financial contraction tends to be 50% deeper than it otherwise would be—and with a much weaker recovery (which is exactly what we've seen with the Financial Crisis of 2007-2009 and its aftermath).

It's a complicated picture—and one further complicated by the effect of the Fed's monetary policy and the government's fiscal policy.[1] Appreciate all the different forces that can affect the stock market, forces that even the best economists in the world can't fully explain, much less predict. **Know what you don't know and be wary of forecasters.** And keep in mind how the cognitive biases and irrationality that were the focus of that last chapter can contribute to and exacerbate the booms and busts of business, financial and market cycles.

Market Cycles and Business Cycles

Before you see how to factor all of these three cycles into your own investment decisions, let's take a closer look at the key features of how market and business cycles relate to one another. While the connection is up to interpretation it's safe to say that, in some cases, the market *reacts* to the business cycle; in others, *anticipates* or predicts it or even *contributes* to its ups and downs.

The clearest instances of the market *reacting* to the business cycle occur when there is an obvious shock to the business world (like a major bellwether company reporting an unexpected drop in earnings) or the financial world (like the failure of Lehman Brothers in 2008 that deepened an already serious banking crisis). Investors typically respond to such shocks to the system with what is called a "flight to quality"—a move from higher-risk investments to lower-

---

[1] The Federal Reserve helps regulate both interests rates and the money supply. Through its *monetary* policies, it is able to partly control *liquidity* and how loose or tight credit is. After the Financial Crisis, the Fed not only kept interest rates at close to zero; it also engaged in a program called *quantitative easing* (or QE). QE is a fancy way of saying the Fed stimulated the economy by purchasing bonds with "electronic cash" that did not previously exist. In recent years, the Fed has phased out of this program.

risk ones. Sometimes this flight is a movement between asset classes (from stocks to bonds, for example). But it can also be a movement *within* a given asset class: from a speculative company with high debt to a more stable "blue chip" company, for example; or from a corporate bond to a government-backed security. Because the lower-risk investments involved in such a shift (like bonds, T-bills and money market funds) also tend to be more liquid, this is sometimes called a "flight to liquidity" as well.

Because of the nature of investors to price in future expectations of the economic fundamentals (those of an individual company, sector, or the entire economy) into stock prices, the stock market can sometimes predict or *anticipate* fluctuations in the business cycle. Declines in the stock market usually occur just before an economic recession and end just before an expansion. Yet the market is just as often a faulty predictor. As George Soros relates, "It is an old joke that the stock market predicted seven of the last two recessions. Markets are often wrong."

Soros goes even further, contending that while the market might correctly (and just as often incorrectly) *anticipate* economic shifts, it can also *precipitate* them. The market's anticipation of an economic downturn might trigger the kind of conservative economic behavior that could prevent a recession from actually materializing, or it could trigger a panic that actually helps turn a slowdown into a downturn. Conversely, an overly optimistic market (recall Alan Greenspan's "irrational exuberance") can cause expectations to rise faster than the fundamentals would indicate. Soros uses the term *reflexivity* to designate the self-reinforcing momentum (up or down) in which, as he says bluntly, "Markets can influence the events that they anticipate."

The relationship between business cycles and market cycles is complex and hotly debated. Some so-called "macroeconomic investors" attempt to profit from them. But this is a risky proposition for the average investor—particularly given the fact that there is no clear, precise, predictable relationship between the two cycles. It's worth noting that in the 1964-1981 bear market, GDP grew by 370%, yet the stock market was flat. Conversely, GDP grew very slowly during the bull market that followed.

Market Cycles: Bulls and Bears

In1999, Warren Buffett expressed skepticism that the hot tech and dot-com driven market of the time was unsustainable—and in doing so, noted the tendency of the stock market to move in roughly 17-year cycles. In the preceding bull market (one that, as Buffett suspected, was on its last legs) that had begun in 1982, the Dow had grown ten-fold. Yet in the 17 years preceding that unprecedented boom had been a long bear running from 1964 to 1981, during which the Dow had essentially been flat. **There is absolutely nothing scientific or inevitable about that 17-year pattern.** In fact, some analysts date that bear market from 1968 to 1982, making it a 14-year stretch. But the intermediate term pattern holds, more or less, in preceding years as well: that bear was preceded by a modest bull period, running from the late 40s to the late 60s, of somewhere between 17 and 19 years; and before that was another bear, beginning with the stock market crash of 1929 and lasting (again, depending on how you date it) from 18 to 20 years.

What are we to make of these long-term bears and bulls (or as Buffett called them, extended "lean" and "fat" periods)?[2]

Again, there is nothing scientific or inevitable about this pattern. But it provides the wise and skeptical investor with a useful way to step back and see the forest for the trees. Because what is deceiving about these long-term cycles is that they contain short-term cycles that seem to send the opposite signal. **In other words, there are rallies within long-term bears, and sharp dips or corrections within long-term bulls—** and investors with short-term horizons and poor memories sometimes lose sight of the big picture and overreact to these temporary fluctuations.

Let's go back to Warren Buffett in 1999. Mindful of these long-term patterns, he was skeptical of the sustainability of the rally: he felt the stock market was overpriced, and refused to jump on the high-tech and dot-com bandwagon. Just as important, even as the stock market began to recover in 2002 and then build up toward a significant rally, he remained skeptical, and kept large cash reserves. **He realized that what looked like a new bull was just a short-term rally in a long-term bear.** And his caution paid off: as he was in a better position to withstand the financial and stock market crisis in 2008.

An example of the reverse: In the midst of the great bull market of 1982 to 1999 was a temporary crash in late 1987:

---

[2] Analysts refer to these stretches as *secular* bulls and bears. To avoid confusion, I will mainly use the adjective *long-term*. We normally think of secular as being the opposite of religious. But this usage harkens back to the Latin root of the word, which is *saeculum*, meaning for a "long period of time."

Black Monday, the single largest one-day drop the Dow has ever experienced. Those who sold in panic while the market was falling were needlessly throwing good money away (unless they were smart enough to buy at the bottom—which few investors are).

Of course, recognizing these patterns in hindsight is one thing; anticipating and profiting from them another thing entirely. Value investors like Buffett and Howard Marks don't pretend to have a crystal ball. Instead, they use certain broad measures to gauge whether the market is overvalued or undervalued, and make their investment decisions accordingly, acting cautiously and skeptically when prices are high, and aggressively and opportunistically when prices are low. And they try to see the forest and not the trees, looking for long-term trends and not overreacting to short-term fluctuations one way or the other.

Rationality Cycles

Contrarian investors, like the behavioral economists we looked at in the previous chapter, believe that psychology and perceptual bias play a significant role in the cyclical movement of the stock market. So we could almost talk about a *fourth* kind of cycle: in addition to movements of expansion and contraction of GDP (the business cycle), credit (the financial cycle), and stock prices (the market cycle), there is a corresponding rise and fall of rational behavior in the market.

The rationality cycle consists of multiple stages. If the economy is in a recession, the rational portion of the population, not bound by fear, believe things will eventually get better.

They buy risky assets at discounts while others continue to flock to low-risk investments. Eventually other investors, realizing that an improvement is actually taking place, begin to purchase risky assets also.

With time, the economy is strong and the market is appreciating. The majority of the population believe that things will only continue to get better, but the rational portion of the population, not bound by greed or complacency, believe that things won't always be so rosy. They sell risky assets, realize gains, and flock to low-risk investments. Eventually other investors, realizing that things are worsening, begin selling risky assets also. With time, the economy is weak and the market declining. The majority of the population, believing things can only get worse leave profitable opportunities on the table for those that remain rational.

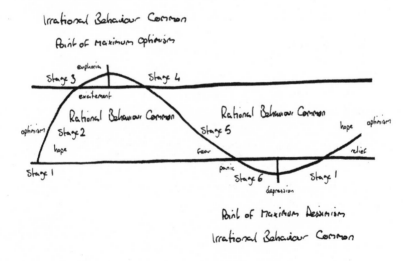

Figure K: The Rationality Cycle

The big takeaway here? Irrationality is highest at the extreme ends of a market cycle (the sky is darkest just before the dawn type of thing), so you want to put the brakes on, stay away from a herd mentality, and avoid getting caught up in an emotional boom or an equally emotionally panic at these points.

Identifying Cycles and Cyclical Behavior

If you could predict these cycles, it would be possible, theoretically, to take advantage of and profit from them. Unfortunately, it's impossible to do so with any precision (although many have tried, and the noisiest financial pundits act as if they can). Behavioral economist Richard Thaler built on the pioneering work of Daniel Kahneman and has this to say on the subject:

Investors should be wary of pouring money into markets that are showing signs of being overheated, but also should not expect to be able to get rich by successfully timing the market. It is much easier to detect that we may be in a bubble than it is to say when it will pop, and investors who attempt to make money by timing market turns are rarely successful.

All of the cycles surveyed above—business, financial, and market—interact with one another in complex ways. There are countless elements that factor into the equation, especially in a global economy where a change in the Chinese *yuan* can immediately send markets in the U.S. tumbling. Moreover, as I hope you're starting to see, human irrationality figures heavily in all of this.

Yet that doesn't mean that the smart investor can't put an awareness of cycles to good use. First, while markets are often driven by human emotion and cognitive bias, that human element is to a certain extent is predictably irrational. Second, there are signs that give a reasonably good indication of the market entering a certain phase or cycle. The most important things to watch for are cyclical extremes since the biggest (and costliest) investing mistakes are made at those extremes.

Note that the signs I'm going to review below won't help you predict the market; they are simply a *reasonably good indication* that extreme behavior exists. Taking the temperature of the market is very different from presuming to predict it. When prices are high, investors are largely risk tolerant and risky behavior is common. At these times, pull back and exercises restraint. When prices are low, investors are largely complacent and risk averse. At these times, specifically when the dominant emotion is fear, jump in and looks for bargains.

Signs that can be used to take the temperature of the market include:

• **Price/Earnings Ratios** – Good times often teach bad lessons and bad times often teach good lessons. Benjamin Graham, father of value investing and mentor to Warren Buffett, who developed his philosophy by analyzing the hard lessons of the stock market crash of 1929 concluded that the most important thing for investors to consider is the relationship between *price* and *value*. If a stock is priced below its intrinsic value, it may very well be an attractive investment. If it is priced above that value, it's a bad bet—even if its price is rising and it appears to be a "hot" investment.

One of the simplest ways to measure the relationship between price and value is the *price-to-earnings ratio* (often written in shorthand as P/E). It is the ratio of a company's current stock price to its per-share earnings, and therefore connects the price to a measure of the company's fundamental value and health[3]. P/E ratios can be used to gauge the relative price of an individual stock or of the market as a whole. The most widely used method of determining the market's overall P/E is that developed by economist Robert Shiller, and is commonly referred to as the Shiller Ratio.[4]

This historical average of the Shiller P/E is around 17— which should act as a reasonable cut-off between overpriced and underpriced stocks. And historically, there has been a remarkable correlation between peaks in the Shiller P/E and subsequent market crashes or sharp downturns. (In other words, a high Shiller P/E is a good sign of over-optimism and, possibly, irrational behavior). It was at 30 before the stock market crash of 1929 and 44 in late 1999, just before the dot-com bubble burst. It is important to note that this indicator shouldn't be used to try to predict the *immediate* future of the stock market. As Shiller himself points out, it was "never intended to indicate exactly when to buy and to sell." And growth-oriented investors argue that P/E ratio isn't necessarily a good criterion for judging an individual stock. **But it is a good measure of the overall mood of the market—a high**

[3] P/E ratios can also reflect expectations about future growth—or, to put it another way, the market's optimism about a company's long-term prospects. The stock of a company committed to aggressive long-term growth (such as a tech-oriented company like Google) may have a high P/E ratio but still be a sound investment. Proponents of *growth investing* argue that P/E ratios shouldn't be the main measure of value, while at the same time acknowledging that growth stocks generally carry a higher risk.

[4] You will also see it referred to as the CAPE (or Cyclically Adjusted Price-to-Earning Ratio).

Shiller P/E likely indicating an overpriced market in which investors should be cautious and a low P/E indicating an underpriced market where good bargains can be found.

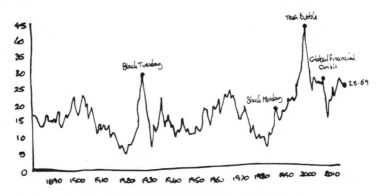

Figure L: Representation of the Schiller P/E Ratio
(For Illustration Purposes Only)

• **The "Buffett Indicator"** – Value investors like Howard Marks and Frank Martin are big proponents of the Shiller P/E as a way to take the temperature of the market. The most famous Value investor, Warren Buffett, has helped popularize another measure: the ratio of Total Market Value to Gross Domestic Product. In principle, the Buffett Indicator and the Shiller P/E have something in common—both are a way to establish a relationship between stock market prices and a fundamental measure of economic health. One recent study concludes the Buffett Indicator is somewhat more accurate in predicting long-term trends. But the behavior of both indicators is remarkably similar. The Buffett Indicator peaked at a historic high of 148% in early 2000, just before the dot-com bubble burst and just after the Shiller P/E peaked. The historic average of the

Buffett Indicator is 85%. It hit an all-time low in 1982 at 35%--just before stocks began their longest sustained bull market.

• **The "Fear & Greed Index"** – CNN Money tracks seven indicators of investor sentiment and combines them into an overall measure of whether the market is greedy (and likely to be overpriced) or fearful (and likely to be underpriced).

• **NYSE Margin Debt** – This is a measure of the extent to which investors are borrowing against their brokerage accounts (i.e., the stocks and other investments they already own) in order to buy additional stocks. In other words, they are using their existing investments as collateral to make additional investments. This is a tricky matter for the average investor: while it multiplies or amplifies your potential returns by allowing you to expand your portfolio, it also multiplies potential losses and adds a new layer of risk.

The pros and cons of buying on margin are too complicated to get into here. But keeping an eye on the total margin debt in the market can be a useful way to gauge the current risk temperature. Rising margin debt can be a sign that investors are overly complacent about risk, even reckless. As you can see in the chart that follows, the crashes of 2000 and 2008 were both preceded by peaks in margin debt. (Yet debt margin debt hit an all-time high in April of 2015, and although there were significant corrections in the months to come, there was no crisis.) Similarly, a sudden drop in margin debt can in some cases indicate a shift from risk-taking to risk-avoidance, and in turn the start of a bear market. (Yet it can also reflect a healthy degree of caution, which might actually prevent or delay a downturn.)

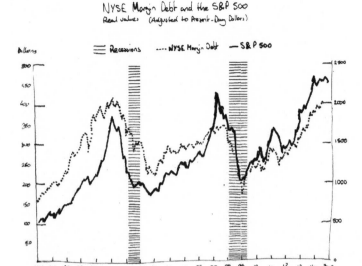

Figure M –Margin Debt on the NYSE (For Illustration Purposes Only)

The bottom line: margin debt is hardly a sure-fire way to predict the ups and downs of the market. But as a general rule, **when margin debt is well above its historic average, you should probably tread carefully; and when it drops well below that average, it might be a good time to look for bargains and value opportunities.**

• **Bond Market Yield Spreads** – For a number of reasons, the bond market can also be a useful way to take the risk temperature of the stock market. First, the bond market is larger than the stock market. Second, because bonds have a fixed maturity and their return or yield is easy to calculate, there are fewer variables and uncertainties—making bonds a kind of weathervane telling you which way the 'risk wind' is blowing.

A QUICK LESSON ON BONDS: YIELD VS. PRICE

Yield is a complicated and confusing topic when it comes to bonds, especially for beginning investors. Bonds have a fixed face value, and a fixed amount of interest (or coupon) the investor will earn based on that face value. But its actual price on the market, and thus its effective yield, will go up and down depending on demand and overall credit conditions. For example, a $1,000 bond with a 10% coupon will generate $100 in coupon payments each year—giving you a 10% yield if you bought it at face (or par) value. But if demand increases, and the price drops, and you buy that same bond for $800, its annual yield is 12.5%. Conversely, if demand drops, and the price rises to $1200, the annual yield would only be 8.33%.

With *zero-coupon bonds* (which includes T-bills), there is no interest, so the investor's yield comes entirely from buying the bonds at a "discount" below the face value. (For example, a $1,000 one-year T-bill purchased for $952 would return an effective yield of 5%.) Since there is no coupon payment, the price of a zero-coupon bond is more sensitive to interest rate changes than a similar coupon bond. But in either case, yield and price are inversely related. Like a see-saw, when one is up, the other is down.

Specifically, market observers look at various *yield spreads*—the difference between the effective yield on two different kinds of bonds. Two in particular bear watching. One is the difference between yields of Treasuries of varying maturities. (Short-term Treasuries, or T-bills, have maturities of a year or less. Mid-length Treasury notes are from 2 to 10 years. And long-term Treasury bonds are from 10 to 30 years.) Under most conditions, if you plot short-, mid- and long-term Treasuries on a chart, you will get an upward-sloping pattern, or what is called a *normal yield curve*. This is a healthy sign, in that long-term investments are being rewarded with higher returns. When the spread between short- and long-term Treasuries narrows (reflecting a *flat yield curve*), that can indicate concern about the long-term health of the economy. An *inverted yield curve* (where long-term rates drop below short-term ones) is a rare event that in many cases has signaled an imminent recession.

The other type of yield spread worth watching are credit spreads between high-risk, high-yield corporate bonds and low-risk Government bonds. (Typically, the comparison is between high-yield "junk" bonds and Treasuries, and is termed either the *junk-bond spread or the high-yield spread.*) Because Treasuries are seen as having no risk of default, this spread is a good measure of how tight or loose credit is in the private sector, and of how creditworthy the private sector is seen as. In the case of a very narrow spread, investors aren't asking for a high premium on higher-risk investments, which can indicate unhealthy complacency about risk. A wide spread, on the other hand, indicates tightening credit, and general fear in the market. A moderate credit spread likely reflects a balance between adequate credit and a healthly respect for risk.

Staying Smart With Cycles

How is the average investor to sort through all these cycles, and the complex interactions between them when even the world's greatest economists can't agree what it all means? **When in doubt, keep it simple, keep it straightforward, and avoid the big mistake.**

Below is a simple graphic in which I've charted the full range of an individual investor's response to the ups and downs of market cycles. At one end is *aggressively active*, at the other end is *inactive* or *neutral*, and in the middle is *selectively active*. I've rated these strategies according to the results I think they are likely to produce.

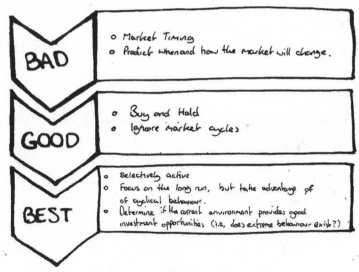

BAD
- Market Timing
- Predict when and how the market will change.

GOOD
- Buy and Hold
- Ignore market cycles

BEST
- Selectively active
- Focus on the long run, but take advantage of of cyclical behaviour.
- Determine if the current environment provides good investment opportunities (i.e. does extreme behaviour exist?)

Figure N

Because one of the cardinal themes of this book is to first and foremost avoid disastrous mistakes, let's start with BAD, the worst of the three strategies: trying to "time" the market.

This aggressive approach can produce big hits, but also big losses. Some investors have had success with it and the daily chatter of the financial media (*jump on this stock! dump this one before it's too late ...*) will appeal to your competitive desire to try and outsmart the market. My advice? Stay humble. Know what you don't know. And remember a central cautionary lesson from the previous chapter: Those who trade most frequently tend to underperform in the long run. The more you trade, the more you become vulnerable to the cognitive biases discussed earlier.

In the middle is a largely inactive or neutral approach: basically, a "buy and hold" strategy that forgoes forecasting and timing, and assumes it is foolhardy to take advantage of market and business cycles. This is certainly not an optimal strategy: going this route will prevent you from earning abnormal returns. But it protects you, in most cases, from major disaster. And it protects you from yourself and your tendency to think you can outsmart the market. In the big picture, it's an acceptable approach.

BEST, I feel, is a *selectively active* strategy that isn't passive but doesn't pretend to be able to outsmart the market either. It comes down to *recognizing* where we are in a market or business cycle; then assessing the threats or *pitfalls* that come with that position along with the *opportunities*.

Opportunity and Risk in Market Cycles

Another way to look at cycles is in terms of a changing relationship between the opportunity to gain and the risk of loss. The greatest irrationality and, the worst investment mistakes, comes at the extremes of the market cycle when the opportunity to gain or the risk of loss is perceived to be high. At the high end, investors overestimate both the duration of the boom and the extent of their own investing prowess— and as a consequence tend to overbuy. Avoid this mistake. At the low end, investors tend to join the general panic and sell off assets. Remember the phrase "buy low, sell high." Think twice, especially when a market cycle seems to be approaching a trough.

If the greatest pitfalls come just before the market has hit either a high or a low, so do the greatest opportunities. Rather than reacting when the market reverses itself, do your best to remain rational and protect your capital in the midst of the extreme. While the bull may have more room to run, it may be wise to hedge against a possible downturn by shifting your portfolio slightly away from more speculative investments and increasing your share of safer, more liquid assets like bonds, T-bills, and cash. If the bull market continues, you will have temporarily lost ground to those who are convinced the market will remain hot. But the important thing is this: You will be protected against disaster when the extreme behavior reverses.

As George Soros says: "Missing an opportunity is painful. Fortunately I did not miss the market: I merely failed to take maximum advantage of it. My caution may cost me dearly, but it will also ensure my survival." **Missed opportunity is a cost, and a form of risk—but a small cost and a small risk compared to permanent loss.**

At the other end, remember that, while the average investor over-buys at the top, he is unduly afraid of buying at the bottom. Don't be shy about looking for value bargains when the market is down.

Against the Cycle: The Loneliness of the Value Investor

I've suggested before that, if you have the stomach for it, Value Investing is the most fundamentally sound contrarian approach, and the most sustainable way to beat the market over the long term. So let's close this chapter by taking a look at how value investors navigate the ups and downs of market cycles, and at how their contrarian approach reveals a very different perspective on things like opportunity and risk.

Value investing is a philosophy that dates back to Ben Graham, and to his protégé Warren Buffett, and continues on to noted contemporary value investors like Howard Marks. The essence of the approach is simple: to attempt to buy stocks or other investments when they are undervalued, and then wait out the market until the price at the very least returns to the asset's intrinsic value. Thus, value investing is also about cycles: the volatility cycle that almost every asset goes through as it fluctuates up and down, eventually settling on or near its intrinsic value in a process known as *regression to the mean*. The tricky part is this: You are generally betting on a stock when the rest of the market is betting against it, and therefore have to conduct the necessary research (or "due diligence" as we say in the industry) to separate a stock that is only temporarily neglected or undervalued from one that is just a losing cause (or what insiders call a "value dump").

But if you have done your homework and successfully found an attractive investment, the difference between the (discounted) price you pay and the stock's intrinsic value will provide you with a built-in *margin of safety*. That margin is crucial in two respects. First, even if you have somewhat misjudged the asset's underlying value, you are still likely to come out ahead. Second, you are not basing your bet on beating the market: you are simply waiting for the market to come to its senses and the prices of that security to revert to its intrinsic value. An undervalued stock that later becomes fairly priced is a winner—and, if it should become overvalued, then all the better.

This highlights one way that the Value investing philosophy departs from the mainstream. **Whereas Modern Portfolio Theory views volatility as risk, Value investing views it as opportunity.** The up and down fluctuations of any one investment, and of the market as a whole, create moments when individual stocks (and the market in general) will be undervalued and underpriced.

Yet where there is opportunity when prices are low so there is risk when prices are high. Modern Portfolio Theory (and its central tactic of diversification) measures risk as volatility, regardless of price. Value Investing, by contrast, views a hot stock or a hot market as inherently risky. High prices often come with high risk. No matter how solid a company's fundamentals, if it is overpriced you are taking on unnecessary risk. Two kinds of risk, in fact. One is that the price will stall or actually drop and you will be holding an under performing stock (and here reversion to the mean is no longer your friend but your enemy). Even worse, the stock's overpricing could be a symptom of a bubble in the market in general, leaving you vulnerable to substantial and permanent loss.

So how do Value investors go about navigating the various cycles we surveyed earlier in the chapter? What they *don't do* is try to predict the ups and downs of those cycles and "time" or outsmart the market based on those predictions. Instead, they take the overall pulse or temperature of the market, and try to assess its riskiness.

And here's where the loneliness (and strong stomach) comes in: It's not easy to sell when everyone is buying, and harder still to buy when everyone is selling. In 1999, Warren Buffett characterized the risk mood of the hot bull market as one of "unsupportable optimism." In December of that year, *Forbes even* ran an opinion piece entitled "Buffett: What Went Wrong?", criticizing him for being slow to jump on the high-tech bandwagon. But, when the bubble burst the following March, Buffett had the last laugh.

Value investors also have to accept that their portfolios may often underperform during hot bull markets. Buffett and other value investors held back from going all in on tech stocks, and as a result missed out on some short-term gains. And even as the market bounced back after 2002, Buffett remained cautious and held larger cash reserves than many. The Value investor reluctantly accepts the cost and risk of such missed opportunity—realizing, as Frank Martin writes, "There is a difference between opportunities missed and capital lost."

• • •

Not everyone has the temperament and the stomach to be a contrarian investor. But, at the very least, I hope that you walk away from this chapter aware of the dangers of following the herd at either the top or the bottom of market cycles. A conservative buy-and-hold approach—while it generally won't result in superior performance—is infinitely preferable to getting caught up in the manic-depressive moods swings of the market. And if you can go a bit further and bring yourself to make some well-placed strategic moves at both the top and the bottom of market cycles, you'll be all the more ahead of the game.

Chapter 10

The Active vs. Passive Debate

Early on, I introduced you to two different schools of thought about investing and the market: One is the school that sees the market as essentially rational and efficient. According to this view, prices represent intrinsic value and fluctuations in the market are impossible to predict, and therefore impossible to exploit. In this world, the wisest course is to remain passive and *ride the market* through broadly-based index funds.

The other school is convinced that the market is occasionally irrational and inefficient, that it often overreacts. By avoiding those overreactions, and sometimes taking advantage of them, the savvy investor can indeed outperform the market.

The two schools present the investor with a fundamental choice: take a chance by actively trying to beat the market or be content with passively riding it.

One of the things that makes this choice so complicated is that it is *not*, contrary to how many experts portray it, a simple either/or choice. You can (and should, in my opinion) combine both approaches in a way that works best for you—for your individual goals, your financial circumstances, and your temperament as an investor.

Another thwarting factor is that the active vs. passive debate has recently become lopsided. Many respected investors like Warren Buffett are now recommending strictly passive approaches. In his case, it's a classic gap between *do what I do vs. do what I say.* For most of his life, Buffett has been a bold but prudent contrarian investor: going against the grain of popular opinion; making big, concentrated bets; and in the process earning returns that puts the S&P 500 to shame. Yet in his later years, his parting advice to heirs of his fortune has been decidedly cautious and conservative: put the bulk of your inheritance, he says, in a passive index fund.

The "New Normal"

Buffett's advice that his heirs stick to passive indexing is cited by advocates of the ride-the-market approach as evidence that the ongoing debate between passive and active investing has turned in their favor. If the ultimate beat-the-market investor has switched sides and joined the passive investing team, who are we to argue? Yet as I wrote earlier in response to claims that this debate is over: Not so fast…

The underlying concern of Buffett's advice is an important cautionary note we should all pay attention to. Attempts to beat the market can easily go horribly wrong and result in significant losses. Avoiding big losses has always been Buffett's number one rule of investing. Thus, it may be a bad idea for some investors to even try to beat the market. At the very least, anyone making the attempt should do so with extreme care, and a healthy dose of humility. Yet the problem with applying Buffett's advice to the average investor, particularly Millennials, is that Buffett has already made his fortune—so it makes perfect sense that his number one priority would be to protect and preserve that fortune. Millennial investors, on the other hand, are in the very early stages of building long-term wealth. They should be prudent, and careful, to be sure. But in my opinion they can't afford to limit themselves—particularly given the realities of the post-crisis economy.

In 2009, Mohamed El-Erian, who you were introduced to in the last chapter, was the CEO of PIMCO, one of the largest investment management firms in the world. As the world struggled through the early months of the post-crisis recovery, El-Erian tried to get a handle on how to view economic and investing prospects in the coming years. Many assumed that the economies of industrialized countries like the United States would sooner than later bounce back to pre-crisis economic health, as has historically been the pattern after most recessions. But El-Erian and his colleagues felt that the aftershocks of the Great Recession would be deep and long-lasting. **They coined the term "The New Normal" to indicate a prolonged period of sluggish and uncertain growth.** "Our use of the term was an attempt," he wrote, "to move the discussion beyond the notion that the crisis was a mere flesh wound, easily healed with time. Instead, the crisis cut to the bone."

Similarly, in April 2016 the McKinsey Global Institute, a respected analytics group, released a report supporting this idea of The New Normal. "The forces that have driven exceptional investment returns over the past 30 years," the report says (such as low inflation and interest rates, strong global economic growth, and high corporate profits) "are weakening, and even reversing. It may be time for investors to lower their expectations... After an era of stellar performance, investment returns are likely to come back down to earth over the next 20 years." Even a modest decline in average returns, they point out, has serious repercussions for the average investor: to make up for a 2% drop, for instance, "a 30-year-old worker would have to work seven years longer or almost double his or her saving rate."

It was this challenging future I had in mind when, in the Introduction, I wrote about what I called the Millennial Disadvantage. The Financial Crisis of 2008 has left a mark on your financial prospects and will continue to do so. Older Millennials who had already purchased a home and those in debt suffered a significant loss of wealth during the crisis. For younger Millennials just entering the job market, the crisis dealt a sharp blow to job prospects and wages at precisely the time that young workers are usually building up their earnings potential. Millennials are embarking on their lifelong journey to build lasting wealth with a significant handicap. I remain optimistic that your strengths and advantages, and the strength and dynamism of the economy, will ultimately allow you to overcome that slow start. But an overly cautious approach to building wealth is unlikely, in my opinion, to meet the challenges posed by The New Normal. As I've stated before, Millennials, more than any previous generation, must take responsibility for their own long-term financial well-being.

Pros and Cons of Riding the Market

The same things that make this a great time to be an investor—a varied menu of options, the ease of buying into different asset classes via ETFs and other vehicles, and ready access to a wealth of research and information—also make this a very *dangerous* time to be an investor. Today's investor is bombarded with overwhelming amounts of information and choices. All this information, and all these choices can easily collude investors to do the wrong thing at the wrong time.

Perhaps this is why David Swensen – an aggressive contrarian investor in his capacity as head of Yale University's Endowment Fund – urges a cautious, passive indexing strategy for the average investor. And a keen awareness of the pitfalls of trying to time the market is surely behind Warren Buffett's conservative advice to his heirs. I share their caution... up to a point. It's all too easy for investors to be their own worst enemies. And the high turnover rates and short holding periods typical of many investors is evidence that aggressive, beat-the-market strategies may not be wise or appropriate for some.

Yet a strict ride-the-market approach has its pitfalls as well—particularly in today's uncertain economic environment:

- Proponents of index investing often cite a sample 10- or 15-year period from the past to demonstrate how much, say, $10,000 invested at the start of that period would be worth at the end if you were able to just keep pace with the S&P 500. But the problem is that **there is no such thing as an average 10-year period.** Yes, there are some periods during which you would have enjoyed healthy double-digit returns. During others, however, you would have been better off with cash and fixed-income investments. And, even more so, uneven returns may well be the rule in the New Normal.

- **Index funds provide no downside protection in the event of a major market correction, or worse.** This is especially troublesome if the financial system proves to be increasingly vulnerable to bigger and more frequent bubbles.

- Another way of restating that point: **Index funds actually increase your exposure to market risk and to the emotional ups and downs of the market.** The *cap-weighted formulas*[1] behind most index funds mean that, as the market starts overvaluing certain kinds of stocks, your index funds will become more heavily invested in those very stocks. This happens automatically, without any decision on your part. This "passive drift" is a kin to market timing: your fund is actively chasing growth and exposing you to increased risk, even as you trust it as a passive, low-risk investment vehicle.

In short, while passively managed index funds remove *individual irrationality* **from the equation, they continue to expose you to** *market irrationality*. There is no human element, no adaptability, no ability to protect yourself from the market's irrationality—or maybe even profit from it

---

[1] As I pointed out in Chapter 7, this means that the fund's investment in a given stock is directly proportionate to the size of its market capitalization (the total value of its stock) within the index. So if you own an S&P 500 index fund, for example, and the stock of a certain company soars, and its share of the total value of the index goes up from, say, 2% to 4%, your index fund will mimic the market, and its holdings in the company will increase accordingly.

Not Just What... But When

When we discuss asset allocation, we're talking about the *what*: What asset classes are you going to invest in, and in what proportion? But another key question is how do you know the time is right to buy or sell a given asset?

While the question of timing will be a major focus of **Chapter 13: Putting It All Together**, I just want to touch on one aspect of this question. There is an approach to when that is a natural companion to the passive indexing approach to *what*.

One of the objectives of passive indexing is to take emotion and impulse out of investing decisions, and in the process protect investors from themselves. Don't try to outsmart the market, this philosophy warns, because much of the time it will backfire on you. There is some wisdom to this: while it may not be the optimal approach, the one that helps you maximize your wealth-building potential, it is far preferable to trying to time the market's short-terms ups and downs, and to the overtrading that results from that attempt.

Similarly, one way of taking emotion and impulse out of the *when* decision is to put yourself on a kind of *investing auto-pilot schedule*[2]: you commit to making a regular investment at regular intervals (say monthly), regardless of whether the market, or that particular asset, is up or down. You protect yourself from your own worst decisions by adopting a discipline that prevents you from trying to time the market.

---

[2] Actually, it's two different variations on this basic approach—one called Dollar Cost Averaging, and the other simply Value Averaging. I'll give you a brief overview of both in Chapter 13.

There is wisdom in this approach as well. While not optimal, it saves investors from the most common mistake: overreacting to the short-term ups and downs of the market. It is a common sense "middle path" that is neither the best, nor the worst.

But I would argue that, just like passive indexing, the auto-pilot approach unnecessarily handicaps you as an investor—removing flexibility and adaptability from your toolbox. It saves you from your own worst mistakes but prevents you from avoiding the mistakes made by the market. By selectively employing the following contrarian strategies—even just a little, some of the time—you can build a significant competitive advantage over other investors and the market:

1. **Defense**—pulling back and reallocating when the market is overheated.

2. **Offense**—jumping in when the market is undervalued.

3. **Patience**—not overreacting to short-term ups and downs, and sitting on the sidelines when the options are unclear or unsatisfactory.

Edge #1: Defense

I've mentioned several times how Value investors believe that while it isn't possible to time the market with any precision, it does make sense to take the overall temperature of the market—particularly its risk mood and how that mood might impact our portfolio. When optimism and certainty dominate investor sentiment, and people are more afraid of missing out on potential profits than of possible losses, contrarian investors smell an overheated market. They pull back and adopt a more defensive investing position: protecting themselves from irrational exuberance, and from a possible bubble getting ready to burst.

In practice, defensive investing involves several different strategies. One is simply exercising restraint: refusing to jump on the hot trend of the moment.

Playing defense usually involves shifting some of your asset allocation away from equities for a greater emphasis on cash and cash equivalents, and on fixed-income securities. It can also involve moving the equity portion of your asset allocation toward so-called "blue chip" stocks: older, established companies like IBM and Wal-Mart, that yield steady if modest returns and often pay regular dividends. Such companies tend to weather the storm of a downturn better than other companies, and also tend to rebound more quickly from recessions.

The tricky part about playing defense is that it's impossible to time with any precision. Even George Soros failed to move out of technology stocks before the bubble burst and paid the price. In the last chapter, I offered a few metrics that indicate the market is *probably* overvalued, and may be headed toward a bubble. Yet prices can be high and yet continue to rise for some time, the 1990s bull market being a perfect case in point. Although Buffett declared the market overvalued in 1997, the bull market raged for another two years. (Others called the market overvalued as early as 1992!) As individual investors, you don't need perfect timing to make profitable escape from overvalued markets because high prices eventually revert[3].

Edge #2: Offense

In investing, as in sports, good defense often translates directly into good offense. Offense in investing is the freedom and the courage to jump into a depressed market and take advantage of low prices and good values precisely during those times when investor sentiment is fearful and people are more likely to be selling than buying. Yet you can't take advantage of such bargains if you haven't first shifted some of your money away from stocks and toward more liquid assets like cash, money market funds, and short-term Treasuries. This provides you with what professional investors call *dry powder*: discretionary funds that can quickly be targeted toward attractive buying opportunities.

Many investors are too slow to play defense and too slow to shift from defense to offense. In 1968, Warren Buffett was getting ready to pull out of the market at the time 35% of private U.S. investment was in equities. Investors shifted away from stocks during the stagnant 70s, but then were slow to jump on the ensuing bull market. As late as 1989, a full seven years into the bull market, only 13% of private investment was in equities.

---

[3] There is proverb on Wall Street that being early is equal to being wrong. For money managers, timing is more important than it is for individual investors. If an investment manager becomes overly conservative too early, his inability to keep up with competition may cause investors to flock to a competitor.

Edge #3: Patience

Patience is the common denominator of contrarian investing in both good times and bad. Patience allows you to pull back in an overheated market and continue to show restraint, even while conventional wisdom urges you to buy. And patience enables you to stick with a value stock bought at a bargain price, even in the midst of a panic, and even if it takes the stock years to bounce back.

Patience is also, often, the move you *don't* make. Successful investing requires inactivity. The importance of patience is a theme that contrarian investors return to repeatedly, often using sports analogies to make their point. Warren Buffet once compared investing to stepping up to the plate in baseball. Each pitch we see is a potential purchase. Some are strikes and some are balls; yet, unlike a hitter in baseball, it is difficult for investors to strike out by merely looking.

Even though you *can* strike out in baseball, two of the greatest hitters in the game's history, Babe Ruth and Ted Williams, were legendary for their patience. For every home run that he hit, Williams watched 30 balls go by. In fact Warren Buffett closely read Williams's book *The Science of Hitting* and has made frequent use of it in his investing. The legendary hitter describes how he mentally broke up the strike zone into 77 "cells," each the size of a baseball. Three and a half of those cells represented his "sweet spot"—the pitches he knew he could hit, and hit hard. He felt his success as a hitter was largely due to discipline and patience: letting pitches in the other 73 ½ cells go by, and waiting for the handful in his sweet spot.

Why Beating the Market Often Backfires

While I urge you to pick your sweet spots and selectively go against the grain of the market—thus gaining a significant competitive advantage that will pay sizable dividends over the long run—it is important to keep in mind that many individual investors who try to beat the market end up failing, sometimes spectacularly.

We have already encountered some of the major reasons behind this uneven record back in Chapter 6, when we examined the under performance of many actively managed mutual funds. The same factors that hold back professional fund managers can hold you back as well:

1) Chasing Performance – Although study after study has shown that the top-performing funds or stocks from the last year (or two or three) are unlikely to repeat that performance in the next few years, individual investors alike are frequently unable to resist the temptation to jump on the latest hot pick in the hopes that they will be able to continue to ride the rising tide. More often than not, they are buying an overpriced asset that, sooner or later, will come back to earth.

2) Lack of Conviction – Conviction is the companion virtue to patience. It is the patience and the discipline to stick to your guns, even when the market seems to be telling you you're doing the wrong thing. It is tough to sell when your peers are buying, and even harder to buy when they are selling. Most difficult of all, perhaps, is holding onto an under priced stock when your better instincts tell you it's eventually going to bounce back—but when the mood of panic in the market tempts you to sell.

3) Lack of Concentration – Earlier I quoted Warren Buffett's long-time business partner Charlie Munger: "The idea of excess diversification is madness. Wide diversification, which necessarily includes investment in mediocre businesses, only guarantees ordinary results." We've already seen how excess diversification dooms many professional fund managers to mediocrity: their first, high-conviction picks perform well, but then they water down their portfolio with dozens of lesser holdings. Simply put, an investor can't earn abnormally high returns through wide diversification. The only way to significantly outperform is by making concentrated bets, and by going against the crowd and conventional wisdom. This doesn't mean putting all of your money in one stock, but rather owning a handful of quality investments. You can be diversified without compromising much upside by holding 10-15 securities. If you make diversification the cornerstone of your investing philosophy, you are essentially tying yourself to the crowd and earning near-average returns.

4) Ignoring Anomalies – Even proponents of the Efficient Market Hypothesis (who argue that the market for the most part prices assets correctly) acknowledge that there are certain anomalies, or exceptions to the rule. Various anomaly "effects" have been identified over the years: situations where the market consistently underprices certain kinds of stocks, creating an opportunity for the smart and disciplined investor. As we reviewed in Chapter 4, some of these anomalies (like the Super Bowl effect) are silly; others (like the momentum effect) are in my view unnecessarily risky. Yet there are three – the Small Firm Effect, the Neglected Stock Effect, and the Value Effect – that I believe have stood the test of time. Small stocks, neglected stocks and value stocks have persistently outperformed the market. Ignoring these proven long-term strategies in favor of short-term attempts to "time" the market leads many individual investors to disappointing results. (We'll revisit these anomalies, and how you can use them to practical advantage, in the following chapter.)

5) Overreacting and Overtrading – Undisciplined investors all too often overreact to short-term market fluctuations, and fail to keep their eyes on the long view. Even long bear markets have short-term rallies—luring impatient investors into buying optimistically, only to have to sell when the market goes south again. And even long bull markets experience sharp corrections or temporary downturns—tempting jittery investors to sell prematurely even when the long-term trend is highly favorable. The result of overreacting is overtrading which, in turn, almost always leads to poor performance.

How Contrarian Is Right For You?

To be clear: I am not suggesting that you necessarily try to be the next Warren Buffett, picking the Geico of the future and throwing half of your fortune behind it. And not every investor has the temperament or the discipline to live with a portfolio built significantly around individual stocks (although I'm not discouraging you from doing so if you're up to the challenge).

What I am suggesting is that – even if your inclination is to be cautious and to build a portfolio largely around passive index funds – you would do well to pay attention to the mood of the market, and to be mindful of its tendency to overreact to both good news and bad. If you can do that, and even occasionally go against the grain of conventional wisdom and popular opinion by adopting some of the contrarian strategies I've briefly presented here, you'll be ahead of the game and have an edge on the average investor. You can protect yourself from the market's mood swings and even profit from them.

The metrics I outlined in the last chapter will aid you in taking the temperature of the market, and help you spot irrational behavior and possible bubbles and busts[4]. But keep in mind that being a contrarian investor—protecting yourself from the market's extremes—is, in the end, more about mindset than numbers. To beat the market, you have to act differently than the market.

Just how contrarian you choose to be is also where you choose to come down on the question of riding-the-market vs. beating-the-market. It's not a black and white, either/or question. You have to pick a mix that you are comfortable with, and that matches your situation and your financial goals. Finding that mix, and putting together an appropriate portfolio, will be the topic of the final chapter of the book.

But now that we've set out the terms of the debate between passive and active investing, between riding the market and beating it, let's focus specifically on how – in a prudent and strategic way – you might go about trying to achieve superior performance.

---

[4] Due to space concerns, and also wanting to keep this book accessible and digestible for the beginning investor, I have discussed only a few such metrics. But to truly perform the necessary due diligence (especially if you're going to adopt contrarian strategies) I suggest being a student of other factors as well.

Chapter 11

Beating the Market

n Chapter 10, we discussed whether you should ride the market or try to beat it, concluding that:

✓ It's not an either/or question;

✓ You can blend both approaches in a way that works best for you;

✓ A 100% passive investing strategy is hardly risk-free, and in fact may increase your exposure to overall market risk;

✓ You can adopt a fundamentally conservative and prudent approach to investing while at the same time taking steps to actively avoid the worst effects of the market's periodic mood swings.

With that background in place, it's time to move on to a survey of some ways of achieving above-average returns, emphasis being on sound techniques with a proven track record. Yet those techniques – as we say in the business – are no guarantee of future returns. It is all too easy for winning strategies to become losing ones. The problem almost always is not one of technique, but of temperament. Investors lose their cool and bail out on a solid value investment when everyone else is panicking; or they jump on the bandwagon of a trendy investment when everyone else is buying. The Value investing philosophy is central to most of the strategies I'm going to review in this chapter. And Value investing requires an investor to stay focused on the big picture; to avoid getting swept up in the mood of the moment (whether that be greed or fear); and to feel comfortable going against the grain of popular opinion.

Attempting to beat the market is not something to be taken lightly. It can be done wisely and prudently but remember that many who try fail and lose money in the process. Not everyone is up to the challenge; and for these investors, a largely passive approach might be more appropriate. Also, please keep in mind that I can give you only a broad overview of the topic here. The burden is on you to thoroughly research any potential investment. And depending on factors like your risk tolerance, capacity to bear risk, and your time and ability to do research, it may also be wise to seek the input of a good financial advisor.

Profiting From Anomalies

The Efficient Market Hypothesis (EMH) holds that markets are in general "informationally efficient," meaning stock price, in the long run, will accurately reflect all relevant information about an asset's underlying value. Value will ultimately determine price and any short-term price fluctuations not determined by value are random, unpredictable, and impossible to profit from consistently. Critics argue that the market is efficient some of the time but hardly all of the time. Often enough, they say, there are information gaps that create inaccurate pricing or the market responds irrationally to the information that is available—overreacting to both good news and bad news, resulting in overpricing and underpricing respectively.

According to classical theory, instances where price fails to reflect value should be random and short-lived. Yet even hard-core EMH proponents acknowledge a handful of *anomalies* that don't conform to the theory: exceptions to the rule that have stood the test of time. Some of these anomalies (or "effects" as they are sometimes termed) are based on short-term timing patterns. And while some argue that positive and negative price momentum can be exploited, I recommend staying away from any strategy that involves trying to time the market.

Yet there are three anomalies that have less to do with timing and more to do with a stock's underlying value as compared to its price. These present the savvy investor with an opportunity to purchase stocks at a discount, and to reap above-average yields when the price eventually bounces back and returns to value. This is the heart of *Value investing*, which I feel is the most prudent and low-risk means of beating the market and earning abnormal returns.

So let's look at how you can use them to identify underpriced stocks.

• **The Small Firm Effect** – Sometimes termed the Small-Cap Effect (referring to a company's smaller market capitalization, or the total value of its stock), this describes the historic tendency of smaller companies to outperform larger ones on the stock market. There are a number of theories about why this is true. One is that because a smaller company is generally in the earlier stages of their life cycle, it is therefore likely to have a bigger upside. In other words, a 20% or 30% increase in earnings is easier to achieve in a small company worth millions than in a large one worth billions. The small-cap effect was given a major boost in 1981 when Nobel Prize-winning economist Eugene Fama acknowledged the long-term superior performance of small stocks. After his study, some reports indicated that the small-cap effect began to diminish—supporting a contention by EMH proponents that once an anomaly is discovered and publicized, investors won't find it as easy to use it to their advantage. But a major study in 2015 found that by using simple filters[1] to adjust for the financial health of companies, small stocks continue to hold a considerable advantage over large ones. In other words, over time, **small high-quality stocks seem to outperform large high-quality stocks.**

• **The Neglected Firm Effect** – This anomaly stems from the fact that some stocks – due to smaller size, lower trade volume, or general lack of industry buzz – attract less attention from professional analysts and institutional investors, and are thus less "informationally efficient." This is something on which both EMH proponents and contrarian investors agree: the less attention a given segment of the market attracts, the greater the likelihood of misinformation and mispricing. When that results in a stock being under appreciated and undervalued, it presents a significant opportunity for the patient investor.

---

[1] The authors of the study combined a number of factors (including profitability, growth, and safety) into a metric it dubbed Quality Minus Junk, or QJM. Other analysts have developed slightly different metrics to filter for quality.

There is a certain degree of overlap between the neglected and small firm effects, as small companies will tend to fly under the radar. One study found that the typical small-cap firm is covered by only 6 analysts where a comparable large-cap firm might be covered by 23. The changing nature of the investment landscape also comes into play here. Fifty years ago, 90% of investors were individual and only 10% institutional. Now that ratio has roughly been reversed. Because of the amount of money they need to put into play, institutional investors (such as pension funds) are inherently biased towards large companies, increasing the prevalence of the neglected firm effect.

• **The Value Effect** – In Chapter 9, I explained how economist Robert Shiller uses the Price-to-Earnings ratio – the ratio of total stock prices to total company earnings[2] – to measure whether the market is overpriced or underpriced. This measure can also be applied to individual companies. P/E ratios work as a major indicator of whether or not a stock may be selling at a significant discount. Historically, stocks bought at low P/E ratios have outperformed the rest of the market. This pattern is aligned with Ben Graham's contention that **while the market in the short term might be a voting machine** (or popularity contest), **in the long run it is a weighing machine**. In other words, price will eventually rise up (or come down) to value, depending on whether the stock is under- or overpriced to begin with.

All three of the above effects are more powerful in combination with one another. For example, while the small-cap effect tends to be strongest under certain market conditions

---

[2] In fact, the calculation is somewhat more complicated, and involves a "cyclical adjustment" to smooth out the numbers and correct for short-term fluctuations—hence its formal name of Cyclically Adjusted Price-to-Earnings, or CAPE.

(such as the early stages of a bull market), small-cap value stocks (filtered for both size and value) might outperform in a number of markets. And filters for quality will improve the potency of all three.

Identifying Potential Value Stocks

We now turn to one of the most important techniques of the Value investor: identifying underpriced stocks that *may* present a profitable opportunity. With over 5,000 companies listed on US stock exchanges, it is essential to have useful and reliable means for narrowing the field. Otherwise, the average individual investor will tend to rely on word-of-mouth and hype.

Fortunately, all three of the above anomalies can be translated into statistical filters you can use to screen for potentially worthy investments. Many websites like Yahoo Finance as well as the sites of discount brokerage firms, feature stock screening options. And, for a small annual membership fee ($29 at last check), the American Association of Individual Investors (AAII) offers access to a variety of screeners and reports and studies.

• **Value Effect** – The simplest and most intuitive way to filter for potential value is the Price-to-Earnings or P/E ratio. The Value investor is looking not just for a slight discount but one big enough to come with a significant *margin of safety*. Such a margin ensures that, even if you have erred in your initial estimate of a company's intrinsic value, you will be buying it at a discount large enough to cover that error and still leave you with a profit once the price rebounds and returns to value.

It can also be helpful to invert or flip the P/E ratio. The ratio of Earnings-Per-Share (or EPS) to share price gives you what analysts calls the *earnings yield*, usually expressed as a percentage. For example: a stock trading at $20 per share and with an EPS of $2 would have a P/E of 10 and an earnings yield of 10%. This can help you compare the desirability of the stock as compared to other stocks and also to other asset classes like bonds.

It is important to keep in mind that P/E ratios and earnings yields are just a shorthand indication of price-to-value, and not the final word on the value or merits of a stock. What analysts call "equity valuation" is a complicated subject I can't address fully here. A somewhat more involved alternative to P/E, for example, is the ratio of a company's *Enterprise Value* (how much the company would likely sell for) to its *Earnings Before Interest & Taxes* (or EBIT). Many sites will also allow you to screen for EV/EBIT (and EV/EBITDA)[3]. I suggest further research into equity valuation if you are serious about investing in individual stocks. This more complex fundamental analysis is also where the assistance of a quality investment advisor can come in handy. But a simple screening for P/E is a good start.

• **Small-Cap Effect** – It is very simple to screen or filter for small firms based on total market capitalization. Small-cap companies are generally defined as those with a total market value of less than $2 billion. Some further break that down into the categories of *micro-cap* ($50 million to $300 million) and *nano-cap* (less than $50 million). The smaller the company,

---

[3] An even more precise financial picture comes from Earnings Before Interest, Taxes, Depreciation, and Amortization (or EBITDA).

the harder it is to research—which means that at the lower end of the small-cap spectrum, you'll also be benefiting from the neglected firm effect.

• **Neglected Firm Effect** – There are two simple statistical filters that allow you to screen for neglect. One is the extent of *institutional ownership of the stock*, a factor you can screen for at various websites like *Barron's* and the *Wall Street Journal*. For neglected stocks, that percentage will likely be below 40%. (Because of the way institutional investors dominate the market, stocks neglected by these investors also tend to attract less analysts.) The second filter is the number of analysts following the stock, a number also widely available at financial sites, and through the AAII (American Association of Individual Investors).

Additional Analysis

I recommend doing an initial screening for stocks with a P/E of less than 15 and to identify from the bottom 25% of results for the small-cap and neglected firm filters. This will very quickly help you narrow the field considerably.

Yet it hardly guarantees a winner. **Some stocks may be small, neglected, and underpriced simply because they are bad bets**: struggling companies in bad shape, and with a high risk of failure. These do not represent bargains but what investment professionals call a "value dump." Cheap is good, but not sufficient. The challenge is to pick out the ones that are high quality and neglected or whose trouble is relatively short-term, and whose price will eventually bounce back. It's not easy, and investing in unfashionable stocks isn't for everyone.

Yet the record is clear: stocks with a low P/E have historically outperformed the market in the long run.

A stock is truly a bargain, Benjamin Graham wrote, only if it was selling at about two-thirds of its intrinsic value, *and* "if the earnings record and prospects are reasonably satisfactory." This is key. Companies with underpriced stocks might not be in spectacular shape—but in order to be a prudent investment, they have to be in reasonably good shape. This is why, as discussed earlier, quality filters are an important tool for any value investor[4].

As this kind of filtering makes clear, value investors come to the table with a very particular philosophy. Unlike short-term investors, they are not concerned with the momentum of short-term price fluctuations, or with the factors driving those fluctuations. They are concerned with the business behind the stock symbol, and with whether or not its current price reflects its underlying value. In one of his most famous articles, "The Superinvestors of Graham-and-Doddsville,"[5] Warren Buffett writes about a lineage of value investors beginning with his mentor Benjamin Graham, and continuing on through himself and a new generation. Despite their different styles, what unites them all, he says, is their basic philosophy: they are "buying the business, not buying the stock." Value investors

---

[4] An AAII summary of Graham's valuation methods recommends a simple filter for companies with both positive earnings and a positive cash flow for the previous 12 months. The authors of the study referred to earlier, on filtering small-cap companies for overall financial health, have developed what they call a Quality-Minus-Junk (QJM) metric. The firm that sponsored the study, Applied Qualitative Research, updates those numbers monthly.

[5] David Dodd was a colleague of Benjamin Graham's at Columbia in the years after stock market crash of 1929. The two collaborated on Graham's first book, *Security Analysis*. Buffett posits Graham-and-Doddsville as a kind of imaginary town that the great value investors can all be traced back to.

buy businesses, and they buy them at a discount—"exploiting the gap between the market price of a business and its intrinsic value."

One final note on value investing. Although low P/E stocks are often small-cap companies that are undervalued and under appreciated in part because they fly under the radar, the stock of large, established companies sometimes falls out of favor as well. A company might lose ground to an upstart competitor, go through a difficult restructuring or change in management, or experience an unexpectedly poor quarterly earnings report that Wall Street overreacts to, causing its stock to plummet. During the overheated dot-com boom of the 90s, for example, "old guard" companies like IBM became unfashionable. At one point, its P/E fell as low at 10. IBM was in the process of changing its business model, and the transition wasn't always a smooth one. But it was a solid company, its stock was a better bet, and at a vastly discounted price, as compared to current flavors-of-the-month like Netscape—whose P/E at one point was over 70!

The Value of Growth Investing

Although Benjamin Graham has a reputation as a strict value investor who wasn't a big fan of growth stocks, he realized, as we've seen, that cheapness alone isn't reason enough to buy a stock. He also looked at a company's profitability: its past earnings, and its prospects for future earnings. And when we talk about profitability, aren't we really talking about growth?

Yes and no. *Growth investing* is generally defined as focusing on companies with big upside: with the potential for explosive growth. Yet a number of noted value investors factor profitability and growth potential into their investing decisions. On the other side of the coin, while the cliché about growth investors is that they are willing to pay for a rapidly expanding company regardless of price (and while that may have been true for some during heated bull markets like the 90s), in today's world most realize the importance of price, of relative value. In other words, growth investing and value investing aren't always mutually exclusive.

It's no surprise that, once again, Warren Buffett is a model for incorporating the best of both worlds. As a protégé of Benjamin Graham, his early focus was on bargain-hunting. But his investing philosophy evolved, and he came to realize that it is "far better to buy a wonderful business at a fair price than to buy a fair business at a wonderful price." In other words, strong growth at a reasonable price was just a different kind of value. Buffett's recent purchase of the railroad company Burlington Northern Santa Fe is a perfect case in point. He bought it at a P/E ratio of 20—supposedly a high price for a value investor. But the company's earnings had been growing an average of 19% in recent years; and some analysts are saying that, even at a hefty price tag of $26.5 billion, he "stole" the company. As a column about the sale in *Forbes* puts it, "To Buffett all investing is about value. Assessing a company's growth prospects is simply one part of gauging value... The distinction between growth and value is flawed."

Another star investor who has successfully mixed both styles is Peter Lynch, best known for thirteen record-breaking years running Fidelity's Magellan mutual fund. Between 1977 and 1990, Lynch outperformed the market by over 13% a year, turning Magellan into the largest mutual fund in the world.

During the stagnant economy of the late 70s, Lynch was able to buy solid companies at bargain prices—sometimes with P/E ratios of well below 10. But as the market heated up in the 1980s, and pure value bargains became harder to find, Lynch adapted to the times, focusing on companies with big upside, but which he could still get at a reasonable price. He remained flexible; or as he put it in his book *Beating the Street*, he was a "chameleon," never tied to any one investing style. The phrase that best captures his approach, "Growth at a Reasonable Price" (or GARP), is a really a hybrid of value and growth[6].

Earlier I mentioned how, even for the strict value investor, it is important to filter for quality. Recently, there has been an increasing amount of attention on quality filters that involve profitability—further eroding the false distinction between growth and value investing. A metric now being adopted by a number of top investors and funds is *gross profitability*—the ratio of a company's gross profits to its assets. The author of a paper documenting the usefulness of this quality metric says he sees it as just a different way of looking at value. Cliff Asness, who also uses profitability in his Quality-Minus-Junk metric, also rejects the outdated notion of seeing growth investing as "simply the opposite of value... Including measures of profitability along with measures of value in the same portfolio effectively makes [for] a better value strategy."

Although books about investing and rating services like Morningstar often pit growth and value against one another, I hope you can see that this is another aspect of investing

---

[6] One metric that Lynch pays a lot of attention to is the PEG ratio: the relationship of a company's P/E number to its growth numbers (as measured by earnings per share). In general, he doesn't like paying for a company with a PEG greater than 1. (Buffett's purchase of Burlington is a perfect example of how an apparently high P/E isn't so high if you compare it to growth.) Fidelity offers a GARP screen that includes PEG and other measures favored by Lynch.

where the choice isn't black and white, isn't either/or. The best investors mix both styles, based on the opportunities available to them at the time. While I am convinced that value investing remains the best long-term strategy, providing a crucial margin of safety to protect you from capital losses, growth investing also has a place. And there are certainly times when growth-based investing will outperform value-based investing. But even in growth investing, price should always be the starting point.

Concentration and Diversification

Here we return to the debate about whether to try to beat the market or simply ride it. As I explained earlier, passive indexing is really the principle of diversification taken to its ultimate logical conclusion. The aim is to eliminate everything but overall market risk. Instead of investing in individual companies, you are essentially trying to "buy the market" as a whole and capture your fair share of its long-term upward trend.

At the opposite end of the spectrum is the investor who puts all of his money in a single stock: the ultimate in a concentrated portfolio, with no diversification.

In practice, most investors fall somewhere between those two extremes, and one of your challenges is to find the mix that works best for you. In a world where conventional wisdom seems to be leaning toward passive indexing, I am encouraging you not to be entirely married to the market. And when you do choose to chart an independent course and go against the grain of whatever trend is driving the market at a given time,

I suggest you incorporate some degree of concentration in your portfolio. **Without some concentration, you greatly reduce your chances of achieving superior returns. It's hard to earn abnormal returns holding a portfolio of over 20 stocks.**

You will recall that, in our examination of research on the mixed success of active mutual fund managers, those who successfully beat the market employed a higher degree of concentration in their portfolios: they chose a smaller number of high-conviction stocks (ones they had researched thoroughly and believed in strongly) and avoided over-diversification.

In a 2004 paper, Louis Lowenstein of Columbia University published the results of a study that confirmed the merits of concentration and Value investing. Although a tough critic of the mutual fund industry (he later wrote a book on the topic), Lowenstein studied those active managers who went against the grain of popular opinion and did not simply follow the herd. Focusing on the "disorderly boom-crash-rebound years of 1999-2003," he studied ten value funds run by managers who had clear investing philosophies and stuck to them. These funds did not "suffer the permanent loss of capital of so many who invested in telecom, media and tech stocks." Every one of them beat the index for this volatile five-year period, by an average of 11% per year.

They did so by following the core principles I have suggested here and in previous chapters:

1. They had the discipline to refrain from jumping on the dot-com bandwagon.

2. They stuck with highly selective, concentrated portfolios, with an average of 34 stocks as opposed to the industry average of 160.

3. They remained true to their convictions and avoided the temptation to constantly tinker with their portfolios, in spite of the ups and downs of the market—turning over their portfolios at one-sixth the rate of the average fund.

The bottom line: concentration works, if pursued in a disciplined and well-researched manner.

Maintaining A Healthy Stock Portfolio

Yet concentration doesn't mean abandoning diversification altogether. You don't want to purchase all your stocks from the same industry or sector, for example. **The indisputable truth at the heart of diversification is the benefit of owning investments that respond differently to given market conditions.** This can be a struggle for individual investors who tend to invest only in areas they are familiar with—either professionally or as consumers. (We call this the trap of "lifestyle investing.")

On the other hand, a properly diversified portfolio doesn't require that you own dozens of different stocks. Studies have shown that most of the benefits of diversification can be achieved with as few as 10 stocks and that additional benefits are minimal once you hit 20 stocks. And if at first you are comfortable owning just a few stocks (or aren't financially able to go beyond that), complement those individual stocks with a broadly-based index fund or ETF in order to obtain the necessary diversification.

Regarding your portfolio of individual stocks, however large, diversification and variety will often mean that some of the stocks will be going up while others are going down. This is a good thing; but it can be difficult for a beginning investor to get used to. It is of course the case as well with any mutual fund or ETF you might own—but, in that case, the ups and downs of individual stocks are invisible and out of sight.

I have three tips for helping you stay calm with the inevitable ups and downs of individual stocks in your portfolio.

1. Measure the success of your investing strategy *by the performance of your portfolio as a whole over 10-year periods.* Don't get caught up in the short-terms fluctuations of individual stocks.

2. Don't monitor your portfolio's performance on a daily basis or you're likely to get caught up in what we call the "noise" of short-term price movements, and the speculation in the financial press that goes along with them. Establish a schedule whereby you check the portfolio on a periodic basis that works for you.

3. Keep a long-term focus and stick to longer holding periods. Generally, it makes sense to hold a stock for at least 5-10 years and, in some cases, even longer. With value stocks in particular, it can take a while for the price to reflect underlying value, and you have to be patient.

Weathering Bear Markets

Entire books have been written about surviving bear markets, and I'll include a couple in my Suggested Reading at the end of the book. Many books about investing, especially those that in my view paint an overly rosy picture of the stock market, make much of long-term historical returns. There is some truth to those historical averages: over the long haul, the U.S. economy has been a good bet, and will likely be so in the future; and stocks have been and likely will remain your best means of building long-term wealth. But those historical averages can be misleading as well: within every 30-year period of healthy average returns is a 10-year period of poor or negative returns.

In other words, not every 10-year stretch is created equal. Let's say, for example, you had listened to the optimists at the end of 1999 and assumed that annual returns of at least 10% were a near sure thing for the foreseeable future. You inherited $10,000, invested it in a stock fund and, using a handy compound interest calculator, counted on having $27,000 at the end of 2009 to put towards a child's education or the down payment on a house. Given market returns during the "lost decade," you'd be lucky if you still had the original $10,000. You'd have been better off putting your money into bonds and keeping a substantial portion in cash, and liquid investments like short-term Treasuries and money market accounts.

Keep in mind the cruel math of how hard it is to re-coup big losses: You need a 25% gain to make up for a 20% loss; a 100% gain to make up for a 50% loss. Because it's so difficult to dig yourself out of a hole, better to avoid one in the first place. Often, it isn't how much you gain in the good markets but how much you don't lose in the bad ones.

Complicating matters is the fact that strategies that work in a bull market won't necessarily work in a bear market. **Riding a bull and riding a bear are two different things entirely**. As in any facet of investing, there are no hard-and-fast rules that will work in every situation. But here are some general principles to keep in mind in an extended bear market:

o **Strategically shift asset allocation.** As a general rule of thumb, deep into a bull market, you want to be less exposed to stocks or equities and have a portfolio weighted more toward cash and fixed-income securities like bonds and short-term Treasuries.

o **Shift within equities as well.** Small, upstart companies tend to fare less well in a bear market. Conversely, established blue-chip companies like IBM and Wal-Mart, often dismissed as unfashionable or behind-the-times during bull markets, generally do a solid job of weathering bear markets. Other "defensive" investments include companies in so-called "counter-cyclical" sectors of the economy like utilities, health care, and consumer staples.

o **Exercise patience and selective offense.** Sometimes the best moves you make during a bad market are the ones you don't make: like Ted Williams keeping his bat on his shoulder until he sees a pitch he knows he can hit. Yet the companion to patience is selective offense, and here's where a shift toward cash and liquid assets figures in: giving you the reserves, the "dry powder," to step in and take advantage of the bargains offered by severely underpriced stocks. The greatest investors have made a good deal of their wealth this way: being decisive when everyone else is acting scared and cautious.

o **Don't abandon your regular investing routine.** One of the biggest mistakes average investors make during down markets is getting out of the market entirely. In this sense, maintaining a consistent, auto-pilot approach is preferable if it helps you stick to a discipline of saving and investing on a regular basis.

o **The best bear strategies begin early, late in a bull**. Bubbles can burst and turn into panics in a heartbeat. By the time prices really start tumbling, it may be too late, and you'll find yourself in unflattering company: that unfortunate majority of investors who buy high and sell low. Be like Warren Buffet, who distrusted the dot-com boom, stayed away from trendy internet stocks, and shifted early into cash and bonds; and not like many other investors who suspected a bubble was coming, but didn't get out until it had already burst.

Finally, let me repeat: the greatest danger for the individual investor is overreacting to short-term market fluctuations. The risk in adopting a special strategy for bear markets – as opposed to maintaining a constant, auto-pilot approach – is that you'll misread every short-term dip as a bear; or, within a bear, misread every short-term rally as a sign that the bear is over and a bull has started. And as a consequence you'll engage in the losing game of overtrading, and of excessively tinkering with your portfolio.

So, keep your cool and don't pay too much attention to the daily noise of the financial media. Focus on the big picture, the big questions: Is the market overvalued or undervalued? Is it ruled by greed and excessive optimism, or fear and undue pessimism? Know yourself, and your tendencies. If you're likely to overreact during difficult markets, lean toward the constant, auto-pilot approach; or use a financial advisor as a kind of buffer to protect yourself from your own worst impulses.

Anomalies, Mutual Funds and ETFs

Individual stocks remain the best way to take advantage of anomalies and pursue a value strategy. Index funds, because they track and mirror the market, obviously aren't a good way to go against the grain of the market and take advantage of its mispricings and overreactions. And as we've seen, a large number of supposedly active funds don't differ a whole lot from index funds. Even in the case of more focused sector funds, mispricings for a whole basket of stocks are likely to cancel one another out, and the case for a bargain discount harder to define and pin down.

Having said that, there are value-oriented mutual funds and ETFs that can be a solid contrarian investment, especially for those just getting their feet wet in individual stocks. These include funds that target companies with a low P/E—even better if they also screen for quality and financial health. There are well-designed small-cap funds as well. Additionally, in bear markets, funds in the *growth & income* category allow you to buy into a stable of the kind of unglamorous but steady and solid blue-chip companies that are good at withstanding market downturns. Other funds that are bear-friendly include *balanced funds*, which hold a conservative mix of stocks, bonds, short-term Treasuries.

Yet in general, as I've mentioned before, be wary of a growing array of "smart beta" funds that try to gain an edge on the rest of the market through technical and timing advantages. The more specialized and complicated their approach, the more skeptical you should probably be. The smart-beta trend is especially pronounced in the world of ETFs, where a new generation of funds, as Ben Carlson puts it in his book about the value of simplicity in investing, "slice and dice" the market according to a range of risk factors, sectors, regions, and asset classes.

In the "New Normal" of uncertain returns, investors are understandably looking for ways to improve their odds while minimizing risk, and the proliferation of specialized ETFs is directed at such anxious investors. They are heavily marketed, and increasingly popular: accounting for over 20% of ETF offerings, and over 30% of new money coming into the industry. Yet they are sold to consumers as if they were in keeping with a low-risk, passive index approach—when in fact they are a hybrid of active and passive strategies. A CNBC report, "Smart Beta and Stupid Fund Tricks," concludes: "There are thousands of factors and combinations of factors that might arguably generate investment returns better than the market, but very few of them have track records that can support that claim." James Montier is even more blunt in his assessment, calling the new breed of funds a mix of "dumb beta plus marketing." As I stated earlier in a section on the pros and cons of ETFs, they are a great addition to the investing menu, but best employed in the service of a broadly-based, index approach.

Chapter 12

Keeping Your Costs Low

Superstar investors like Warren Buffett and George Soros combine what might seem like contradictory qualities. They're willing to take certain calculated (and well-researched) gambles: to go in big on one stock; to depart from a classically diversified portfolio; to go against conventional wisdom. They're definitely out to try and beat the market and, in that sense, are anything but conservative.

Yet they balance that boldness with decidedly conservative qualities. Both are adamant that the successful investor does the following:

1) Avoid big mistakes;

2) Protect against market major downturns;

3) Keep costs to a minimum.

The last few chapters have, in one way or another, addressed the first two. Now it's time to move onto #3.

The reason that a smart investor can build long-term wealth is largely due to the *miracle of compound interest*:

even modest returns can, over time, produce an impressive nest egg down the road. The self-reinforcing dynamic of compound interest is the basic building block of any sound investment strategy. **But working against that strategy, and eating away at that building block, is the phenomenon of what we might call *compound cost*.** What appears to be a solid annual return of 10% might, upon closer inspection, be several percentage points lower once you've added up all the costs that take a bite out of your return. Most of those bites are so small that you won't feel them individually. Even taken together, they may not feel too devastating in any given year. But cumulatively, and over time, those costs will significantly undermine your long-term returns and leave you with a much small nest egg in the end.

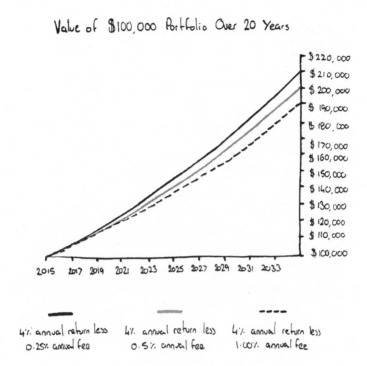

Value of $100,000 Portfolio Over 20 Years

4% annual return less 0.25% annual fee

4% annual return less 0.5% annual fee

4% annual return less 1.00% annual fee

Figure O

"Who The Heck is FICA?"

The biggest bite out of both your investment returns and your income is going to come courtesy of the taxman. It's a lesson we all learn on our first payday and the sting of that lesson is felt by everyone from the average working person to superstar athletes.

> *Last time I looked at a paycheck, I said to myself, 'Who the hell is FICA? And when I meet him, I'm going to punch him in the face.'*
>
> - Shaquille O'Neal

FICA (short for the Federal Insurance Contributions Act) is a payroll tax automatically deducted from our wages. As of the writing of this book in 2016, the rate is 7.65%--with 6.2% of income going toward Social Security and 1.45% going toward Medicare. There's nothing you can do to reduce your FICA tax: deductions and exemptions don't count against it. And your investment strategy will have no effect on your FICA taxes, so we won't go into it too much other than to note a few salient facts.

First, because the Social Security component of FICA is applied to only the first $118,500 of wages earned, it is viewed by some as a *regressive tax* that actually contributes to income inequality—as opposed to the rest of the federal tax code which is, for the most part, constructed *progressively* to counter income inequality. (The Medicare rate actually goes up to 2.35% for income over $200,000.)

Second, because there are no deductions or exemptions for FICA, some U.S. taxpayers will pay more in payroll taxes than they do in income taxes.

Finally, due to changing demographics (basically, an aging population), the benefits most workers receive down the line is expected to fall well short of their contributions. And that's not the end of the bad news: neither Social Security nor Medicare (as presently constituted) is fully sustainable in the long run. To make up for revenue shortfalls, tough reforms that will probably involve a mix of tax hikes and benefit cuts will almost certainly be necessary at some point. Which makes it all the more urgent for young investors to take control of their own long-term financial security.

Retirement Plans: A Brief History

Because retirement plans, either of the IRA or 401(k) variety, have emerged as your best option for both building a nest egg *and* saving on taxes, it's important to see where they came from and how the retirement plan landscape has changed over the years.

In hindsight, it was perhaps never realistic the Social Security system implemented by FDR in 1935 in response to the Great Depression would make for a comprehensive retirement package; it was more of a "safety net" for those without other options, and a supplement for those who had them. Employer-funded pension plans were not the norm at the time. But, in the prosperous years following WWII, a growing number of companies, led by the booming auto industry, did start offering pensions. So, by the 1960s, a new expectation had set in: that between Social Security and pension benefits, the average American worker would be able to retire at 65 or thereabouts and enjoy his "golden years" in relative comfort.

But cracks were already appearing in the system, and it was a case involving an automaker that brought the issue to the public eye. In 1963, Studebaker declared bankruptcy and revealed that its pension system was insolvent as well: the company had been promising workers more than it was setting aside for the plan. This early pension crisis generated calls for reform that culminated in 1974 with the Employment Retirement Income Security Act, or ERISA.

ERISA was first and foremost focused on pension reform—mandating employers to adequately fund their plans and requiring them to take out pension insurance. It also regulated other benefits such as health care plans. Yet many now associate it mainly with the creation of the Individual Retirement Account, or IRA. Initially intended only for workers not covered by an employer-funded pension, the IRA provisions introduced two important policy innovations: allowing workers to deduct their contributions from their taxable income; and allowing those funds to grow tax-free until withdrawal (so-called "tax deferral").

The concept of the IRA was also the beginning of a move away from the defined benefit model of traditional pensions (where benefits were guaranteed, and both the responsibility and risk of funding those benefits fell on the employer) to a *defined contribution* model where that responsibility and risk was increasingly shifted to the employee. That shift intensified in the 1980s. First, an obscure provision of a 1978 tax reform bill, *section 401(k)*, began to be used as a tool for the creation of a new generation of retirement plans that were an interesting hybrid: established and monitored by the employer, who would often also match an employee's contributions (up to a point), but with the investment burden falling on the employee, and no guarantee of benefits. Then, in 1981, IRAs were opened up to all workers.

Since then, defined benefit plans, which once covered nearly 40% of the workforce, have slowly but surely been replaced by defined contribution plans. **Yet most experts** agree that, despite all the options available, the new defined contribution model has not adequately replaced the old pension model, and that the country is facing an imminent retirement crisis:

- According to a recent study by the PEW Charitable Trusts, only 58% of all full-time workers have access to company-sponsored plan, and 20% of those don't choose to participate. So overall, just under half of all full-time workers participate in such a plan.

- Another study, by the Center for Retirement Research, paints a somber picture as well. Due to longer life expectancies, rising health care costs, and low interest rates, retirement income needs are growing. On the other hand, because of declining Social Security benefits and uneven participation in retirement plans, actual retirement income is shrinking.

- That same study finds that only 10% of 401(k) participants make the maximum contribution allowed. As a result, even for those who do participate in a retirement plan, the typical household approaching retirement has a total nest egg of only about $111,000—well below the amount experts say will guarantee a comfortable retirement, and which translates into less than $400 of income per month.

- An Employee Benefits Research Institute survey found that over half of all workers report total household savings and investments of less than $25,000—with 26% of workers having saved less than $1,000.

To address the fact that so many Americans are woefully underprepared for retirement, the federal government launched a new *my*RA program in 2014: a Roth-style IRA account run by the Treasury Department that consists entirely of conservative savings bonds. While the plan is simple, risk-free, and charges no fees, it is really designed as a kind of "starter account" to be rolled over into a traditional IRA or 401(k) once it reaches $15,000. But it's a good start for those without other options. The federal government also offers a Savers Credit providing low-to moderate-income households with an additional tax break on contributions to any retirement account—yet only about a quarter of targeted households are aware of it. Finally, there are a number of state initiatives in the works to extend retirement plans to those without access to an employer-based plan.

The Double Tax Benefit of IRAs and 401(k)s

So, no... The overall picture of Americans and their retirement security isn't a rosy one. On a public policy level, there is no consensus about what can be done to address the problem. On a private level, it means that more and more Americans will be postponing their retirement and working at least part time well into their "golden years." And, on a societal level, we will all have to adjust our picture and expectations of what retirement means.

At the very least that the above picture underscores the urgency of taking control of your long-term financial wellbeing, even if you're getting a late start to retirement planning (a common issue for Millennials whose biggest and most immediate financial challenge is overcoming large student debt). Whatever their imperfections, the benefits of defined contribution retirement plans are just too good to pass up. IRA and 401(k) plans of the traditional variety provide both an immediate and a long-term tax break: you can deduct (up to certain limits) your contribution from your annual taxable income *and* your invested retirement assets grow tax-free until you begin withdrawing them.

The big difference between them is that a **401(k)** is employer-sponsored and often involves a employer match: you agree to have a pre-set amount deducted from your paycheck, and your employer matches that contribution up to certain limits. (Employer matches vary greatly, but a common formula is 50% of the first 6% of income contributed with a certain ceiling). 401(k) plans also allow for a much higher annual contribution: in 2016, up to $18,000 for workers under the age of 50 (older workers can make higher, "catch-up" contributions). On the downside, because the retirement fund is employer-sponsored, employees will have a limited range of investment options. Also, the employer match can't be withdrawn until the employee has worked a certain number of years and is said to be "vested" in the plan. (Vesting requirements vary, but 5 years is fairly typical.)

Yet not all workers will have access to a 401(k). For those that don't or expect to change jobs frequently, the **IRA** offers great flexibility and freedom[1]. Because it is entirely self-managed, you don't have the ease of an automatic paycheck deduction. More important, you don't get a matching contribution from your employer. The annual contribution limit is also a good deal lower: $5,500 for workers under 50.

---

[1] In addition to the traditional IRA, there are lesser-known alternatives designed for small business owners, entrepreneurs, and the self-employed. These include the SEP (Simplified Employee Pension) IRA, the SIMPLE (Savings Incentive Match Plan for Employees) IRA, and the Solo 401(k).

On the other hand, anyone with taxable income can set up and contribute to an IRA, and you have total control over the assets you invest in.

It's important to note that you don't have to choose between the two. If your employer offers a 401(k), it's foolish not to take advantage of that option—especially because the employer match is the closest thing to "free money" you're ever going to see. But if you've contributed enough to receive the full match and can afford to do so, contributing to an IRA is a great idea (although if you're in an employer-sponsored plan and you exceed certain income limits, you may not be able to take the full IRA deduction). And if you "vest" in your employer's plan and later move on elsewhere in your career, converting or "rolling over" your 401(k) into an IRA may be your best option.

Pay the Taxman Now or Later: the Roth Option

In 1997, a bill sponsored by Senator William Roth was passed creating a new option for those with Individual Retirement Accounts: they could forgo the immediate tax deduction on their contribution and, in return, their future withdrawals from the fund would be tax-free (instead of, as with the traditional IRA, being taxed as ordinary income). The argument for the new option was two-fold: for some workers, a tax break down the road might be more valuable than one in the present plus it would increase current tax revenues and help reduce the deficit. In 2001, a similar option was added for 401(k) plans.

The Roth option is akin to a farmer having the option of paying a tax on his seeds, instead of on the final harvest. While some farmers may want to delay paying taxes until they are assured the seeds will yield a healthy crop, some would rather pay tax on the seeds. Although it costs the farmer more today, the potential profits from the harvest become greater.

While the main distinction between Roth and traditional retirement plans is the timing of the tax break, there are other differences as well. Those with higher incomes may not be able to contribute to a Roth IRA, while the traditional IRA has no income cap (but the ability to take a tax deduction does). On the other hand, an investor can make an early withdrawal from all previous contributions to a Roth IRA without penalty, while doing so with a traditional IRA carries a stiff penalty.

There are a lot of articles analyzing the pros and cons of traditional vs. Roth retirement plans. Generally, if you expect to be in a much lower tax bracket in the future, the upfront deduction of a traditional plan might be more valuable. However, if you expect your future bracket to be comparable to your current one, the benefits of being able to make your withdrawals tax-free down the road might outweigh the immediate tax hit you'll take with the Roth alternative. For most Millennials, the Roth is the better option, since your income is likely to rise. Also, the U.S. is in about $20 trillion of debt, which will likely be paid off through spending cuts and higher taxes (something the Roth protects against). But the larger point is this: **The difference between the two types of accounts is not as important as the benefits of using either.** And just as you can have both an IRA and a 401(k), you can also have a mix of Roth and traditional accounts.

Other Investment Tax Considerations

The financial hit you take from your federal income taxes (and state, depending on where you live) is the biggest and most noticeable drag on your effort to build long-term wealth—so trying to reduce that hit with tax-savvy investment decisions should be a major priority. But there are other, more subtle tax consequences to your investment choices. So let's take a moment to review some of them as well.

Earlier, we discussed some of the disadvantages of the typical "actively managed" mutual fund: with some notable exceptions, they charge higher fees without superior performance. But there are also hidden tax consequences for that more active style: the higher volume of buying and selling that comes with active management can generate capital gains (often of the more taxable, short-term variety) that you, the investor, will have to pay taxes on. **Actively managed mutual funds are thus said to be "tax inefficient" as compared to index funds and ETFs.**

Does that mean you should categorically avoid actively managed mutual funds? Not necessarily. If you've done your research and found one you feel consistently performs well, by all means invest in it. **But do so in a tax-protected plan like an IRA.**

TAX EFFICIENCY AND ASSET LOCATION

In the chapter on diversification, we spoke about *asset allocation*: splitting your total "investing pie" among different asset classes. As we focus here on taxes and controlling costs, we turn to the question of *asset location*: being smart, tax-smart, about which assets you put where. Any asset that might expose you to a higher tax burden — such as an actively managed mutual fund — is termed tax *inefficient* and should be located in a tax-protected account. In general, it makes sense to place tax inefficient investments first, tucking them away in your tax-protected plans. Once you have maxed out your IRA and/or 401(k), the remaining, more tax efficient investments will go in brokerage or other accounts that are not tax protected.

- Most tax inefficient: active stock funds; high-yield bonds; TIPS; REITs

- Moderately tax efficient: balanced mutual funds; international stocks; index funds

- Most tax efficient: passive ETFs; savings bonds; municipal bonds

Keep in mind that your taxable accounts have one crucial advantage: the ability to withdraw from them without penalty—giving you flexibility for short-term financial needs. So liquidity is also an element to consider in asset location.

Pay attention to how long you've held an asset before you sell it. If you've held it for less than a year and you're selling it for a profit, it will be taxed as ordinary income, not at the more forgiving long-term capital gains rate.

Finally, I should at least mention a technique called *tax-loss harvesting*. While buying high and selling low is generally a bad idea, if you're expecting a higher than normal capital gains tax for the coming year, it can be good strategy to sell another asset at a loss you can use to offset that gain. Some high-volume investors turn this into a bit of a game: selling a poorly performing stock at the end of the year for tax purposes, and then immediately buying a comparable stock or even the same stock back after 30 days (the IRS has what it called a "wash-sale rule" to prevent too much gaming of the tax system). Some studies show this tactic produces minimal savings, while incurring additional transaction costs. I don't recommend making a habit of it. But if you've got a poor stock you're going to sell sooner or later, then using those losses to offset other gains might make sense. The cost-benefit analysis of tax-loss harvesting can be complicated, so it's a good idea to consult a financial advisor or accountant first.

Fees and Charges... Some Obvious, Others Not

Many of the subtler fees you will incur as an investor are so small they are measured in hundreds of a percent, or what are called *basis points*. (Thus, 20 basis points would be equivalent to .20%.) But, again, it all adds up.

Not to make them out to be the bad guys all the time... But mutual funds, especially actively managed ones, are a frequent offender here. It used to be common for mutual funds to charge what is called a *load*—sometimes upon purchase (front-load), sometimes upon redemption (back-load). So many "no-load" options are now available to the investor that there is no longer an excuse to bear these additional costs.

Some mutual funds also charge what are called *12b-1 fees* that cover marketing and distribution costs. A study by one financial analyst found that funds that charged such fees typically had an expense ratio of 1.45% (as opposed to the industry average of 1.19%) *and* actually underperformed their competition.

One last note on mutual funds: A study of 1,800 equity funds found that the true aggregate trading cost was, in many cases, more than .3% higher than the advertised expense ratio. In general, funds that traded more actively were guilty of the highest "hidden" costs.

ETFs and Costs

Exchange Traded Funds or ETFs are marketed to investors as a low-cost alternative to mutual funds; and that's mostly true—with a few important caveats.

The good news is that expense ratios for ETFs are even lower than those for passive index funds: 0.44% on average compared to 0.74% for index funds, according to Morningstar. Also, for reasons that are too technical to go into here, ETFs are often even more tax-efficient than index funds.

On the other hand, because ETFs trade directly on the stock market, in most cases you will pay a commission or brokerage fee every time you buy and sell—something to factor in, depending on your investing schedule. If you have a single lump-sum amount to invest, that commission may not offset the lower expense ratio. However if you're going to be investing a smaller, fixed amount every month, an index fund might make a better option.

Additionally, as with any other security bought or sold directly on the stock market, you will encounter certain costs entailed with what is called the *bid-ask spread*: the gap between the price of the highest buyer and the lowest seller. The more actively traded and liquid an asset, the smaller that spread will be. But if that spread is significant, you can end up overpaying for an ETF. Therefore, even though some brokerage firms have begun to introduce commission-fee ETFs, that savings might not be worth it if the fund isn't sufficiently liquid. A good financial advisor can help you structure your purchase in a way to minimize being hurt by bid-ask spreads.

Online Tools for Researching Fees

Because even a 1% change in the fees you are charged can make such a huge difference over time (buying or costing you up to 10 years worth of retirement!), it pays to be a smart shopper—to pull out the magnifying glass and take a very careful look at the fees and other costs associated with a given investment. Shave off a little here, and a little there, and you'll be rewarded handsomely down the road.

o   FINRA, the Financial Industry Regulatory Authority, is a nonprofit watchdog agency, authorized by Congress but wholly independent. Its mission is to protect and educate American investors. They offer a number of free online tools and resources to help you become a more savvy investor. One of them, the **Fund Analyzer**, estimates fees and expenses for over 18,000 mutual funds and ETFs. (On that same page, you will also find savings calculators, tutorials, and other resources.)

o **FeeX** (which bills itself as "The Robin Hood of Fees") is a free service that helps you find and reduce fees in retirement funds, and in other investment accounts.

o And **BrightScope,** also mentioned in the section on 401(k) plans, provides analytics and rankings of other financial services as well.

Holding the Line on Costs

To sum up:

✓ Costs compound and add up just as quickly and invisibly as compound interest. Especially in a "new normal" where future returns may not match past returns, being extra vigilant about costs is more important than ever.

✓ Resisting the urge to overtrade will not only protect you from overreacting to the market's short-terms ups and downs, it will keep your transaction costs low.

✓ Be tax-smart when it comes to asset location— prioritizing potentially tax-inefficient investments for your tax-protected retirement accounts.

✓ Bid-ask spreads are yet another reason to avoid narrow, specialized ETFs.

Finally, a few words on the fees charged by financial advisors …

Compensation for financial advice falls under three broad categories: a commission on the purchase of a particular investment; an annual percentage of the total value of the investments the advisor is managing for you (Assets Under Management, or AUM); or flat or hourly "advice-only" fees.

In general, the industry trend is toward the second arrangement: a percentage of assets under management (this is sometimes called the "fee" model). But here, as in all areas of investing, there is no one-size-fits-all right answer. As a *Wall Street Journal* column points out, there are cases where commission-based advice is preferable. Fee-only advisors often have an account minimum of $50,000 or more assets under management, pricing out the small investor. And if you're only looking for targeted advice on a particular investment, as opposed to comprehensive financial planning, paying a commission may work out better for you.

Flat or hourly fees can be good for someone who wants to largely handle their own investing, but just needs help putting together a strategy. On the other hand, such fees can discourage investors from seeking advice when they need it.

With the annual percentage model, you're paying for more than simply investing advice. If you do your homework and choose the right advisor, you're getting someone to help you attain life and financial goals, and set the appropriate timeline for those goals; plus education and coaching on a range of financial issues (college savings, taxes, estate planning, etc.).

Most important, perhaps, you're getting someone to act as a buffer between yourself and your investments: someone to protect you from your own worst mistakes, to help you cultivate and stick to good financial habits. As one financial advisor puts it: "The dominant determinants of long-term, real-life investment returns are not market behavior, but investment behavior."

Successful investor Howard Marks stresses to occasionally go against the grain of popular opinion—learning to "react differently and behave differently." And the biggest investing errors, he goes on to say, are psychological in nature. If having the right coach at your side can help you avoid those errors, and help you escape the worst mood swings of the market, a reasonable fee for advice can be a solid investment in itself.

Chapter 13

Putting It All Together

We've covered a lot of ground so far. Among other things, we've seen:

- Economic inequality in America is increasing, and the ripple effects of the 2008 Financial Crisis are deep and still with us;

- The market in the long term may be a rational weighing machine, but in the short term is all too often an irrational voting machine;

- Risk is a slippery concept, and the biggest risks can't be neatly quantified;

- Diversification is a useful tool, but not a magic bullet, and won't protect you from an irrational market;

- Beating the market is possible, but not easy, and should be approached with caution;

- Even if you choose mostly to try to ride the market, you don't have to be entirely at the mercy of its mood swings;

- Costs can silently eat away at your attempts to build wealth.

Yet the question remains: What do you do with all this information? As I stressed at the beginning of the book, it is more imperative than ever that Americans take their long-term financial security into their own hands. While I hoped to educate and inform you, and maybe entertain you a little along the way, most of all I want to inspire you to take positive action.

So in this final chapter we'll deal with the three central questions faced by every investor:

✓ **What do I invest in?**

✓ **When do I invest?**

✓ **How do I monitor and modify my portfolio?**

What Is Your Investor 'Personality'?

At one point or another, most of us have taken the Meyers-Briggs Personality Test. Some people take it just for fun. Sometimes companies have their employees take the test to determine their "type" and work style. It's a set of simple questions designed to gauge your preferences in four broad areas. At the end, you can declare yourself an ESTJ, or an INFP[1], or fourteen other possible combinations. People disagree about just how useful it is, but it can reveal a person's broad tendencies.

---

[1]   For example, an INFJ (Introvert-Intuitive-Feeling-Judging) person, an "Advocate," is a quiet idealist; an ESTP (Extravert-Sensing-Thinking-Perceiving), an "Entrepreneur," enjoys living on the edge.

I'm not going to give you a test with a simple cut-and-dry answer at the end. But, just as Meyers-Briggs measures your tendencies along four different lines (for example, if you tend to be introverted or extraverted), I'm going to suggest that investors display certain tendencies in four broad areas as well. Some of these preferences have to do with your basic personality or temperament. Others are dictated more by your financial situation, your financial and life goals, and the time frame for those goals.

As I see it, there are four possible objectives an investor might have for his or her portfolio. Some investors might have all four objectives, and it's a matter of which are more or less important. For other investors, one or two of these objectives will be dominant.

1. Preserving Capital for the Short-Term – This should probably be part of the mix for all investors. Financial advisors recommend having three to six months of expenses available in assets that are both *liquid* and *extremely low risk*: cash, money market funds, short-term bonds, etc.

2. Preserving Capital for the Mid- to Long-Term – This might be money for goals that aren't immediate but come with a relatively short time frame. (For example: a recently-married couple who wants to make a down payment on a house in five years.) This category might also apply to people with a decent nest egg who would like additional growth, but most of all want to avoid significant loss. Here, the objective is modest returns with low to moderate risk: perhaps a conservative mix of index funds and bonds.

3. Accumulating Capital for the Long-Term – This is the "in it for the long haul" objective of most young investors.

This is about patiently and methodically building wealth for relatively long-term goals: your child's college education in 20 years or your own retirement in 40 years. An investor whose goals fall primarily in this category will have a classically diversified portfolio weighted toward stocks, but not featuring any big gambles. Here the objective is to ride the general long-term upward trend of the market but not necessarily to beat it.

4. Building a Fortune – There's no getting around it: to build a fortune, to beat the market, you need to be willing to take some chances. A classically diversified portfolio built around mutual funds or ETFs won't get you there. Investors who have successfully built a fortune do so by taking aggressive positions on individual stocks and have a portfolio characterized by a good deal of concentration.

It's important to note two things before we move on. First, very few investors' goals will fall exclusively under just one of these categories. An exception would be someone who's already retired, in great financial shape, and just wants to protect himself against disaster. The goals of someone nearing retirement might fall largely under the first two categories. The typical young investor will have some stake in all four objectives. Your circumstances and personality will determine the exact mix. Even superstar investors, while placing a good deal of emphasis on the fourth objective, especially early in life, balance that aggressiveness with caution and are sure to hedge against the possibility of a major and unexpected market downturn.

The other thing to note is that your mix of these objectives, your investor personality, will change and evolve over time. For example, once you've saved up money to make a down payment on a house, you might be free to be a little more aggressive and concentrate primarily on the third objective. As you near retirement, your objectives will, in most cases, grow more conservative. (We've seen how Warren Buffett, having accumulated a substantial fortune, is recommending that his heirs use a conservative, passive strategy to manage that fortune.)

Risk Tolerance and Risk Capacity

As you probably noticed, the above four investing objectives are listed in order of increasing aggressiveness: from extremely low risk to high risk. So your "investor personality" is on some level a matter of what is commonly referred to as your *tolerance for risk*. But, as we've seen in previous chapters, risk is a tricky and slippery concept and it's important to define our relationship to risk in precise terms.

Risk tolerance is a useful notion—but should be seen as subjective and variable. It is largely a question of temperament, of your individual psychological make-up. **To put it very simply: How well can you sleep at night when the stock market is going on a roller coaster ride?** That quality varies from individual to individual and often depends on circumstances. In a bull market, for example, an investor might describe themselves as having a fairly high tolerance for risk. But, in a bear market, that same investor will give a very different answer. **Risk tolerance, in other words, is subjective, individual, and often emotion-driven.**

It's good to know your psychological make-up and the degree to which you can or cannot tolerate risk. But, in most cases it is more important to understand your capacity for risk. *Risk capacity* **is a much more objective question.** Basically, it comes down to this: Given your current financial condition, your goals, and the time frame for those goals, how much risk can you afford to expose yourself to? For example, psychologically you may be very tolerant of risk—but if you're hoping to buy a house in two years, your wife is pregnant, and you're going to be the primary wage earner for a while, you can't afford to adopt an investment strategy with too much risk of short-term loss. In other words, while you as individual might able to handle a good deal of risk, your real-life circumstances dictate a strategy with less risk and lower volatility.

Note the interplay between the two ideas of risk. Take a contrasting example: You might be a young unmarried investor with no foreseeable major financial obligations so your *risk capacity* is quite high. Yet if you're not the type of person who deals well with the inevitable ups and downs of the market (i.e., you have low *risk tolerance*), you might still want to pursue a largely conservative investment strategy.

Bottom line: Know yourself, know your goals, know your time frames, and act accordingly.

When to Invest

So you've assessed your financial situation, your goals, and your time frames. You know your tendencies, how much risk you as an individual can tolerate, and how much risk your portfolio can withstand. Your answers to these questions will determine your appropriate asset allocation, the *what* of investing. Now the question is: **when?**

Some experts will tell you the simple answer is TODAY because you can never hope to time the market perfectly, so this argument goes, just get in there and start investing, in something—now. There's a certain truth to that: As I've stated from the beginning, Millennial investors in particular (many of whom have been reluctant to jump into the market) need to do so sooner than later. Yet, as in most areas of investing, the truth is not so simple.

What is clear is that you should, if you haven't already, start saving in a deliberate and disciplined manner, and setting that money aside. What *isn't* clear is that you should immediately put that money in the market. As we've seen, one of the secret weapons of great investors is patience: knowing when to sit on the sidelines and hold cash and liquid assets like short-term Treasuries. Knowing when, like Ted Williams, to keep the bat on your shoulder and wait for a pitch in your sweet spot.

So there's a lot to be said for "taking the temperature" of the market before you jump in. If the market is overheated and overvalued, you might want to steer your savings toward fixed-income investments and cash; or to follow some of the bear market strategies outlined in the previous chapter. It is unrealistic to think that the same investments that work in a bull market will also work in a bear market.

On the other hand, the matter of when to invest, and how much, is one that is always full of uncertainty and question marks: Is the market about to go up, or down? When is the "right" time? Do I jump into the market, or wait and hold back? As we've seen in previous chapters, the higher the degree of uncertainty, the greater the likelihood that emotion, cognitive bias, and irrational behavior will kick in.

In view of this reality, **some argue that the best way to avoid those bad decisions, to take emotion and bias out of the equation, is to trust in a simple process that essentially ignores the question of when is the "right" time.** This is what might be called the *auto-pilot* approach to investing. It has its merits, and comes in two different variations.

Dollar Cost Averaging

It sounds complicated and abstract (some call it the "Constant Dollar Plan" instead), but the idea is simple: Invest a fixed amount in a fixed investment at a fixed time.

For example, say you've decided to adopt an investment strategy of 70% stocks and 30% bonds, and that your portfolio consists of an index stock fund and a bond fund. And say you've decided you can afford to invest a total of $4,000 over the course of a year. A Dollar Cost Averaging (DCA) strategy would be to invest $1,000 on the first of every quarter, $700 into the index fund and $300 into the bond fund. (That's a very simple example, and it gets a little more complicated in practice the more investments you have, but you get the basic idea.)

Dollar Cost Averaging isn't a perfect strategy by any means and has its critics. (We'll get to that in a second.) But it does have several clear and compelling advantages. First, it is a protection against volatility. The risk of a large, lump-sum investment is the possibility of a sudden drop in price right after your purchase. This is the risk, in general, of any attempt to "time" the market: such an attempt is always, at best, an educated guess, and there's always the chance your guess could go horribly wrong. DCA essentially forgoes any effort to time the market by scheduling your investments ahead of time, and breaking them up into installments as opposed to large lump sums.

This method thus takes emotion, impulse, and irrationality out of the equation, thereby protecting investors from themselves. And, on a related point, it helps risk-averse investors take healthy risks they wouldn't otherwise take (such as buying when the market is falling) and makes it easier to stomach volatility.

Value Averaging

One weakness of Dollar Cost Averaging is that it is a static and not a dynamic approach. It doesn't respond to changing market conditions. While it tends to perform well during moderately volatile times, it may not do so well during a prolonged market run or slump. It also offers the investor no guidance on when to sell as opposed to buy.

A more dynamic and somewhat more complicated method, called Value Averaging or Dollar Value Averaging (DVA), was developed by Harvard professor Michael Edleson as a refinement of Dollar Cost Averaging. As with DCA, you invest (or sell) according to a predetermined schedule. But, instead of choosing a fixed sum to invest, you choose a fixed rate of return and vary your investment accordingly.

That's a mouthful so let's illustrate with a simple example. Let's say your targeted rate of return is 8% a year, or 2% per quarter. If, at the end of the first quarter, your return is holding at 2%, you don't invest anything. But if your return has shot up to 4%, then (to maintain the 2% target) you would actually *sell off* 2% of your portfolio. Conversely, if your portfolio *declined* by 3%, you would contribute an amount equal to 5% so that the portfolio continues to meet the 2% target.

Still sound complicated? It is, a little. But Edleson's book, *Value Averaging*, provides simple worksheets to guide you through the process, and any good financial advisor can talk you through it as well.

Like Dollar Cost Averaging, Value Averaging isn't a perfect system. But it has one striking advantage. It's essentially a trigger to get you to sell when the market is high (and when your investments are quite possibly overpriced) and buy when the market is low (and assets are likely underpriced). DCA also encourages investors to buy more than they otherwise would when the market is low but DVA takes it a step further.

The Downside of DCA and DVA

The strength of both of the above DCA and DVA is that they protect against volatility, and will generally give you decent performance (and help protect against big losses) in volatile times. Their downside is that certain problems arise when the market is either in a sustained slump or a prolonged upswing.

For example, if you have $2,000 to invest but only invest $1,000 under DCA and the market continues to go up, that same $1,000 will buy you fewer shares in the same investment three months from now. And DVA might actually trigger you to sell shares well before the market peaks. Conversely, in a long slump, both methods might trigger you to buy well before the market hits bottom.

Value Averaging, because of the larger investments triggered when the market is down, also requires you to have a substantial cash reserve. This method probably works best under the scenario initially outlined by Edleson in his book: where you have a 401(k) split between a stock fund and a money market fund, and invest in each according to what the formula dictates.

Both methods have been criticized in studies that compare staggered investments to lump-sum investments. But this assumes a false choice: the average Millennial investor doesn't usually have a large lump-sum to invest at any given time, and is just looking for a reasonable system for steadily growing his or her portfolio.

Yet it should be pointed out that, because both of these staggered investment methods work because they protect against volatility, they are more applicable to investment vehicles like stocks and stock-based funds and less relevant for lower-risk, fixed-income assets. So if you inherit a substantial lump sum, you don't necessarily need to hold onto it, even if you're committed to a staggered schedule. It may very well make sense to invest some of it in a low-risk bond or money market fund.

Auto-Pilot vs. Adaptability

Whatever their flaws, these "auto-pilot" approaches to investing have two undeniable advantages:

1. They protect investors from themselves, from the tendency of most investors to overreact to the inevitable daily ups and downs of the market;

2. They get you in the habit of regular savings, and of setting that money aside for the future.

Yet it's also undeniable that a 100% auto-pilot approach, just like a 100% ride-the-market approach, ties your hands and doesn't allow you to protect yourself against the manic-depressive moods of the market. **It may protect you from your own individual irrationality but not from the market's collective irrationality.**

Earlier, I argued that you needn't view the issue of whether to ride or beat the market as an either/or question. You can lean on the passive indexing approach for some or most of your investing while, at the same time, maintaining some flexibility to go against the grain of the market. Mix and match in a way that works best for you.

Similarly, you can set up an auto-pilot schedule to get yourself into the habit of regular savings and investing, and stick with that during periods of moderate market volatility. But you can also make a habit of taking the temperature of the market from time to time, and give yourself the flexibility to adapt accordingly.

Going back to our Dollar Cost Averaging example, for instance: In 1999, sensing an overheated market and the possibility of the dot-com bubble bursting, you might have moved away from your standard monthly 70/30 stock/bond investment and directed your savings toward cash and short-term Treasuries. Or, in a cheap market gripped by panic and fear (such as was the case in 2009) you might have bought into undervalued stocks more aggressively than normal.

To put all this in perspective, let's revisit the spectrum of BAD to BEST investing approaches I introduced in Chapter 10—with a slight altering of the terms to reflect the concepts we've covered since then:

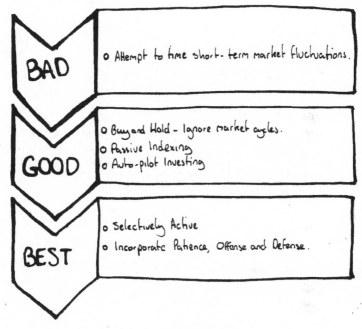

BAD
o Attempt to time short-term market fluctuations.

GOOD
o Buy and Hold - Ignore market cycles.
o Passive Indexing
o Auto-pilot Investing

BEST
o Selectively Active
o Incorporate Patience, Offense and Defense.

Figure P

As I wrote earlier, the middle path, while it won't get you the best results, is greatly preferable to an undisciplined, emotion-driven attempt to time the market. Yet if you stay humble, disciplined and prudent, I think you can do better than just good, and have tried, throughout the book, to present you with some straightforward principles for doing so.

Lockbox vs Sandbox.

Another way of developing your own unique investing philosophy, taking some chances, and going against the grain of the market and conventional wisdom is to combine the ideas of Nassim Nicholas Taleb, who joked that investors should try to be "90% accountant and 10% rock star", and Jason Zweig, who suggested that investors have a *lockbox* and a *sandbox.*

The *lockbox* is where you maintain a disciplined, regular system of investing on auto-pilot. You pick one of the methods above, a variation on either, or a system you develop with the help of a financial advisor and you stick with it. Outside of making small, periodic adjustments to your portfolio (what advisors call "rebalancing," which I'll cover in the next section), you refrain from the temptation to constantly tinker with your investments—i.e., you don't try to time or outsmart the market.

Yet there's also something to be said for having a *sandbox* where you can step outside of that system and try to take advantage of unique opportunities as they present themselves. This would be your 10% rock star: where you take a calculated bet on an emerging tech company, or maybe buy low on an established company that has just seen a sudden drop in price but which you think has good long-term fundamentals. The sandbox concept gives you a way to add a bit of flexibility to the auto-pilot of either the DCA or DVA approaches.

If you're a conservative investor, you might want to stick with a 100% lockbox strategy, at least to start. Even if you like taking the occasional risk, your sandbox investments, in most cases, should be a small part of your overall portfolio. As with anything having to do with your money, it's about your individual comfort level and following common sense. And it's about finding your own personality as in investor. To what extent are you comfortable being a contrarian? Do you want to simply try to ride the market? Or do you want to pick your spots and sometimes bet against the market?

Monitoring (and Modifying) Your Portfolio

Even the best strategy requires the occasional adjustment. And, to continue with the auto-pilot analogy, even a pilot making use of an automatic flight system would be wise to monitor it periodically to make sure the plane stays on course.

In the world of investing, we call this "rebalancing" and the basic principle is fairly straightforward. Let's say (to make things very simple) the *asset allocation* you've chosen for your portfolio is 70% stocks and 30% bonds. If over the course of the year your stock funds have gained 10% and your bond funds only 3%, your asset allocation will change as one piece of the pie grows faster than the other. As a result, your portfolio balance might have shifted to, 75% stocks and 25% bonds. (In the business we call this "portfolio drift.") Rebalancing your portfolio would require you to sell off some of your stocks and reinvest them in bonds or another low-risk vehicle like a money market fund, bringing you back to your target 70/30 split.

If the market is riding high and everyone seems to be making money, the temptation is to allow your portfolio to remain imbalanced so your stock funds can continue to realize the benefits of a hot market. But as you'll recall from the chapter on human behavior, investors tend to be driven by greed when the market is up, and by fear when the market is down. Periodic rebalancing is a technique that is, in a sense, very similar in result to the strategies described above: **an automatic method for avoiding irrational behavior at market extremes.** A 2012 report by Columbia Business School professor Andrew Ang even found that periodically rebalanced portfolios outperform fixed ones, especially during volatile markets.

How often should you adjust your portfolio? While some experts advise doing so quarterly, one study found that investors who rebalanced annually slightly outperformed those who did so quarterly. (And both, it should be noted, outperformed those who did not rebalance at all.)

The important thing is to pick a schedule and stick to it and to avoid the temptation to constantly tinker with your investments. One of the many benefits of a regular schedule is that it protects you from being swayed by the daily reports of financial pundits either warning of imminent disaster or promising quick profits. There are a handful of business journals and financial websites worth reading; but my general rule of thumb is to not pay too much attention to the day-to-day up and downs of the market or to the daily forecasts of the financial press. Instead, focus on long-term trends and fundamentals.

On the other hand, just because you begin with a given asset allocation formula (again, for the sake of simplicity, say a 70/30 stock-bonds allocation), doesn't mean you have to stick with it through thick and thin, regardless of market conditions. While you don't want to tinker with it repeatedly, if you take the temperature of the market and sense, for example, a major downturn on the horizon, it may be wise to go beyond rebalancing, and to adjust your asset allocation strategy as well. As I've stated several times already, strategies that work in a bull market can't always be expected to work in a bear market—and the difference between bull and bear strategies often comes down to differences in asset allocation.

Asset Allocation and Investing Life Cycles

You may want to adjust your asset allocation in response to changing market conditions. You will definitely want to do so in response to changing life conditions.

In general, the younger you are and the more modest your immediate financial obligations, the more you can afford to invest in a portfolio more heavily weighted towards stocks. Going back to the four broad investing objectives introduced at the start of the chapter, you are likely at this stage of your life to be focused on *long-term capital accumulation*. Yet, at some point, you may also have some significant short- and mid-term goals on the horizon: a down payment on a home, for example. This will call for a mix of objectives. You will still be trying to build long-term wealth for retirement but, at the same time, *capital preservation* will also be a major goal. Later, with your house paid for, you might once again focus largely on accumulating wealth. Even later in life, as you approach retirement, you will want to be more conservative with your investments and focus on preserving and protecting the nest egg you've built up.

All of which is to say: Because your life and financial goals and thus your asset allocation strategy, will go through different cycles over the course of your life, you will need to continually adapt your portfolio. One old rule of thumb (when most people's portfolios were split between stocks and bonds) was that the percentage of assets devoted to bonds should be roughly equal to your age. This simplistic formula is seen by many as outdated but you can see the thinking behind it

In recent years, so-called "life-cycle" investing has become more sophisticated and more prevalent. College savings plans start out weighted toward stocks in the early years, then shift gradually toward bonds as the target date (the time your child actually begins school) approaches. And *target-date mutual funds* following the same principle have become an increasingly popular offering, especially in many 401(k) plans. The target-date concept is also being incorporated into many of the algorithms used by robo-advising services.

First, your asset allocation should evolve over the course of your life, and if it doesn't, that can be a problem—leaving you, for example, over-exposed to the volatility of stocks as you approach retirement. In one study of one of the nation's largest retirement funds, more than half of the participants did not adjust their asset allocation as they got older. That's not good.

Second, it is often wise to protect investors from themselves, and their tendency, when left to their own devices, to sometimes over-manage their investments and excessively tinker with their portfolios in response to the short-term ups and downs of the market. So, in a sense, target-date investing goes hand in hand with passive indexing and auto-pilot investing schedules: the idea is to set up a rules-based strategy that takes emotion and impulse out of the equation—a kind of "set it and forget it" approach to investing.

While I understand the thinking behind such automatic strategies, I also think you can be prudent and responsible without locking yourself into a rigid approach that doesn't allow for flexibility and adaptability. What if your auto-pilot formula calls for your portfolio to be heavily weighted towards stocks at a time when stocks are overvalued and the market is headed towards a bubble? Auto-pilot approaches tend to assume stable markets with a normal range of volatility, and that may or may not be the case in coming years. Bear markets and bull markets demand different approaches and different kinds of asset allocation—and purely automatic strategies won't allow you to adjust accordingly.

Moreover, automatic strategies, by fostering a "set it and forget it" mentality, can instill a false sense of security. One survey found that participants in target-date funds had unrealistic expectations about their rate of return and their exposure to the possibility of loss.

My advice on the matter of adjusting your asset allocation is similar to my advice on other questions: Make use of automatic strategies to the extent that they help you develop a habit of saving and investing and offer peace of mind. But try not to fall into the "set it and forget it" trap and allow your investing choices to be made out of sight, out of mind. With or without the help of a professional, the best option is to make conscious and active choices.

The Value of Professional Advice

I've tried to keep things as simple as possible throughout this book. But economics, finance, and investing aren't easy. There are a lot of factors to consider in putting together a long-term plan that not only works for you and helps you meet your goals, but is one you are comfortable with and allows you to sleep at night.

This is where the value of a financial advisor can come into play. You will notice that, while I have presented what I feel are the essential principles of putting together a solid portfolio and outlined a range of options, I have chosen *not* to recommend a specific investment strategy. If you've been reading this book and eagerly awaiting the moment when I pull back the curtain to reveal my Fool-Proof System, you're going to be disappointed. In the end, I feel it's dishonest to do so. While certain basic principles are universal, each individual needs to find a customized plan tailored to his or her unique situation, goals, and comfort levels.

Some of you will take the principles I've outlined, check out my recommended reading, and want to put together an investment strategy on your own. If so, that's great. Others might feel overwhelmed by the amount of information and the sheer variety of investment alternatives available, and not know where to start. If that describes you, seeking out a qualified financial advisor to help you sort through the options might be a good first step.

And that's the most important thing: Whatever way suits your situation and your temperament, **take that first step and get started.**

Saving Comes First

At the risk of stating the obvious: that first step is saving. Unless you're the fortunate recipient of a sizable inheritance, you can't invest what you haven't saved in the first place. And having some goals in mind can be helpful in instilling the discipline of saving and investing.

You'll likely have short-term savings goals (say, for the down payment on a house); mid-term goals (a college fund for your kids); and long-term goals (retirement). Exactly how much you'll need for retirement is extremely variable, depending on the age you hope to retire, whether you plan to work part-time beyond the traditional retirement age (a growing reality for most of us), and the lifestyle you hope to maintain. There are a number of tools available, online or in print, which can get you started with this planning. Among them is a free Guide to Retirement that J.P. Morgan publishes every year. It includes milestones of how much you ideally should have saved by a given age.

While the Morgan guide assumes a 5% annual contribution to a retirement account, other experts advise trying to save 10% or more of your annual income. What is realistic for you will depend on a number of factors—including the amount of student debt you have to pay down. But however rough the math you use for establishing initial goals, setting them can be crucial.

We have seen that the insights of behavioral economists can help us identify, anticipate, and sometimes avoid the irrational mood swings of the market. **That same research can also be applied to the development of good financial habits**. In his book of the same name, co-written with Cass Sunstein,

271

Richard Thaler writes about "nudges" that can prompt us to make better decisions. Focusing specifically on the question of retirement savings, Thaler helped develop the **Save More Tomorrow** program to encourage wider participation in 401(k) plans, and at higher levels.

A key finding of Thaler and his colleagues was that the pain of having to sacrifice current consumption for future saving can be minimized greatly if employees agree ahead of time to automatically commit pay increases to their retirement fund. Even if your employer doesn't offer a 401(k) or participate in Save More Tomorrow (SMarT, as it is known, has now been implemented in hundreds of workplaces), you can make use of such "nudges" on your own.

The Most Important Thing(s)

Throughout this book, I've cited and quoted *The Most Important Thing* by Howard Marks, in my view one of a handful of books every serious investor should read. As he explains in the book's Introduction, the title is a bit of an inside joke. In meetings with current or prospective clients, he constantly found himself emphasizing a key principle by saying, 'The most important thing is X,' or 'The most important thing is Y.' So he put together a memo collecting the most important of those most important things, ending up with 18 of them. He has modified the list somewhat over the years, but it formed the basis for the book and for his core philosophy. What hasn't changed is that there is no one most important thing.

They're all important. Successful investing requires thoughtful attention to many separate aspects, all at the same time. Omit any one and the result is likely to be less than satisfactory. That is why I have built this book around the idea of the most important things—each is a brick in what I hope will be a solid wall, and none is dispensable.

David Swensen, whose book *Unconventional Success* I've also cited numerous times, has his own take on the most important thing. He points to studies finding that asset allocation is the most important determinant of returns—more important than stock selection, or market timing. In other words, in his view, figuring out how to split up the pie chart of your portfolio – the correct proportion of stocks, fixed-income assets, cash, and other assets – is the key to long-term success.

William Bernstein, a neurologist turned successful writer and investing advisor, takes almost the opposite point of view: "Discipline matters more than allocation," he writes. "Almost all advisors tell you that what separates successful from unsuccessful investors is the ability to stay the course, irrespective of what that precise course is."

So who is right? In keeping with Marks' belief that there is no one most important thing, I'd say they're all right, in their own way.

As you begin you're investing journey, you don't want to get too caught up on researching the perfect plan. The good news is that most of you will start out simply – perhaps with a stock fund and a bond fund – and so advanced theories about proper asset allocation won't really matter at that point. Just get in the habit of saving and investing on a regular basis.

But as your finances improve and you have more to invest, and once you've grown more knowledgeable about the world of investing, I encourage you to explore the full range of options we surveyed in Chapter 6. And as you do so, it will make sense to look more deeply into the question of asset allocation, and to determine a strategy best suited to you and your situation. A key question you'll have to consider at that point is whether to settle on a given asset allocation and stick with it, modifying it only slightly over time (an approach known as *static allocation*); or whether you want to give yourself the freedom to adjust your pie chart based on prevailing market conditions (*dynamic allocation*).

Thus it comes down to yet another variation on the essential choice you face as an investor: the extent to which you're willing and able to make active decisions and to at times go against the grain of the market and of popular opinion; or whether you want to largely ride the market and lean towards an automatic approach. My advice, as always, is that there is no one-size-fits-all answer. Some asset allocation strategies, some portfolios, work fine in bull markets, but not in bears; and the reverse holds true as well. If you're comfortable taking on the role of an independent, contrarian investor, then adapting to changing market conditions can allow you to optimize your returns. Yet if you're not comfortable with that role, and concerned about overreacting to market fluctuations and becoming your own worst enemy, then a more passive, automatic approach might be best for you.

The good news, again, is that you don't have to decide all of this at once. You can start simple, build your confidence and your knowledge, and investigate the deeper questions of investing down the road. You will evolve and grow as an investor, just as you evolve and grow in other areas of life.

Conclusion

Building Your Own American Dream

We began with the idea of the American Dream facing a series of unprecedented challenges in the 21st century—challenges that Millennials are taking the brunt of.

In the last century, following the social, economic and political crisis of the Great Depression, the federal government put in place a series of programs and reforms to prevent that kind of devastation from ever happening again. A safety net was established in the form of Social Security and Medicaid and new regulations were imposed to create stability in the banking and finance industries. The economy slowly recovered, and then took off after World War II—generating widespread prosperity and making things like home ownership a reality for an ever-growing middle class.

But in the new century, the American economy—and with it, the American Dream—has taken a couple of stiff blows to the gut. The longest bull market in the history of the stock market ballooned into a bubble, and in 2000, that bubble burst. A housing bubble built up soon after that, and the bursting of that bubble in 2008 set off a worldwide financial crisis and recession. The crisis not only destroyed wealth and devastated retirement accounts but, also, stalled and hobbled the ability of young people to build earning potential and begin generating wealth.

The economy and the market have bounced back (for now). For those who are enterprising and can adapt to an ever-changing economy, the possibilities are endless. Yet the old certainties of previous generations are gone. The likelihood that you will stay in one job, or even one career, is slim. The employer-funded pension plans that used to promise an early and comfortable retirement are the exception rather than the rule. Workers increasingly must take steer their own retirement plans, and can expect less from the safety net of Social Security.

At a time when the immediate prospects for the economy and the stock market are unclear, Millennials, more than any previous generation, must take responsibility for their own long-term financial health.

Time Is On Your Side... For Now

Time is indeed on your side, and is in some ways your greatest asset. *Time, time, time... is on my side,* the Rolling Stones sang. But they also sang, *Time waits for no one.* In other words, time won't remain on your side forever.

Let me illustrate with an example.

Say Sheila begins saving for retirement at the age of 23, investing $250 every month in an IRA that averages an 8% annual return. She continues to do so for 17 years, until the age of 40, and then stops.

Ted, on the other hand, also puts away $250 a month, but doesn't begin until he's 40. He continues to do so until the age of 67, for a total of 27 years, 10 years longer than Sheila.

Who comes out ahead? Sheila, and it's not even close. At the age of 67, having invested a total of $51,000, she has a nest egg of nearly a million bucks. Ted, despite investing $81,000 ($27,000 more than Sheila) has just over a quarter of a million.

Sheila has a 4 to 1 advantage. **Because she got an early start. Because she tapped into the power of** *compound interest* **and because she tapped into the power of time.**

Start Early, Start Now, Start Simple

That doesn't mean you should throw your hands up in the air and give up if you're 27, 30 or older and haven't yet seriously started saving for retirement. For a variety of reasons, a lot of Millennials are getting a late start in building long-term wealth. There are ways of catching up and making up for lost time. But I hope this example drives home the urgency of getting an early start.

Exactly where you should start depends on the kind of investing philosophy you decide to adopt. I've given you the pros and cons of trying to beat the market vs. simply riding it, of active vs. passive strategies. But when in doubt, start simple. Even if you think you'd later like to pursue a more nuanced approach, it can be wise to begin with a straightforward, broadly-based index fund or ETF; or with a low-cost "balanced" mutual fund that mixes stocks and bonds.

The important thing is just to start. As a Prussian military expert once said: "***The greatest enemy of a good plan is the dream of a perfect plan.***"

Begin With Saving

While obvious, I'll say it once again. Any plan begins with saving. You can't invest what you haven't saved in the first place.

If, like many Millennials, you have significant student debt, you'll want to put together a plan to intelligently pay it off, the right amounts at the right times. But if you have high interest credit card debt, pay it down as soon as possible! The power of compound interest can work against you as well as for you. You may have to split every dollar you save between paying off debt and investing in your future. But even if that split is 80/20, start setting something aside for the long run.

As with anything in life, saving is easier if you set specific goals. You can work backwards, using a *retirement calculator* to estimate how much you'll need to save in order to have a certain amount put away by a certain age. Or you can begin with a fixed percentage of your income. While many experts recommend eventually trying to put away 10-15% of your income, even 5% is a solid start.

And take advantage of the insights of behavioral economics, and of the Save More Tomorrow plan. Make your saving routine as automatic as possible. If your employer offers a way for you to automatically deduct a portion of your paycheck and direct it toward a retirement or savings plan, take advantage of it. Even if you're self-employed or a freelancer, you can set up automatic transfers with your bank. Commit ahead of time to devote at least a portion of any future raises or bonuses toward long-term savings.

Motivation: Money as a Means, Not an End

Keeping up a consistent routine of saving and investing isn't easy. There will be times when you're tempted to stray from the course. The science of motivation and habit-building tells us that remembering the big picture, keeping our eyes on the prize, can help us stay on course.

Most of us aren't driven by a desire to accumulate money just for the sake of it. Money is a means to a bigger end: the ability to live a certain kind of life, the capacity to take care of loved ones, the free time to follow creative pursuits or charitable endeavors.

So, hand in hand with your financial goals, write down your non-financial goals as well. You'll find you will be better able to stick with your plan when it is driven by *purpose* and *values* and not just numbers. Also it may help not to think of your nest egg as simply as your retirement fund but, instead, as your LIFE fund.

The Millennial Disadvantage

I remain an optimist at heart—both about the American economy, and about the long-term prospects for Millennials. But it's important to take a cold hard look at the special challenges facing our generation:

o   A slow start to building wealth

o   Stagnant wage growth

o   High student debt

o   A "new normal" of a more volatile and uncertain stock market

I point out these realities not to discourage you but to light a fire. As I've repeated over and over, Millennials, more than any previous generation, have to take charge of their long-term financial health. **And to get where you want to go, you're going to have to** *save smarter, earn smarter, and invest smarter.* And in spite of the tough hand you've been dealt economically, the Millennial Advantage is that time is on your side and the opportunities and tools for doing so have never been greater.

Save More

It's important to start a program of saving and investing however imperfect or incomplete the plan. But once you've done so you'll find, if you project the numbers out into the future, that at some point you're going to have to step up and take it to a different level. If you can set aside 5% of your income to start, you can eventually double that—whether you do so by committing pay advances ahead of time or by seeking out additional ways to save.

You can't improve on what you don't measure, so if you need to save more, I urge you to track your expenses and look for opportunities to cut back. You may find, for example, that you're spending more than you realize on eating out—whether that be a $4 latte at Starbucks, a deli sandwich for lunch, or drinks and appetizers after work. Cutting back $50 a month may not seem like much, but it adds up.

I advise identifying every potential expenditure in terms of future and not present value. That same $50 in today's money, if saved and invested, can turn into ten times that in twenty years.

There are a bunch of creative ways to save and set aside more for the future. These include accelerating payments on your mortgage to save thousands in interest and considering a move to an area with lower taxes and living expenses (such as Florida, or even somewhere abroad). There are dozens of books and websites with tips on saving. Put it all on the table and figure out what's right for you. Unless you're extremely fortunate, the odds are you're going to have to be creative and learn how to save more, and save smarter.

Earn More

Saving more and saving smarter will only get you so far. It also pays to get creative and figure out ways to increase your earnings. You can't invest what you don't save, but you only save what you've earned. And in a world where the Financial Crisis has had a dampening effect on wages and wage growth, taking the initiative to improve your earnings is critical.

This isn't a book about career building or self-development. **But I want to plant a seed and encourage you to continually search for ways to make yourself more valuable.** This is a point Tony Robbins makes in all his books: In the long run, success and wealth flow from making yourself valuable to others—offering a service or a set of skills that makes you stand out from the crowd. Warren Buffett is fond of saying that the most powerful investments he ever made were those he made in himself: "Invest in as much of yourself as you can," he says, "you are your own biggest asset by far."

Entrepreneur and speaker Jim Rohn, who mentored countless businessmen, put it this way: "If you want to have more, you have to *become* more. Success is something you attract by the person you become."

The effort to increase your value can come in many forms: reading, attending classes, adding new skills to your toolbox, or just taking better care of yourself and developing a better daily routine. (We'll explore habit more just below.)

A big part of increasing your value is understanding where your present value comes from and then improving upon it. This is the power of focus. You may have learned about the Pareto Principle, also known as the 80/20 Rule: 20 percent of your tasks contribute 80 percent or more of your value. So, understand your unique strengths, where your value comes from; focus ruthlessly on that 20 percent; refine it; simplify and don't let minor distractions dilute your focus.

Invest Smarter

One of the main choices you will face as an investor is whether to try to ride the market through a largely passive approach, or to try to beat it by selectively going against the grain of conventional wisdom and the current mood of the market. I've suggested you not see this as an either/or choice and that you combine passive and active strategies in a way that best suits your situation and your temperament.

Regardless of which route you choose, I encourage you to maintain a certain degree of independence and not tie yourself completely to the market. There are long stretches when being married to the market is sound and profitable. But there are other stretches when it can be disastrous.

Summarizing points I've made in previous chapters, maintaining independence of thought and action involves, among other things, the following:

o Take the temperature of the market from time to time. Avoid getting swept up in greedy bubbles, or fearful panics.

o Protect yourself from big losses and big mistakes. Remember that big mistakes come in two forms: individual mistakes and those made by the market.

o Never overlook risk. Any investing decision should involve considering potential downside.

o Never overlook cost. Be ruthless in determining any and all fees that come with any investment—and that includes your company's 401(k). Work with an accountant or financial advisor to make sure your portfolio is as tax-efficient as possible.

o Stay humble. Know what you don't and can't know. If you're going to try to beat the market, approach doing so with caution, keeping in mind that many who try end up failing. Seek out good advice.

o Part of staying humble involves knowing what Buffett calls your "circle of competence": the investment areas you have researched and understand.

o Ignore the daily noise of the financial press. Keep your eyes on the prize: long-term trends and your own long-term goals.

o Adjust your strategy as needed, and rebalance your portfolio periodically. But don't excessively tinker with it, and avoid overtrading.

Compound Habits

One of the tricky things about developing a disciplined routine of saving and investing is that it will take a while to bear substantial fruit. You'll recall that, in Chapter 3, I illustrated the miracle of compounding through a mental exercise where you are given two choices: $3 million in cash upfront; or a single penny that doubles every day for a month.

The magically doubling penny wins in the end...but it takes a while. More than half-way through, on Day 16, you've got only $327.68 while your friend who took the cash has the $3 million. You don't even hit six figures and break $100,000 until Day 25. And as late as Day 29, you still fall short of the $3 million. But then on Day 30 you break through, and on Day 31 you're over $10 million—a decisive victory over the upfront cash.

Building long-term wealth can feel like that. In the book *The Compound Effect*, Darren Hardy likens it to an old-fashioned steam-powered locomotive: it takes a lot of energy at first just to get the thing going, and progress at first seems minimal; but once it picks up momentum (a head of steam, as they say) it becomes a nearly unstoppable force.

Only with consistency, and only over time, do compound habits reveal their true power. Consistent progress plus time equals massive accomplishments.

Over the long haul, Hardy writes, **you will reap "huge rewards from a series of small, smart choices."**

The most successful (and happiest) people in life are usually those with productive and healthy routines. And good habits are the building block of good routines. I recommend taking the time to read up on the growing science of habit formation. Charles Duhigg's *The Power of Habit* is a good place to start. He writes about what he calls "keystone habits" that spark "chain reactions that help other good habits take hold." Gretchen Rubin's *Better Than Before* is also worth a look.

Compound Advantages

One way of understanding how small smart choices can compound over time and give you an advantage over competitors or the market is to return to a sports analogy we've touched on previously. "Moneyball" is the name given to Oakland A's general manager Billy Beane's use of a new generation of statistical measures, or metrics, to build a competitive advantage over teams with higher payrolls. Analyst Bill James made a compelling case that too much attention was paid to stats like batting average and runs-batted-in (RBIs), and not enough to lesser-known stats like on-base percentage and slugging percentage. If a player got on base more often than another player with a higher batting average simply because he was more patient and drew more walks that, in the long run, would contribute more to winning. So Beane stacked his line-up with players with a slightly higher on-base percentage and over the course of a long season that small advantage compounded and translated into a poorer team significantly outperforming many teams with higher payrolls.

This is also a theme of Jeff Olson's book *The Slight Edge*. He writes that the small differences that over time will give you an advantage over others (and over your old self as well) are easy to overlook and may seem insignificant. He calls them "simple daily disciplines...Little things that seem insignificant in the doing yet, when compounded over time, yield very big results."

Think back to the chapter on costs, where I pointed out that while interest compounds in a way that works for you, costs and fees compound in a way that works against you. It's not always easy to beat the market and some of that comes down to luck and other factors out of your control. But cost is something you always can and should control. If you achieve simply average or slightly above average returns, but are scrupulous in controlling costs, you will be a winner in the long term. Shaving 1% off your costs may not seem like much—and it's certainly not as glamorous or exciting as picking a winning stock. But over time, that small advantage, that slight edge, can make the difference between superior and average performance.

Compound Learning

One of the habits that will compound over time is that of learning: about yourself and your goals and values; the world of economics and investing; your tendencies, strengths and weaknesses as an investor.

The enemy of a good plan is the dream of a perfect plan, so I've suggested you start out with something simple and manageable—but, however imperfect, to start and set a plan in motion.

But I also encourage you to constantly evolve as an investor, just as you evolve as a human being. On the one hand, you don't want to impulsively change course in response to every dip and dive, every swoop and swoon the market takes. Yet your understanding of the finer points of investing should deepen over the years. You'll have to adjust to the changing circumstances of your own life. And the market and the economy are likely to present all of us with new, unforeseen challenges *and* opportunities. The financial services industry will surely come up with new investing tools and products— some of them helpful, others to be avoided. Tax codes will change.

Even if you choose to pursue a largely passive investing strategy, it pays to stay alert, to make conscious choices, and to avoid sleepwalking through the decisions that will shape your future.

Investing Is Complicated. Your Plan Shouldn't Be.

That may seem like a bit of a contradiction. I think of it as more of a creative tension.

Yes, the world of investing is far from simple and you should distrust anyone who tells you different and promises sure-fire, risk-free, set-it-and-forget-it results. Every investment and every course of action comes with pros and cons, upside and downside. And without confusing you, I've tried to present you with a diversity of options and a range of points of view.

Yet the world's most successful investors, while never fooling themselves that investing is easy, don't get lost in the endless detail of the trees, but keep their focus on the big picture of the forest. They use certain broad principles as their guiding stars. For example, predicting whether the market is about to go up or down is no easy matter and not a good idea. But investors like Howard Marks and Warren Buffett take the general temperature of the market by asking basic, essential questions: Is the dominant mood one of greed? Or is it one of fear?

One thing that can help you navigate this tension between complexity and simplicity is to adopt a process that is consistent and repeatable, but also flexible and adaptable. And one of the best tools for keeping that *process* on course is the humble *checklist*. Behavioral economists have shed light on the power of the checklist to assist us in making clear-headed decisions in complex situations. Atul Gawande's *The Checklist Manifesto* details the usefulness of checklists in fields as varied as medicine and airline safety. Inspired by Gawande's research, a number of high-profile hedge-fund managers began incorporating checklists into their investing process. And *Wall Street Journal* columnist Jason Zweig declares checklists "one of the most reliable ways to improve the quality of your portfolio."

Notable investors who have adopted checklists include Charlie Munger, Warren Buffett's long-time friend and business partner. These high-level investors mainly use checklists in researching individual stocks. For the beginning investor, the point, Zweig writes, is to come up with "a standardized set of questions you must answer before you commit to any investment decision." And as one such investor puts it, it's important to keep in mind that a checklist "is not a shopping list of desirable attributes. It's a list of predictable errors."

So I urge you, perhaps in consultation with a financial advisor, to develop a series of checklists that helps you stick to a regular routine of:

✓ Making regular and consistent investments

✓ Monitoring and maintaining a target asset allocation

✓ Assessing short-, mid- and long-term goals, and aligning your investment strategy to those goals

✓ Periodically taking the temperature of the market to gauge whether it is overvalued or undervalued

✓ Assessing the upside and downside of existing and future investment options

Finally, remember that not all your investments are going to be winners. You'll make mistakes, but the important thing is to learn from them. The best way to build a checklist that works for you is by looking at your past mistakes. So when you make a new investment, think it through and write down your rationale for making the choice you made. That will allow you to revisit bad decisions and learn from them.

A Holistic Approach to Financial Health

I'm a big believer in the idea of *financial fitness*, and as a financial advisor I see myself as a coach helping clients get and remain on the path to financial health. I take a very holistic view of financial fitness and of my calling as a financial coach. I encourage clients, and I encourage you the reader, not to separate your financial self from the rest of your life.

When he coached the Los Angeles Lakers, Phil Jackson was famous for handing out books to his players. These were customized reading assignments, sometimes having to do with sports but, just as often, they would be about history or philosophy. His choices sometimes left players and observers scratching their heads. What was he up to?

His point was simply that if they continued to evolve as human beings, they would also evolve and improve as basketball players. Jackson was taking a holistic approach to what it means to be a professional athlete and I think that's a lesson we can all apply to our own lives—including our financial lives. Cultivating a rich and varied and meaningful life will ultimately make you a better and more motivated investor.

In addition to offering some keen insights into investing, Guy Spier's book *The Education of a Value Investor* shares how his personal journey and his financial journey intersected and eventually became one. He confesses that he started out as a "Gordon Gekko wannabe," but his early success as an investor couldn't hide an inner emptiness. He relocated from New York to Zurich, devoted himself to value investing instead of swinging for home runs, and became a disciple of Warren Buffett. In return for a donation to Buffett's favorite charity, he and a friend had a memorable lunch with the great investor, who shared a key piece of advice: "It's very important always to live your life by an inner scorecard, not an outer scorecard."

According to those who know him well, these are words Buffett lives by. "I don't work to collect money," he says in a recent profile. "I work because I love what I'm doing." He plans to give away most of his fortune to the Bill and Melinda Gates Foundation, and still lives in the same modest house he bought in 1958 for $31,500. Even at the age of 85, he likes to say he still "tap dances to work."

As a financial advisor, I obviously realize that money and financial freedom are important. But in the end, you're likely to be happier, and probably more successful, if you see those things as a means toward an end—if you can develop your own inner scorecard and live by it.

The Journey Is The Reward

This is the title of the first biography of Steve Jobs, written in 1986: a year after he was forced out of Apple, the company he had founded; and eleven years before his triumphant return to the company, which he would lead to some of its most important innovations (the iMac, iTunes, and the iPod) and its wildly successful "Think Different" advertising campaign. But even then, so much of his journey still ahead of him, Jobs was relentlessly focused on process—on the path, not the destination. After dropping out of college, he traveled to India, where he developed an interest in Zen meditation and Eastern spiritual traditions. He practiced meditation his whole life, praising how it helped him "see a tremendous expanse in the moment."

Phil Jackson—not coincidentally nicknamed 'The Zen Master' for his philosophical inclinations—preached the same approach to his players. "At the start of every season I always encouraged players to focus on the journey rather than the goal. What matters most is playing the game the right way and having the courage to grow, as human beings as well as basketball players. When you do that, the ring takes care of itself."

It is uncanny how many successful coaches and athletes have uttered a variation on that last line. In his book about his leadership philosophy, *The Score Takes Care Of Itself*, three-time Super Bowl winning coach Bill Walsh says: "I directed our focus less to the prize of victory than to the process of improving—obsessing, perhaps, about the quality of our execution and the content of our thinking; that is, our actions and attitude. I knew that if I did that, winning would take care of itself."

An almost extreme example of this devotion to process is college football coach Nick Saban, who has won five national championships at two different schools, and has for a number of years been the nation's highest-paid college coach. His approach is somewhat mysteriously referred to as, simply, The Process. But there's nothing mysterious about how he and others describe it.

Saban was inspired by a psychiatry professor who put together two essential insights. One is that football is so complex – with so many moving parts, and variables, and unpredictable elements – that it is impossible to get your head around all the details at any given time. But he also saw that the average play in football lasts just seven seconds. Although the complexity of the game as a whole might be overwhelming, seven seconds was manageable. So the theme of The Process, according to Saban's biographer, was that the players "would concentrate only on winning those seconds, take a rest between plays, then do it all over again. There would be no focus at all on the scoreboard or on the end results."

In his book *The Obstacle Is The Way*, entrepreneur and author Ryan Holiday draws great inspiration from Saban's radical focus on process. "In the chaos of sport, as in life, process provides a way[2]. A way to turn something very complex into something simple... Seven seconds. Sticking to the situation at hand. Focusing on what's immediately in front of you."

Goals and dreams are important—but as student of human performance Brad Stulberg writes, they are best viewed as a kind of distant guiding light, a "north star." On a daily basis, he and other researchers find, those who have a "process mindset" are more likely to succeed. A Harvard Business School report titled "Goals Gone Wild" finds that being overly fixated on goals can backfire. Life is more unpredictable and subject to chance than we like to acknowledge, and events beyond our control might derail certain goals, or force us to modify them or find new ones. When we embrace the journey as its own reward, we focus on what we can control, and celebrate the small victories that come with each small step.

And it's in small steps that great things are achieved. It's how Steve Jobs reinvented personal computing. It's how Warren Buffett became a billionaire. And it's how I managed to write this book.

So I urge you to find your own process; to develop routines and habits that feed and nourish your process; and to embrace the journey. If this modest book can provide you with a little guidance along the way, I will be more than pleased.

---

[2] One could easily say this of investing as well.

Appendix A

ONLINE RESOURCES

⇒ The **American Association of Individual Investors (AAII)** is an independent non-profit whose mission is to educate and assist individual investors. There is some free information on their website. And for a modest yearly fee of $29, you can access to newsletters, online tutorials, and a number of screening and research tools. Their "Best of the Web" feature regularly reviews new online resources.

http://www.aaii.com/

⇒ The **Financial Industry Regulatory Authority (FINRA)** is an independent non-profit authorized by Congress to protect America's investors. At their website you can find a wealth of information, as well as tools for financial planning and evaluating investment options.

http://www.finra.org/investors/tools

⇒ **BrightScope** is a financial information and technology firm designed to bring transparency to markets and financial services. You can find rankings of   401(k) plans among other things:

https://www.brightscope.com/ratings/

⇒ **FeeX** (which calls itself the "Robin Hood of Fees") is another way of researching fees for retirement plans, mutual funds, and other services.

https://www.feex.com/

⇒ The **U.S. Department of Labor** publishes guides to 401(k) plan fees and other helpful guides.

https://www.dol.gov/ebsa/publications/401k_employee.html

⇒ If your employer doesn't offer a 401(k) plan, the **U.S. Treasury Department's MyRA** is a good option as a kind of "starter" retirement plan

https://myra.gov/about/

⇒ The **J.P. Morgan Guide to Retirement** is a helpful introduction to the challenges of retirement planning.

https://am.jpmorgan.com/us/en/asset-management/gim/adv/insights/guide-to-retirement

⇒ This article in the *New York Times*, "A Nudge to Save a Bit More," reviews online savings and retirements tools along the lines of the **Save More Tomorrow** plan.

http://www.nytimes.com/2014/06/28/your-money/for-retirement-online-tools-can-encourage-greater-saving.html

⇒ **CNN'S "Fear and Greed Index"** is a quick way to gauge the "temperature" of the market.

http://money.cnn.com/data/fear-and-greed/

Appendix B

RECOMMENDED READING

OVERVIEW

Howard Marks, *The Most Important Thing: Uncommon Sense for the Thoughtful Investor* (Columbia University Press)

> A good introduction to the philosophy of value investing. Just as important, this is a model of clear thinking about the market, and its risks and opportunities. A later edition of the book, *The Most Important Thing: Illuminated,* contains additional comments from other noted value investors. At the website of Marks's investment firm, Oaktree Capital, you can sign up to subscribe to his occasional memos.

John Bogle, *The Little Book of Common Sense Investing* (John Wiley & Sons)

> Though I find his advice to stick to passive index funds a bit conservative, the Vanguard founder's cautious and skeptical views on investing are worth a look

David F. Swensen, *Unconventional Success: A Fundamental Approach to Personal Investment* (Free Press)

As Chief Investment Officer of the Yale Endowment fund for over 30 years, Swensen is one of the most successful institutional investors. His thoughts on asset allocation are especially useful.

Ben Carlson, *A Wealth of Common Sense: Why Simplicity Trumps Complexity in Any Investment Plan* (Bloomberg Press)

It's easy to get lost in the complexity of the world of investing. Carlson's book is a helpful guide through that complexity.

Frank Martin, *A Decade of Delusions: From Speculative Contagion to the Great Recession* (John Wiley & Sons)

Avoiding mistakes is a big part of successful investing. And Martin offers a wealth of insight into the many expensive mistakes investors made during the "lost decade."

BEHAVIORAL ECONOMICS

Daniel Kahneman, *Thinking, Fast and Slow* (Farrar, Straus and Giroux)

Not an easy read. But if you're interested in the world of behavioral economics, this is where it all began.

Dan Ariely, *Predictably Irrational: The Hidden Forces That Shape Our Decisions* (Harper Collins)

A more accessible book, from a Duke Professor of Psychology and Behavioral Economics.

VALUE INVESTING

Benjamin Graham, *The Intelligent Investor: The Definitive Book on Value Investing* (Harper Collins)

Graham's 1949 classic is the bible of value investing, and still relevant. The most recent edition features updates and new commentary by *Wall Street Journal* columnist Jason Zweig, and a preface and appendix by Warren Buffett.

Thomas Howard, *The Vest Pocket Guide to Value Investing* (Dearborn Financial Publications)

An older book you'll probably have to get used or from the library. But a compact and accessible introduction to value investing.

Guy Spier, *Education of a Value Investor: My Transformative Quest for Wealth, Wisdom, and Enlightenment* (St. Martins Press)

Spier recounts his evolution from ambitious Gordon Gekko wanna-be to Warren Buffett disciple.

Jeremy Miller, *Warren Buffett's Ground Rules: Words of Wisdom from the Partnership Letters of the World's Greatest Investor* (Harper Collins)

Buffett entrusted Miller with the letters he wrote to the partners in his first investment partnership, and in this new book, Miller uses those letters to elucidate Buffett's philosophy and document the rationale behind some of his biggest investing decisions.

PERSONAL DEVELOPMENT

Richard Thaler and Cass Sunstein, *Nudge: Improving Decisions About Health, Wealth, and Happiness* (Penguin Books)

A good introduction to practical ways to apply the insights of behavioral economics to everyday decisions. Thaler is also the man behind the Save More Tomorrow plan.

Charles Duhigg, *The Power of Habit: Why We Do What We Do in Life and Business* (Random House)

A well-researched but accessible summary of the new science of habit formation.

Appendix C
QUOTES

You don't gamble, you grind it out.

- Matt Damon in the film "Rounders"

∞

It's tough to make predictions, especially about the future.

- Yogi Berra

∞

There are two kinds of forecasters: those who don't know, and those who don't know they don't know.

- John Kenneth Galbraith

∞

Everything in the investing environment conspires to make investors do the wrong thing at the wrong time.

We're all only human, so the challenge is to perform better than other investors even though we start with the same wiring.

The biggest investing errors come not from factors that are informational or analytical, but from those that are psychological.

For a value investor, price has to be the starting point.

- Howard Marks

∞

Price is a liar.

- John Burbank

∞

Investing isn't about beating others at their game. It's about controlling yourself at your game.

People who invest make money for themselves; people who speculate make money for their brokers.

- Benjamin Graham

∞

Occasionally, successful investing requires inactivity.

It is better to be approximately right than precisely wrong.

In financial markets, almost anything that can happen does happen.

Predicting rain doesn't count. Building arks does.

- Warren Buffett

∞

The biggest risks cannot be reduced to a hard number.

We like to rely on history to justify our forecasts of the long run, but history tells us over and over again that the unexpected and the unthinkable are the norm, not an anomaly.

Survival is the only road to riches.

- Richard Bernstein

∞

Sometimes it's not how much you gain in the good markets but how much you don't lose in the ugly markets that separates the winners from the wannabes.

- Frank Martin

∞

The greatest enemy of a good plan is the dream of a perfect plan.

- Carl von Clausewitz

∞

Everyone has a plan until they get punched in the mouth.

- Mike Tyson

∞

Don't aim at success—the more you aim at it and make it a target, the more you are going to miss it.

- Viktor Frankl

Notes

Introduction

stoke the fires of class warfare
Tami Luhby, "Romney: Income Inequality is Just 'Envy'," CNN Money, Jan. 12, 2012
http://money.cnn.com/2012/01/12/news/economy/romney_envy/index.htm

on being a classless society
David Frum, "Requiem for American Exceptionalism," *The Atlantic*, March 2015
http://www.theatlantic.com/politics/archive/2015/03/
requiem-for-american-exceptionalism/388381/

Five years later
Joseph Stiglitz, "Of the 1%, By the 1%, For the 1%', *Vanity Fair,* May 2001
http://www.vanityfair.com/news/2011/05/top-one-percent-201105

A number of recent studies
Pedro Nicolaci Da Costa, "Janet Yellen Decries Widening Income Inequality,"
Wall Street Journal, Oct. 17 2014
http://www.wsj.com/articles/feds-yellen-says-extreme-inequality-coul
d-be-un-american-1413549684

Census.gov. *Historical Income Tables - Income Inequality - U.S Census Bureau*
https://www.census.gov/hhes/www/income/data/historical/inequality/

Richard Fry and Rakesh Kochhar, "America's Wealth Gap Between
Middle-Income and Upper-Income Families is Widest on Record," Pew Research
Center, December 2014
http://www.pewresearch.org/fact-tank/2014/12/17/wealth-gap-upper-middle-in-
come/

As a result, it seems clear
The Editors, "17 Things We Learned About Income Inequality in 2014," *The Atlantic*, December 2014
http://www.theatlantic.com/business/archive/2014/12/17-things-we-learned-about-income-inequality-in-2014/383917/

Josh Sanburn, "The Loss of Upward Mobility in the U.S." *Time*, Jan. 5 2012
http://business.time.com/2012/01/05/the-loss-of-upward-mobility-in-the-u-s/

several fascinating studies
Nicholas Fitz, "Economic Inequality: It's Far Worse Than you Think," *Scientific American*, March 31, 2015
http://www.scientificamerican.com/article/economic-inequality-it-s-far-worse-than-you-think/

In a paper for the National Bureau of Economic Research
Edward N. Wolff, "Household Wealth Trends in the United States, 1962-2013: What Happened Over the Great Recession?" National Bureau of Economic Research, December 2014
http://www.marineconomicconsulting.com/w20733.pdf

Edward N. Wolff, "The Asset Price Melt-Down and the Wealth of the Middle Class," The US2010 Project, May 2013 (nearly the identical study, but in a more readable format, and with additional charts and graphs)
http://www.s4.brown.edu/us2010/Data/Report/report05012013.pdf

A good summary of Wolff's work on wealth trends in the U.S. can be found here:
Josh Zumbrun, "How to Save Like the Rich and the Upper Middle Class (Hint: It's Not With Your House)" *Wall Street Journal*, December 26, 2014
http://blogs.wsj.com/economics/2014/12/26/how-to-save-like-the-rich-and-the-upper-middle-class-hint-its-not-with-your-house/

Chapter 1

which generation is which?
Josh Sanburn, "How Every Generation of the Last Century Got Its Nickname," *Time Magazine*, Dec. 1 2015
http://time.com/4131982/generations-names-Millennials-founders/

This historical trend was reversed

Chad Stone, et. al., "A Guide to Statistics on Historical Trends in Income Inequality," Center on Budget and Policy Priorities, Feb 20 2015
http://www.cbpp.org/research/poverty-and-inequality/a-guide-to-statistics-on-historical-trends-in-income-inequality

But, starting in the early 70s
Andrew Taylor, "Top 1 percent has nearly quadrupled income since 1979," *The Christian Science Monitor*, Oct 28 2011
http://www.csmonitor.com/Business/Latest-News-Wires/2011/1028/Top-1-percent-has-nearly-quadrupled-income-since-1979

likely to be "unbanked"
"The Unbanked Generation," First Data
https://www.firstdata.com/en_us/all-features/Millennials.html

describe themselves as "conservative investors"
Christine Dugas, "Millennials are tech savvy, tightfisted savers," *USA Today*, April 24 2013
http://www.usatoday.com/story/money/personalfinance/2013/04/23/Millennials-stock-market-averse/1970937/

This new generation is different
Karl Moore, "Millennials Work for Purpose, Not Paycheck," *Forbes*, Oct 2 2014
http://www.forbes.com/sites/karlmoore/2014/10/02/Millennials-work-for-purpose-not-paycheck/

Millennials are big on giving back
Connie Cass, "Millennials Are Volunteering More Than Past Generations," *Huffington Post*, Dec 29 2014
http://www.huffingtonpost.com/2014/12/29/Millennials-volunteering_n_6390446.html

The financial education firm Financial Finesse
Tom Anderson, "Gen Xers Are Doing the Worst Job with Money," CNBC, March 4 2015
http://www.cnbc.com/2015/03/04/money-the-best.html

"The preference for cash…"
Blake Ellis, "Millennials love cash," July 21 2014, CNN *Money*
http://money.cnn.com/2014/07/21/pf/Millennials-cash/index.html

wealth gap between the generations
Phillip Longman, "Wealth and Generations," *Washington Monthly*, August 2015

http://www.washingtonmonthly.com/magazine/junejulyaugust_2015/features/
wealth_and_generations055898.php

the year 1952
Eugene Steuerle, et al, "Lost Generations? Wealth Building Among Americans," Urban Institute, March 2013
http://www.urban.org/sites/default/files/alfresco/publication-pdfs/412766-Lost-G
enerations-Wealth-Building-among-Young-Americans.PDF

had grown to 14.7 times
Ana Swanson, "The Growing Wealth Gap That Nobody is Talking About," *Washington* Post, July 29 2015
https://www.washingtonpost.com/news/wonk/wp/2015/07/29/
Millennials-should-no-longer-dream-of-ever-becoming-millionaires/

under a fifth of the richest Americans
Robert Frank, "Not So Fast, 1 Percent Whippersnappers," *New York Times*, Nov. 20 2015
http://www.nytimes.com/2015/11/22/business/
not-so-fast-1-percent-whippersnappers.html

peaking for each successive generation
Longman, "Wealth and Generations"

zero net loss during the Recession
John Gist, "Retirement Security Across Generations," Pew Charitable Trusts, May 2013
http://www.pewtrusts.org/~/media/legacy/uploadedfiles/pcs_assets/2013/empre-
tirementv4051013finalforwebpdf.pdf

Gen X lost 45% of its wealth in just a few years
ibid

those aged 25 to 49
Lori Trawinski, "Assets and Debt Across Generations," AARP, January 2013
http://www.aarp.org/content/dam/aarp/research/public_policy_institute/securi-
ty/2013/middle-class-balance-sheet-1989-2010-AARP-ppi-sec-pdf.pdf

average earnings loss was 12%
Andrew Flowers, "Bad News for the Class of 2008," FiveThirtyEight, March 2 2015
http://fivethirtyeight.com/features/bad-news-for-the-class-of-2008/

As late as the 1970s
Sylvester Schieber, *The Predictable Surprise: The Unraveling of the U.S. Retirement System*, Oxford University Press, July 2015

goes toward health care
Longman, "Wealth and Generations"

In 1980, the average family
Margaret Cahalan, et al, "Indicators of Higher Education Equity in the United States," Pell Institute, 2015
http://www.pellinstitute.org/downloads/
publications-Indicators_of_Higher_Education_Equity_
in_the_US_45_Year_Trend_Report.pdf

Gen Xers in their thirties and forties
Gist, "Retirement Security Across Generations"

just before the Recession hit
William Emmons and Ray Boshara, "A Life-Cycle and Generational Perspective on the Wealth and Income of Millennials," New America Foundation, 2014
https://www.newamerica.org/down-
loads/A_Life-Cycle_and_Generational_Perspective_on_
the_Wealth_and_Income_of_Millennials.pdf

in very plain language
ibid

An economist at Yale University
Flowers, "Bad News for the Class of 2008"

"Millennials seem to have learned…"
Emmons, "A Life-Cycle and Generational Perspective…" 2014

Chapter 2

Federal Reserve chairman Ben Bernanke
Matt Egan, "2008: Worse than the Great Depression?" *CNN Money,* Aug 8 2014
http://money.cnn.com/2014/08/27/news/economy/ben-bernanke-great-depression/

Lessons from "The Lost Decade"
Frank K. Martin, *A Decade of Delusions: From Speculative Contagion to the Great Recession,* Wiley & Sons (NY: 2011)

[NOTE: unless otherwise indicated, quotes and figures cited in this section are from this book]

... "an almost Biblical symmetry"
Warren Buffet, Carol Loomis, "Mr. Buffett on the Stock Market," *Fortune Magazine*, Nov 22 1999
http://archive.fortune.com/magazines/fortune/fortune_archive/1999/11/22/269071/index.htm

only 48% of American adults
Heather Long, "Over half of Americans have $0 in stock market," *CNN Money*, April 10 2015 http://money.cnn.com/2015/04/10/investing/investing-52-percent-americans-have-no-money-in-stocks/

decline in stock ownership
Lisa Dettling and Joanne Hsu, "The State of Young Adults' Balance Sheets: Evidence from the Survey of Consumer Finances," Federal Reserve Bank of St. Louis, 2014
https://research.stlouisfed.org/publications/review/2014/q4/dettling.pdf

Millennials have actually resorted
Kelli B. Grant, "Under a mattress, in the freezer: Why so many are hiding cash," CNBC, Jan 29 2015
http://www.cnbc.com/id/102377632

in that same 1999 address
Buffett, Loomis, "Mr. Buffett on the Stock Market"

As of the late 1970s
Sylvester Schieber, *The Predictable Surprise: The Unraveling of the U.S. Retirement System,* Oxford University Press
(New York: 2012)

2015 Social Security Trustees Report
Social Security and Medicare Boards of Trustees, "A Summary of the 2015 Annual Reports,"
https://www.ssa.gov/oact/trsum/

Chapter 3

Currently, robo-advisors
Matt Egan, "Robo Advisors: The Next Big Thing in Investing," *CNN Money*, June 18 2015
http://money.cnn.com/2015/06/18/investing/robo-advisor-millennials-wealthfront/

But a recent report predicts
"Millennial Personal Finance—The Fin Tech Startups Targeting Millennials," *CB Insights*, May 24 2015
https://www.cbinsights.com/blog/fin-tech-startups-millennials/

As one New York Times writer
Tara Siegel Bernard, "The Pros and Cons of Using a Robot as an Investment Advisor," *New York Times*, April 29 2016
http://www.nytimes.com/2016/04/30/your-money/the-pros-and-cons-of-usin g-a-robot-as-an-investment-adviser.html

over a given 10-year stretch
Zachary Karabell, "Solving the Active Vs. Passive Investing Debate," *Barron's*, January 26 2016
http://www.barrons.com/articles/solving-the-active-vs-passive-investin g-debate-1422304950

A recent Standard & Poor's study
Jeff Sommer, "How Many Mutual Funds Routinely Rout the Market? Zero" *New York Times*, March 14 2015
http://www.nytimes.com/2015/03/15/your-money/
how-many-mutual-funds-routinely-rout-the-market-zero.html

the average return on the S&P 500
"Historical Returns on Stock, T. Bonds and T. Bills"
http://pages.stern.nyu.edu/~adamodar/New_Home_Page/datafile/histretSP.html

a more modest example
Kathleen Murphy, "If I Were 22: Get a Financial Head Start," LinkedIn Pulse
https://www.linkedin.com/pulse/20140527113349-330990956-if-i
-were-22-get-a-financial-head-start

Chapter 4

In a 1965 article
Eugene Fama, "Random Walks in Stock Prices," *Financial Analysts Journal,*
Sept. 1965 (reprinted in *Financial Analysts Journal,* Vol. 51, No. 1, 50 Years in
Review)
available online courtesy of the University of Chicago School of Business:
https://www.chicagobooth.edu/~/media/34F68FFD9CC04EF1A76901F6C-
61C0A76.PDF

One of the leaders
Daniel Kahneman, *Thinking, Fast and Slow*, Farrar, Straus and Giroux (New
York: 2011)

building on his work
Robert Shiller, *Irrational Exuberance*
Richard Thaler, *Misbehaving: The Making of Behavioral Economics*
Justin Fox, *The Myth of the Rational Market*

In 1973, economist Burton
Burton Malkiel, *A Random Walk Down Wall Street* (now in its 11th edition), W.W.
Norton (New York: 2016)

institutional investors were responsible
Donald MacKenzie, *An Engine, Not a Camera*, MIT Press (Cambridge: 2006), p.
74
available online at:
http://uberty.org/wp-content/uploads/2015/02/
MacKenzie-An-Engine-Not-a-Camera.pdf

The Problem (and Opportunity) of Anomalies
Stephen Simpson, "Seven Market Anomalies Investors Should Know," Investopedia
http://www.investopedia.com/articles/financial-theory/11/
trading-with-market-anomalies.asp

Tisa Silver, "Making Sense of Market Anomalies, Investopedia
http://www.investopedia.com/articles/stocks/08/market-anomaly-efficient-market.
asp

the human response to them

Dan Ariely, *Predictably Irrational: The Hidden Forces That Shape Our Decisions,* Harper Collins (New York: 2008)

and the tough lessons he learned
Benjamin Graham, *The Intelligent Investor* (now in its 4th edition), HarperCollins (New York: 2006)

prominent value investors
Howard Marks, *The Most Important Thing,* Columbia University Press (New York: 2011)

the more diversified your portfolio
see, for example, Frank Martin, *A Decade of Delusions,* pg. 266: "As you increase diversification, you concurrently increase your exposure to market risk—namely, the tendency of your portfolio, like an index fund, to mirror the performance of the market."

Chapter 5

A Brief History of Risk - see Bernstein, *Against the Gods*

Markowitz proposed - Harry Markowitz, "Portfolio Selection," *The Journal of Finance*, March 1952
http://www.efalken.com/LowVolClassics/markowitz_JF1952.pdf

developed into a formula - Eugene Fama and Kenneth French, "The Capital Asset Pricing Model," *Journal of Economic Perspectives*, Summer 2004
http://www.maths.usyd.edu.au/u/UG/IM/MATH2070/r/FamaFrench_JEP2004.pdf

"prevalence of surprise" - Bernstein, *Against the Gods*

in a different way - Christopher Farrell, "Philosopher of Risk" (interview with Peter Bernstein), Bloomberg, April 8 2007
http://www.bloomberg.com/news/articles/2007-04-08/philospher-of-risk

Howard Marks sees this - Marks, *The Most Important Thing,* pg 58

"mismeasurement of risk" - Jack Schwager, *Market Wizards: Interviews with Top Traders,* John Wiley & Sons (Hoboken: 2012)

"a stock that has dropped" - quoted in Tom Beevers, "Everything You Were Taught About Risk Is Wrong," Stockviews, January 16 2015

https://blog.stockviews.com/2015/01/16/everything-you-were-taught-about-ris
k-is-wrong/

Marks restates the EMH thesis - Marks, *The Most Important Thing*, pg 9

Value investors sees volatility - Martin, A Decade of Delusions, pg 407

little stock in beta scores - Buttonwood, "The Secrets of Buffett's Success," *The Economist*, Sept 29 2012
http://www.economist.com/node/21563735

"Awareness of the Pendulum" Marks, *The Most Important Thing*, Chapter 9

"sentiment-based risk" - see Preface to Hersh Shefrin, *Beyond Greed and Fear: Understanding Behavioral Finance and the Psychology of Investing*, Oxford University Press (New York: 2002)

"we have to consider the risk" - Howard Marks, "Investing in an Unknowable Future," *Barron's*, June 8 2015 [This is a long but very worthwhile memo that addresses many of the issues covered in this chapter]
http://www.barrons.com/articles/howard-marks-investing-in-an-unknowabl
e-future-1433802168

has responded to its critics - Jonathan Burton, "Revisiting the Capital Asset Pricing Model," *Dow Jones Asset Manager*, May/June 1998, reprinted here:
https://web.stanford.edu/~wfsharpe/art/djam/djam.htm

Chapter 6

variety of mutual funds - "A Guide to Understanding Mutual Funds," Investment Company Institute
https://www.ici.org/pdf/bro_understanding_mfs_p.pdf

43% of U.S. households - "2015 Investment Company Fact Book," Investment Company Institute
https://www.ici.org/pdf/2015_factbook.pdf

active funds lost - Sarah Krouse and Corrie Driebusch, "Investors Snub Money Managers for Market Clones," *Wall Street Journal*, Jan. 13 2016
http://www.wsj.com/articles/morningstar-says-actively-managed-mutual-fund
s-saw-outflows-in-2015-1452701873

in the past fifteen years – "2015 Investment Company Fact Book," *op. cit.*

has been arguing for passive investing - John Bogle, "The First Index Mutual Fund"
http://johncbogle.com/speeches/JCB_first_index_mf.pdf
world's largest mutual fund company - Colin Barr, "Vanguard Dethrones Fidelity," *Fortune*, Sept 30 2010
http://fortune.com/2010/09/30/vanguard-dethrones-fidelity/

most recent scorecard for 2015 - "SPIVA U.S. Scorecard – Year-end 2015," S&P Dow Jones Indices
https://us.spindices.com/documents/spiva/spiva-us-yearend-2015.pdf

678 domestic equity funds - "Does Past Performance Matter? The Persistence Scorecard," S&P Dow Jones Indices
https://us.spindices.com/documents/spiva/persistence-scorecard-january-2016.pdf

"expert" fund managers - Richard Finger, "Five Reasons Your Mutual Fund Probably Underperforms the Market," *Forbes*, April 15 2013
http://www.forbes.com/sites/richardfinger/2013/04/15/five-reasons-your-mutual-fund-probably-underperforms-the-market/#4e3d16b1b6d8

"forced buying" - Marks, *The Most Important Thing*, pg 32

benefits of diversification - Martin, *A Decade of Delusions*, pg 79

passive indexes the winner - Jason Zweig, "The Decline and Fall of Fund Managers," *Wall Street Journal*, Aug 22 2014
http://blogs.wsj.com/moneybeat/2014/08/22/the-decline-and-fall-of-fund-managers/

He and his colleague - Sarah Max, "Is Your Fund Manager Active Enough?" *Barron's*, Jan. 14 2013
http://www.barrons.com/articles/SB50001424052748703792204578221972943824046

published Cremers' rating - Joe Light, "And the Next Star Fund Manager Is…" *Wall Street Journal*, Jan. 17 2014
http://www.wsj.com/articles/SB1000142405270230441910457932487145103892 0

a Portfolio Drag Index - Ky Trang Ho, "Why Most Mutual Funds Underperform and How to Find Ones That Don't," *Forbes*, Feb. 6 2016
http://www.forbes.com/sites/trangho/2016/02/06/
why-most-mutual-funds-underperform-and-how-to-find-ones-that-dont/

Don Phillips has - Don Phillips, "Indexing's Noble Lie," *Morningstar* Advisor, Oct. 5 2015
http://www.morningstar.com/advisor/t/109785936/indexing-s-noble-lie.htm

one financial writer - Zachary Karabell, "Solving the Active Vs. Passive Investing Debate," *Barron's*, Jan. 26 2015
http://www.forbes.com/sites/greggfisher/2013/08/28/in-mutual-funds-is-active-v
s-passive-the-right-question/

A number of high-profile articles:

Michael Pollock, "The Case for Actively Managed Funds," *Wall Street Journal*, Feb. 8 2015
http://www.wsj.com/articles/the-case-for-actively-managed-funds-1423454485

Sarah Max, "Return of the Stockpickers," *Barron's*, Jan. 10 2015
http://www.barrons.com/articles/return-of-the-mutual-fund-stockpickers-142087
0199

Gregg Fisher, "In Mutual Funds, Is Active Vs. Passive the Right Question?" *Forbes*, Aug. 28 2013
http://www.forbes.com/sites/greggfisher/2013/08/28/in-mutual-funds-is-active-v
s-passive-the-right-question

while Vanguard is known - Stan Luxenberg, "At Vanguard, Active Beats Passive—Frequently," WealthManagement Magazine, June 10 2011
http://wealthmanagement.com/mutual-funds/vanguard-active-beats-passive-fre-
quently

balanced guide to ETFs - Richard Ferri, *The ETF Book*, John Wiley & Sons (Hoboken: 2009)

Broad funds now account - John Bogle, *The Little Book of Common Sense Investing*, John Wiley & Sons (Hoboken: 2007), pg. 167

see also: "How John Bogle Really Sees ETFs," ThinkAdvisor, Sept. 25 2012
http://www.thinkadvisor.com/2012/09/25/how-john-bogle-really-sees-etfs

Quite to the contrary – Bogle, *The Little Book of Common Sense Investing*, pg. 169

On August 24 of 2015 - Eric Balchunas, "The ETF Files," Bloomberg Markets, March 7 2016
http://www.bloomberg.com/features/2016-etf-files/

certain commodities - Liam Pleven, "Commodities ETFs Narrow Their Focus," *Wall Street Journal*, Jan. 3 2013
http://www.wsj.com/articles/SB1000142412788732440750457818574320948432064

some robo-advisor services - Tara Siegel Bernard, "Robo-Advisers for Investor Are Not One-Size-Fits-All," *New York Times*, Jan. 22 2016
http://www.nytimes.com/2016/01/23/your-money/robo-advisers-for-investors-are-not-one-size-fits-all.html

"Is a managed ETF" - Tom Lauricella, "'Managed Portfolios' Appear to Be More Like Actively Managed Mutual Funds," *Wall Street Journal*, Sept. 7 2014
http://www.wsj.com/articles/etf-managed-portfolios-are-hot-1410120104

non-ETF portfolios - "Why the Pros Can't Pick ETFs," *Barron's*, Oct. 4 2014
http://www.barrons.com/articles/why-etf-managed-accounts-fail-1412404692#

very particular set of limitations - Melanie L. Fein, "Robo-Advisers Aren't All They're Cracked Up to Be," American Banker, Oct. 7 2015
http://www.morningstar.com/InvGlossary/morningstar_style_box.aspx

see also: Bob Clark, "5 Reasons Most Robo-Advisors Are Not, In Fact, Advisors," ThinkAdvisor, Oct. 21 2015
http://www.thinkadvisor.com/2015/10/21/5-reasons-most-robo-advisors-are-not-in-fact-advis

ETFs are poised - "2015 Trends in Investing Survey," *Journal of Financial Planning*
https://www.onefpa.org/business-success/Documents/2015%20Trends%20in%20Investing%20Survey%20Report%20-%20FIN.pdf

historic returns for stocks - "Annual Returns on Stock, T. Bonds and T. Bills: 1928 – Current"
http://pages.stern.nyu.edu/~adamodar/New_Home_Page/datafile/histretSP.html

"No other asset class" - Swensen, *Unconventional Success*, pg. 37

a widely-used "style box" - "Morningstar Style Box," Morningstar Investing Glossary
http://www.morningstar.com/InvGlossary/morningstar_style_box.asp

Chapter 7

"Whenever one sector" - Jason Zweig, "Probability and Investing: Take That, Murphy," Money Sense, Dec/Jan 2008
http://www.moneysense.ca/magazine-archive/
probability-and-investing-take-that-murphy/

"It would be like flipping" - Harry Markowitz, *Portfolio Selection,* Yale University Press (New Haven: 1959), pg. 5

foreign index equity funds - John Waggoner, "Why Invest in International Funds?" *USA Today,* Jan. 16 2015
http://www.usatoday.com/story/money/2015/01/16/investing-international-funds/
21825245/

In January of 1993 - *Swensen, Unconventional Success,* pg. 59

70% of their assets in domestic equity - "2015 Investment Company Fact Book," Investment Company Institute
https://www.ici.org/pdf/2015_factbook.pdf

the world's largest economy - "Why You May Need More International Stock," Fidelity Viewpoints, Nov. 18 2015
https://www.fidelity.com/viewpoints/investing-ideas/more-international-stock

A Vanguard study agrees - Philips, et al, "Dynamic Correlations: The Implications for Portfolio Construction," Vanguard Research, April 2012
http://www.vanguard.com/pdf/s130.pdf

The low correlation - "Correlation Building Between REITs and Other Stocks," Morningstar, May 21 2015
bit.ly/1Vkdw0h

correlation with stocks - Murray Coleman, "Advisers See REIT Correlations Subsiding," *Wall Street Journal,* Jan 9 2014
http://www.wsj.com/articles/SB10001424052702304347904579310283081100374

23% more volatility - Michael Finke, "Is the Time Right for REITs?" ThinkAdvisor, May 27 2014
http://www.thinkadvisor.com/2014/05/27/finke-is-the-time-right-for-reits?slreturn=1460422622

a sample asset allocation strategy - Barry Barnitz, "David Swensen's Portfolio," Bogleheads Blog, April 21 2014
https://www.bogleheads.org/blog/
david-swensens-portfolio-from-unconventional-success/

Three Views - Chris Arnold, "3 Investment Gurus Share Their Model Portfolios," Oct. 17 2015
http://www.npr.org/2015/10/17/436993646/
three-investment-gurus-share-their-model-portfolios

"new breed of indexers" - Bogle, *Little Book of Commonsense Investing*, pg 156

Quite to the contrary - Martin, *A Decade of Delusions*, pg. 266

"In the long run" - Joel Greenblatt, quoted in Marks, *The Most Important Thing*, pg. 113

As Frank Martin writes - Martin, *A Decade of Delusions*, pg. 410

And in the years - "PIMCO's Former CEO Mohamed El-Erian," Knowledge@ Wharton, April 21 2016
http://knowledge.wharton.upenn.edu/article/pimcos-former-ceo-mohamed-el-eria
n-delusion-liquidity/

the work of David Bell - Bernstein, *Against the Gods*, pg. 285

more likely to feel regret - Jeffrey Bailey and Chris Kinerson, "Regret Avoidance and Risk Tolerance," Association for Financial Counseling and Planning Education, 2005
https://www.afcpe.org/assets/pdf/vol1613.pdf

willing to make trade-offs - David Bell, "Regret in Decision Making Under Uncertainty," *Operations Research*, Harvard University, Oct. 1982
http://www.people.hbs.edu/dbell/regret%20in%20decison%20making%20.pdf

John Rekenthaler - quoted in "Get the Best Out of Active and Index Funds," panel moderated by Christine Benz, Morningstar, April 2015
http://www.morningstar.com/cover/videocenter.aspx?id=693899

In a classic study - Brad Barber and Terrance Odean, "Trading Is Hazardous to Your Wealth," *The Journal of Finance*, April 2000
http://faculty.haas.berkeley.edu/odean/papers%20current%20versions/individual_investor_performance_final.pdf

of the Harvard Business School - Randy Cohen, Christopher Polk, and Bernard Silli, "Best Ideas," Paul Woolley Centre, October 2008
http://eprints.lse.ac.uk/24471/1/Best%20ideas(published).pdf

Beyond a dozen or so - Martin, *A Decade of Delusiosn*, pg. 79

In most strategic - "PIMCO's Former CEO Mohamed El-Erian," Knowledge@ Wharton, April 21 2016
http://knowledge.wharton.upenn.edu/article/pimcos-former-ceo-mohamed-el-erian-delusion-liquidity/

Chapter 8

two styles or modes – see Chapter 1 of Daniel Kahneman, *Thinking, Fast and Slow*, Farrar Straus and Giroux (New York: 2011)

58 different varieties – Gus Lubin and Shana Lebowitz, "58 Cognitive Biases That Screw Up Everything We Do," *Business Insider*, Oct. 29 2015
http://www.businessinsider.com/cognitive-biases-2015-10

"learn to recognize" – Kahneman, *op. cit.*, pg 28

"Emotions complement reason" Meir Statman, *What Investors Really Want*, McGraw-Hill (Columbus: 2011), Introduction, xiv

Former General Electric CEO – "Learn as You Churn," *The Economist*, April 6 2006
http://www.economist.com/node/6776011

sudden financial gains – Patrick O'Shaughnessy, *Millennial Money*, Palgrave MacMillan (New York: 2014), pg 173

"loss aversion" – Kahneman, *op. cit.*, pg 283

"Sometimes our behaviors" – Statman, *op. cit.*, xvii

he openly worried – Robert Shiller in the 2nd edition to *Irrational Exuberance*, cited in Martin, *A Decade of Delusions*, pg 300

"Herds inflate bubbles" – Statman, *op. cit.*

herding dynamics in the market – Robert Armstrong and Jacob Ward, "What Makes Investors Do the Wrong Thing," *Popular Science*, Feb 19 2008
http://www.popsci.com/scitech/article/2008-02/
money-minded-how-psychoanalyze-stock-market

Second-Level Thinking – Marks, *The Most Important Thing*, pg 4

"We have two classes" – quoted in Buttonwood, "The View from Societe Generale," *The Economist*, Jan 11 2012
http://www.economist.com/blogs/buttonwood/2012/01/economics-and-markets

"nonpredictive decision making" – Nassim Nicholas Taleb, *Antifragile: Things That Gain From Disorder*, Random House (New York: 2012), pg 4

tendency to see cause and effect – Kahneman, *Thinking, Fast and Slow*, pg 74

"I'm constantly on watch" – Dan Steinhard, "23 Investing Lessons from George Soros," Casey Research, March 4 2015
https://www.caseyresearch.com/articles/23-investing-lessons-from-george-soros

the most active traders - Brad Barber and Terrance Odean, "Trading Is Hazardous to Your Wealth," *The Journal of Finance*, April 2000
http://faculty.haas.berkeley.edu/odean/papers%20current%20versions/individual_investor_performance_final.pdf

"investing isn't about beating others" – quoted in Chris Leithner, "The Power of Stoic Thinking," Le Quebecois Libre, Jan 15 2016
http://www.quebecoislibre.org/16/160115-2.html

Chapter 9

Economist Joseph Schumpeter – James Cornehlen and Michael Carr, *Conquering the Divide*, W&A Publishing (Cedar Falls: 2010), pg. 85

eleven such cycles – National Bureau of Economic Research, "U.S. Business Cycle Expansions and Contractions"
http://www.nber.org/cycles.html

Economist Joseph Ellis – Joseph Ellis, Ahead of the Curve, Harvard Business Review (Boston: 2005), Chapter 2

since the 1960s – Claudio Borio, "The Financial Cycle and Macroeconomics," BIS Working Papers, pg 3
http://www.nber.org/cycles.html

Economist Hyman Minsky – Hyman Minsky, "The Financial Instability Hypothesis," Jerome Levy Economics Institute of Bard College, May 1992

A contemporary economic analyst – M.C.K., "Claudio Borio on the Financial Cycle," *The Economist*, Dec 14 2012
http://www.economist.com/blogs/freeexchange/2012/12/reforming-macroeconomics

"Markets can influence" – Proinsias O'Mahony, "Buy Bubbles, Bet Big and Backache—Soros's Secrets," *The Irish Times*, Aug 12 2014
http://www.irishtimes.com/business/personal-finance/buy-bubbles-bet-big-and-backache-soros-s-secrets-1.1893639

two widely quoted speeches – Buffet, quoted in Martin, *A Decade of Delusions*, pg 117

Waves vs. Tides – *ibid*, pg 351

the Rationality Cycle – Marks, *The Most Important Thing*, Chapter 9

"Investors should be wary" – Thalker, *Misbehaving*, pg

helped popularize another measure – Doug Short, "Market Cap to GDP: An Updated Look at the Buffett Valuation Indicator," Advisor Perspectives, June 3 2016
http://www.advisorperspectives.com/dshort/updates/Market-Cap-to-GDP

"Fear & Greed Index" – Fear & Greed Index, *CNN Money*
http://money.cnn.com/data/fear-and-greed/

This is a tricky matter – Michael Foster, "Buying on Margin: Costs, Risks and Rewards," Bankrate
http://www.bankrate.com/finance/investing/buying-on-margin-costs-risks-rewards.aspx

useful way to gauge – Doug Short, "NYSE Margin Debt Increased Again in April," Advisor Perspectives, June 1 2016

http://www.advisorperspectives.com/dshort/updates/
NYSE-Margin-Debt-and-the-SPX.php

Pradip Sigdyal, "Investors Are Shying Away from Margin Debt," CNBC, Feb 6 2016
http://www.cnbc.com/2016/02/06/investors-are-shying-away-from-margi
n-debt-why-that-may-not-be-a-good-thing.html

the bond market is huge – Colin Barr, "The New Bond Market," Wall Street Journal, Oct 5 2015
http://www.wsj.com/articles/the-new-bond-market-bigger-riskie
r-and-more-fragile-than-ever-1442808001

A Quick Lesson on Bonds –

Under most conditions – Jonathan Garber, "Yield Curve Great at Predicting Recessions," Business Insider, Dec 10 2015
http://www.businessinsider.com/yield-curve-great-at-predicting-recessions-2015-1
2

The other type of yield spread – Simon Constable, "Why Tighter Yield Spreads Matter to Investors," *Wall Street Journal*, July 6 2014
http://www.wsj.com/articles/why-tighter-credit-spreads-matter-t
o-investors-1404679626

"Missing an opportunity" – George Soros, *The Alchemy of Finance*, John Wiley & Sons (Hoboken: 2003), pg 209

failed to follow his own advice – Martin, *A Decade of Delusions*, pg 110-111

views it as an opportunity – *ibid*, pg 407

"living in optimistic times" – *ibid*, pg 67

ran an opinion piece – Martin Sosnoff, "Buffett: What Went Wrong?" *Forbes*, Dec 13 1999
http://www.forbes.com/global/1999/1213/0225069a.html

"opportunities missed and capital lost" – Martin, *A Decade of Delusions*, pg 415

Chapter 10

Yet in his later years – Mitch Tuchman, "Warren Buffett to Heirs: Just Use Index Funds," NewsMax, June 3 2015
http://www.newsmax.com/Finance/StreetTalk/Warren-Buffett-investing-funds-index/2015/06/02/id/648255/

"Our use of the term" – Mohammed El-Erian, "Navigating the New Normal in Industrial Countries," International Monetary Fund, October 10 2010
https://www.imf.org/external/np/speeches/2010/101010.htm

"weakening, and even reversing" – Dobbs, Koller, Lund, et. al., "Why Investors May Need to Lower Their Sights," McKinsey & Company, April 2016
http://www.mckinsey.com/industries/private-equity-and-principal-investors/our-insights/why-investors-may-need-to-lower-their-sights

"I care deeply" – quoted in Tony Robbins, *Money*, pg 457

worried that the market – quoted in Martin, *A Decade of Delusions*, pg 68

"excess diversification is madness" -

Chapter 11

co-wrote an important paper – John McDermott and Dana D'Auria, "How Much Small Cap Should Be in Your Portfolio," *AAII Journal*, July 2014 (a summary of Fama's original research with updated numbers)
http://www.aaii.com/journal/article/how-much-small-cap-should-be-in-your-portfolio.touch

But a major study in 2015 – Clif Asness, "The Small-Firm Effect Is Real, and It's Spectacular," AQR, January 2015
https://www.aqr.com/cliffs-perspective/the-small-firm-effect-is-real-and-its-spectacular

the typical small-cap firm – "The Blind Spot Part II: The Distortive Impact of Analyst Coverage," Punch Invest, April 2013
http://punchinvest.com/wp-content/uploads/2011/11/The-Blind-Spot-Impact-of-Analyst-Coverage1.pdf

has roughly been reversed – Ben Carlson, *A Wealth of Common Sense*, Bloomberg Press (Hoboken: 2015), pg. 5

while the small-cap effect – John Rothchild, *The Bear Book*, John Wiley & Sons (NY: 1998), pg 135

In his handy - *ibid*

"reasonably satisfactory" – Wayne Thorpe, "Benjamin Graham's Net Current Asset Value Approach," AAII, pg. 2
https://www.aaii.com/computerized-investing/article/benjamin-graham-s-net-current-asset-value-approach.pdf

Graham's valuation methods – *ibid*, pg. 3

Quality-Minus-Junk (QMJ) metric – Asness, "The Small-Firm Effect Is Real"

one of his most famous – Warren Buffett, "The Superinvestors of Graham-and-Doddsville," Columbia University
http://www8.gsb.columbia.edu/rtfiles/cbs/hermes/Buffett1984.pdf

overheated dot-com boom – Howard, *Vest Pocket Guide to Value Investing*, pg. 59

Buffett's recent purchase Noah Buhayar, "Buffett's $15 Billion From BNSF Show Railroad Came Cheap," Bloomberg, Nov. 10 2014
http://www.bloomberg.com/news/articles/2014-11-10/buffetts-15-billion-from-bnsf-show-railroad-came-cheap

"To Buffett all investing" – John Reese, "A Buffett Approach to Buying Growth Stocks," *Forbes*, June 10 2013
http://www.forbes.com/sites/investor/2013/05/23/a-buffett-approach-to-buying-growth-stocks

as he put it in his book – Peter Lynch, *Beating the Street*, Simon & Schuster (New York: 1994)

A metric now being adopted – Phil DeMuth, "The Mysterious Factor 'P'," *Forbes*, June 27 2013
http://www.forbes.com/sites/phildemuth/2013/06/27/the-mysterious-factor-p-charlie-munger-robert-novy-marx-and-the-profitability-factor

of Columbia University – Louis Lowenstein, "Searching for Rational Investors in a Perfect Storm," Columbia Law and Economics Working Paper... for a good summary, see:
https://greenbackd.com/2012/05/25/searching-for-rational-investors-in-a-perfect-storm-value-investing-through-1999-2003/

the bulk of the benefits – Martin, *A Decade of Delusions*, pg 79

Entire books have been written – see, for example: John Rothchild, *The Bear Book*, John Wiley & Sons (NY: 1998)

The smart-beta trend – Ben Carlson, *A Wealth of Common Sense*, Wiley/Bloomberg Press, pg. 2

A CNBC report – Andrew Osterland, "Smart Beta and Stupid Fund Tricks," CNBC, Oct 6 2015
http://www.cnbc.com/2015/10/06/smart-beta-and-stupid-fund-tricks.html

even more blunt – Robert Huebscher, "James Montier on... Smart Beta," Advisor Perspectives, Feb 2016
http://www.advisorperspectives.com/articles/2016/02/01/james-montier-on-fed-induced-bubbles-market-valuations-smart-beta-and-liquid-alts

Chapter 12

'Who the hell' – Laura Saunders, "Five Great Quotes for Tax Day," *Wall St Journal*, April 2015
http://blogs.wsj.com/briefly/2015/04/14/5-great-quotes-for-tax-day/

imminent retirement crisis – Teresa Ghilarducci, "Our Ridiculous Approach to Retirement," *New York Times*, July 21 2012
http://www.nytimes.com/2012/07/22/opinion/sunday/our-ridiculous-approach-to-retirement.html

PEW Charitable Trusts – "Who's In, Who's Out," The PEW Charitable Trusts
http://www.pewtrusts.org/~/media/assets/2016/01/retirement_savings_report_jan16.pdf

Center for Retirement Research – Alicia Munnell, "Falling Short: The Coming Retirement Crisis and What to Do About It," Center for Retirement Research, April 2015 http://crr.bc.edu/wp-content/uploads/2015/04/IB_15-7.pdf

Employee Benefits Research Institute – "The 2016 Retirement Confidence Survey"
https://www.ebri.org/publications/ib/index.cfm?fa=ibDisp&content_id=3328

*my*RA program – Elizabeth O'Brien, "Don't Have a 401(k) at Work? Starter Retirement Accounts Go Live," Market Watch, Nov 4 2015
http://www.marketwatch.com/story/dont-have-a-401k-at-wor
k-starter-retirement-accounts-go-live-2015-11-04

Savers Credit – "Many Eligible Taxpayers Could Benefit from Saver's Credit If They Only Knew About It," Transamerica Center for Retirement Studies
http://www.transamericacenter.org/tools-and-resources/saver's-credit/sav
er's-credit-press-release

state initiatives – "State-Based Retirement Plans for the Private Sector," Pension Rights Center
http://www.pensionrights.org/issues/legislation/
state-based-retirement-plans-private-sector

lesser-known alternatives –

John Hewitt, "SEP IRA vs. SIMPLE IRA," Inc. *Magazine*
http://www.inc.com/john-hewitt/sep-ira-vs-simple-ira-simpl
e-ways-to-determine-which-is-right-for-your-business.html

Ashlea Ebeling, "How Entrepreneurs Can Get Big Tax Breaks for Retirement Savings," *Forbes*, March 4 2013
http://www.forbes.com/sites/ashleaebeling/2013/02/13/
how-entrepreneurs-can-get-big-tax-breaks-for-retirement-savings

of asset location – Laura Dogu, "The Key to Tax-Efficient Investing," *Forbes*, 5/07/2010
http://www.forbes.com/2010/05/06/ira-401k-taxes-loss-harvesting-persona
l-finance-bogleheads-view-dogu.html

see also: Marston, *Investing for a Lifetime*, pg 69

harvesting – Kristin McFarland, "'Tis the Season for Tax-Loss Harvesting," U.S. News, Nov 2015
http://money.usnews.com/money/blogs/the-smarter-mutual-fund-inves-
tor/2015/11/16/tis-the-season-for-tax-loss-harvesting

one financial analyst – Roger Edelen, "Uncovering Hidden Costs of Mutual Fund Investing," Univ of California/Davis, School of Management, Feb 2013
http://gsm.ucdavis.edu/research/uncovering-hidden-costs-mutual-fund-investing

One last note on mutual funds...

A study of 3,000 401(k) plans – Quinn Curtis, "Beyond Diversification: The Pervasive Problem of Excessive Fees in 401(k) Plans," *Yale Law & Economics Research Paper*, February 2014
http://www.law.virginia.edu/html/news/2014_spr/curtis_qa.htm

by the nonprofit Demos – Robert Hiltonsmith, "The Retirement Savings Drain: Hidden & Excessive Costs of 401(k)s," Demos, 2012
http://www.demos.org/publication/retirement-savings-drain-hidden-excessive-costs-401ks

An AARP survey – *ibid*

transparency rules – Jane Wollman Rusoff, ""401(k) Fee Transparency," Think Advisor, Dec 20 2012
http://www.thinkadvisor.com/2012/12/20/401k-fee-transparency-best-worst-providers

helpful consumer guide – "A Look At 401(k) Plan Fees," U.S. Dept of Labor, Employee Benefits Security Administration
https://www.dol.gov/ebsa/publications/401k_employee.html

flurry of lawsuits – Darla Mercado, "As 401(k) Suits Mount, Check Your Own Plan," CNBC, July 6 2016
http://www.cnbc.com/2016/07/06/as-401k-suits-mount-check-your-own-plan.html

also: Greg Iacurci, "Fidelity 401(k) Lawsuit Could Up Ante for Plan Advisers," *Investment News*, June 6 2016
http://www.investmentnews.com/article/20160606/free/160609945/fidelity-401-k-lawsuit-could-up-ante-for-plan-advisers

But critics contend – Jennifer Erickson, "Fixing the Drain on Retirement Savings," Center for American Progress, April 11 2014
https://www.americanprogress.org/issues/economy/report/2014/04/11/87503/fixing-the-drain-on-retirement-savings/

see also: "Quinn Curtis Sheds Light on Costs of 401(k) Retirement Plans," University of Virginia School of Law http://www.law.virginia.edu/html/news/2014_spr/curtis_qa.htm

half of workers surveyed – Stephen Blakely, "Many Haven't Noticed 401(k) Fee Disclosures," Employee Benefit Research Institute, July 25 2013
https://www.ebri.org/pdf/FF.239.FeeDisc.25July13.pdf

the increased scrutiny – Darla Mercado, CNBC, *op cit*
As Tony Robbins – Tony Robbins, "Hidden 401(k) Fees Can Destroy Your Retirement Dreams," CNBC, July 18 2016
http://www.cnbc.com/2016/07/18/hidden-401k-fees-can-destroy-you
r-retirement-dreams.html

expense ratios for ETFs – "How to Choose an Exchange-Traded Fund," *Wall Street Journal*
http://guides.wsj.com/personal-finance/investing/
how-to-choose-an-exchange-traded-fund-etf/

bid-ask spread – Daniel Solin, "The Hidden Risks and Costs of ETFs," U.S. News, October 2014
http://money.usnews.com/money/blogs/the-smarter-mutual-fund-inves-
tor/2014/10/07/the-hidden-risks-and-costs-of-etfs

some brokerage firms – Janet Brown, "Are Commission-Free ETFs Really Cheaper?" *Forbes*, Feb 2013
http://www.forbes.com/sites/investor/2012/02/13/
are-commission-free-etfs-really-cheaper

free online tools – "Tools and Calculators," Financial Industry Regulatory Authority
http://www.finra.org/investors/tools

FeeX –
https://www.feex.com/

BrightScope –
https://www.brightscope.com/

commission-based advice – Karen Damato, "3 Reasons to Pay Commissions, Not Fees, to a Financial Advisor," *Wall Street Journal*, Feb 18 2015
http://blogs.wsj.com/totalreturn/2015/02/18/3-reasons-to-pay-commissio
ns-not-fees-to-a-financial-adviser/

see also: "How to Choose a Financial Planner," *Wall Street Journal*

http://guides.wsj.com/personal-finance/managing-your-money/
how-to-choose-a-financial-planner/

one financial advisor – Rick Kahler, "A Financial Planner's Most Important Job Isn't What You Think It Is," *Money*, Dec 10 2014
http://time.com/money/3589232/financial-planners-real-job/

Howard Marks stresses – Marks, *The Most Important Thing*, pg 3; pg 98

Chapter 13

***Risk capacity* is a much** – Christine Benz, "Is Your Risk Tolerance at War with Your Risk Capacity?", Yahoo Finance, Jan 13 2014
http://finance.yahoo.com/news/risk-tolerance-war-risk-capacity-120000769.html

Dollar Cost Averaging – Ryan Campbell, "Taking the Long View with Your Investments," Ticker Tape, July 26 2016
https://tickertape.tdameritrade.com/investing/2016/07/
long-term-investing-dca-drip-56738

Value Averaging – Michael Edleson, *Value Averaging*, John Wiley & Sons (Hoboken: 1993)

Both methods have been criticized – Dan Kadlec, "Is Dollar-Cost Averaging Dumb?" *Time*, Nov 15 2012
http://business.time.com/2012/11/15/is-dollar-cost-averaging-dumb/

Even the cautious John Bogle – Bogle, *Little Book of Common Sense Investing*, pg 202

A 2012 report – Brett Arends, "How to Rebalance Your Portfolio," *Wall Street Journal*, June 27 2014
http://www.wsj.com/articles/how-to-rebalance-your-portfolio-1403895865

investors who rebalanced annually – *ibid*

target-date strategies – Deborah Jacobs, "The Trouble with Target Date Mutual Funds," *Forbes*, Nov 11 2013
http://www.forbes.com/sites/deborahljacobs/2013/11/11/
the-trouble-with-target-date-mutual-funds/#5ec97f742fec

also: Melanie Hicken, "Is Your Target-Date Fund Ripping You Off?" *CNN Money*, Jan 26 2015 http://money.cnn.com/2015/01/25/retirement/target-date-fund/

A survey conducted by – Emily Brandon, "Employee Misperceptions About Target Date Funds," *U.S. News*, May 7 2009
http://money.usnews.com/money/blogs/planning-to-retire/2009/05/07/employees-have-misperceptions-about-target-date-funds

free Guide to Retirement – J.P. Morgan
https://am.jpmorgan.com/us/en/asset-management/gim/adv/insights/guide-to-retirement

prompt us to make better decisions – Richard Thaler, Cass Sunstein, *Nudge: Improving Decisions About Health, Wealth, and Happiness*, Penguin Books (New York: 2008)

A key finding of Thaler – John Nofsinger, "Will You Save More Tomorrow?" *Psychology Today*, Sept 1 2009
https://www.psychologytoday.com/blog/mind-my-money/200909/will-you-save-more-tomorrow

They're all important – Marks, *The Most Important Thing*, pg *xii*

He points to studies – Swensen, *Unconventional Success*, pg 11

"Discipline matters more" – William Bernstein, quoted in Tara Siegel Bernard, "Robo-Advisors for Investors Are Not One-Size-Fits-All," *New York Times*, Jan 22 2016
http://www.nytimes.com/2016/01/23/your-money/robo-advisers-for-investors-are-not-one-size-fits-all.html

"The greatest enemy" – quoted in Bogle, *op cit*, pg 161

Conclusion

Sheila begins saving – example modeled on one in Hardy, *The Compound Effect*, pg 47-49

Prussian military expert – Carl von Clausewitz

retirement calculators – Liz Moyer, *"Will You Be Able to Retire?"*, Wall Street Journal, May 23 2014
http://www.wsj.com/articles/will-you-be-able-to-retire-1400880527

Save More Tomorrow – for more on retirement calculators, and other online savings tools, see: Ron Lieber, "A Nudge to Save a Bit More," *New York Times*, June 27 2014
http://www.nytimes.com/2014/06/28/your-money/for-retirement-online-tools-can-encourage-greater-saving.html

"Invest in as much of yourself" – Chris Winfield, "This Is Warren Buffett's Best Investment Advice," *Time*, July 23 2015
http://time.com/3968806/warren-buffett-investment-advice/

"you have to *become* more" – quoted in Hardy, pg 72

magically doubling penny – example taken from Hardy, pg 10

"small, smart choices" – Hardy, pg 9

"keystone habits" – Steven Benna, "8 Keystone Habits That Can Transform Your Life," *Business Insider*, Aug 6 2015
http://www.businessinsider.com/keystone-habits-that-transform-your-life-2015-8

"simple daily disciplines" – Jeff Olson, *The Slight Edge*, Greenleaf Book Group (Austin: 2005), Chapter 1

Inspired by Gawande's research – Jason Zweig, "A Checklist for Investors," *Wall Street Journal*, Dec 13 2013
http://www.wsj.com/articles/SB10001424052702304202204579254793231267408

"not a shopping list" – Clayton Browne, "Guy Spier's Nine Rules to be a Better Investor," Value Walk, July 8 2015
http://www.valuewalk.com/2015/07/guy-spier-better-investor/

"an inner scorecard" – William Green, "I've Followed Warren Buffett for Decades and Keep Coming Back to These 10 Quotes," Observer, May 4 2015
http://observer.com/2015/05/ive-followed-warren-buffett-for-decades-and-keep-coming-back-to-these-10-quotes/

Buffett lives by - *ibid*

"a tremendous expanse" – Drake Baer, "How Zen Meditation Changed Steve Jobs," *Business Insider*, Jan 9 2015
http://www.businessinsider.com/steve-jobs-zen-meditation-buddhism-2015-1

focus on the journey – quoted in Ryan Holiday, "21 Life Lessons Learned From Some of the World's Greatest Sports Coaches," Thought Catalogue, Aug 3 2016

http://thoughtcatalog.com/ryan-holiday/2016/08/21-life-lessons-learne
d-from-some-of-the-worlds-greatest-sports-coaches/

three-time Super Bowl – Bill Walsh, *The Score Takes Care of Itself*, pg 21
http://www.thought-management.com/bill-walsh-leadership-lessons/

theme of The Process – Richard Feloni, "How Alabama Coach Nick Saban Used
Psychology to Build a Football Dynasty," *Business Insider*, Aug 12 2015
http://www.businessinsider.com/alabama-coach-nick-saban-process-2015-8

"chaos of sport" – Ryan Holiday, "Here's the Strategy Elite Athletes Follow to
Perform at the Highest Level," March 1 2016
http://ryanholiday.net/heres-the-strategy-elite-athletes-follo
w-to-perform-at-the-highest-level/

a "north star" – Brad Stulberg, "Why Having Big Goals Can Backfire," New
York Magazine, Aug 3 2016
http://nymag.com/scienceofus/2016/08/why-having-big-goals-can-backfire.html

The Millennial Advantage

Made in the USA
Lexington, KY
29 December 2016